Same Same, but Different

A Life Beyond Certainty

Robert Pokorski, MD

To Liam:

My friend and colleague at
The Hartford.

Bob Pokorski

Park East Press

Printed in the United States of America.

For information address:

Park East Press
The Graybar Building
420 Lexington Avenue, Suite 300
New York, NY 10170

Library of Congress Cataloging-in-Publication Data

Pokorski, Robert

Same Same, but Different/Robert Pokorski

Library of Congress Control Number: 2011933457

p. cm.

ISBN: 978-1-935764-24-3

10 9 8 7 6 5 4 3 2 1

Acknowledgments

I would like to thank my family for the wonderful life we've shared together, and especially my wife, Chris, who has had the understanding and patience to put up with forty years of my eccentricities. I would also like to thank my mother, who was my role model for a successful life, my brother Bill for the good times we shared together as children, and my many friends from around the world who have greatly enriched my life. Finally, special thanks to the children and staff at the orphanage in Seoul, South Korea, where I worked as a volunteer English teacher for three years. They helped me find the path to a meaningful life.

Contents

Finding The Middle Way......273

Preface

As I look back on more than a half-century of life, I realize that I've been happy—truly, deeply happy—almost all of the time. My good fortune has made me ask: "Why me? Why have I had such a happy and fulfilling life? Was it luck? Good genes? My conservative upbringing? Or something that I did or learned later in life?"

And why has it been difficult for me to accept beliefs that seem to come so easily to others? Even now, well into middle age, I'm still not sure about some of the issues that have long since been decided by most people, including questions about God, religion, complex political and social problems, and the best way to live one's life.

Finally, why am I so comfortable with "differences," particularly the differences in belief that cause discord worldwide? I've learned to stand between opinions, not at the extremes, in order to see all sides of an issue, and this approach, if applied on a global scale, would undoubtedly lead to greater peace, tolerance, and concern for everyone. Yet this philosophy of life—choosing the middle ground rather than a position closer to one of the extremes—is rare. Why?

This book answers these questions—and more. It was written mainly during a three-year period when I worked in South Korea (2006 to 2009), and it describes the long journey I've taken from my roots as a conservative Christian American to a centrist Buddhist and citizen of the world. The format comprises short narratives, all of which are true, followed by a brief discussion of the lessons that I learned, and as often as not, the mistakes that I made. The events involve some of the most memorable times of my life—organized not chronologically, but rather by the lessons I learned—and they take in my experiences as a child and then as a husband and father, physician, businessman, and world traveler. The cast of characters includes my wife, Chris; our three children, Michael, Lisa, and Elizabeth; my parents and in-laws; and my brother Bill. Also appearing are friends and acquaintances from around the world (all of whose names have been changed).

As a point of clarification, there is no intent to convince readers that they're wrong about some of their most fundamental beliefs. Rather, the goal is to suggest that, in many cases, they may not be right. This is a subtle distinction, to be sure, but one that has far-reaching implications for how we view the world and our place in it.

The Search for a Spiritual Life

When you are inspired by some great purpose, all your thoughts break their bonds. Your mind transcends limitations, your consciousness expands in every direction, and you find yourself in a new, great, and wonderful world. Dormant forces, faculties, and talents become alive, and you discover yourself to be a greater person by far than you ever dreamed yourself to be.

—Patanjala (c.200 BCE), India[1]

1

The Koan of Everyday Life

How to Live a Spiritual Life Every Moment of the Day

Whoever would be a teacher of men let him begin by teaching himself before teaching others, and let him teach by example before teaching by word. For he who teaches himself and rectifies his own ways is more deserving of respect and reverence than he who would teach others and rectify their ways.

—Kahlil Gibran (1883-1931), Lebanon[2]

When I first met Mark, I didn't know what to make of him. He seemed too good to be true, but as I learned, he was the real deal. During the nine years that we worked together, he became a close friend and an influential person in my life. Every day he'd stop by my office—as well as the offices of many of our co-workers—to give me a pleasant "Good morning" and to wish me well. Somehow he knew everyone's birthday, and once a year we all received a special online greeting from him.

Volunteering was a way of life for him. He and his friends from a nonsectarian spiritual* group were always helping out where

---

* In this book I often use the word "spiritual" instead of "religious" because some of the kindest people I've met during my life were not affiliated with any of the world's organized religions. They got their inner strength, ethical principles, and purpose in life from a belief that all people have a right to respect, dignity, and happiness.

needed, especially with the less fortunate. One of the highlights of his year was Christmas Eve, when he and others of his group would take the train into New York City and distribute food to the homeless.

Mark developed an unusual form of cancer—slow growing, but incurable. He had surgery after surgery, and so many courses of chemotherapy that we lost count. On many occasions he almost died, and everyone prayed while his life hung in the balance. Here's the thing: through it all, he didn't change. True, his pace was slower and he didn't have his old stamina. But he'd still stop by every day with the same cheerful message, maybe show us the peach fuzz that was growing back on his head, tell us the latest medical test results, or matter-of-factly recount his ongoing volunteer efforts despite the illness. To the rest of us who felt like mere mortals, it was a bit unnerving. He kept setting the bar higher and higher, and we wondered how well we'd do when our time came.

I never asked in so many words, "Mark, how do you do it? What keeps you going?" I didn't have to. It was all about people. He lived each day to the fullest, aware of what was happening around him, remaining generous, patient, kind, and wise in a way that most people would never know. Through it all, he was happy and at peace. When the cancer finally overwhelmed him and he moved on to whatever lay on the other side of this life, he was sorely missed by everyone who was fortunate to have known him.

Zen Buddhists are famous for their riddles, called koans, that ask unanswerable questions. In one of them, known as "the koan of everyday life," the following exchange takes place:

Novice monk: "Master, what is the Buddha?"

Senior monk: "The cypress tree in the garden."

It means that the practice of one's spiritual beliefs is not reserved for a special time (Friday for Muslims, Sunday for Christians), place (a temple for Buddhists and Hindus, a synagogue for Jews), or ritual (Mass for Catholics, a worship service for Protestants). Rather, like the cypress tree that the monks would see many times each day, spiritual practice is an ordinary part of one's life from morning until night.

Mark solved the koan of everyday life. A spiritual life wasn't something that he did once a week at a place of worship, but what he did every day, all day long. Like most of us, he spent a lot of time at work, but it wasn't just a job for him. There was nothing ordinary about his greetings of "Good morning"; for him, they were a chance to practice kindness and to be mindful of the world around him.

Everyone needs their own cypress tree. At home, it might be our dining room table or the coffee pot in the kitchen. When I worked in Seoul, it was a fire extinguisher in the hallway near my office. Whenever I walked past it I made a mental note, something like *Remember: be patient and kind today*—or whatever my goal for the day happened to be. It reminded me that the ordinary activities of daily life—commuting, work, and leisure time—were not distractions from spiritual practice. Rather, these were the times and the places when and where it was done.

As a child I used to read a Christian book called *Lives of the Saints* that chronicled the experiences of some very special people. All faiths, including organized religions and secular belief systems, have similar stories of spiritual giants who changed the world by helping others in small ways. These people—quiet, unassuming, and radiating a sense of inner peace—are still with us today, and like Mark, they change the world around them by putting their faith into practice every moment of the day.

2

The Foundering Physician Who Waited Too Long

Finding the Answers Where You Are

In the middle of the journey of our life, I found myself again in a dark wood, so dark that the straight way was utterly lost.

—Dante Alighieri (1265-1321), Italy[3]

I was in the middle of my specialty training in internal medicine and looking for a mentor to steer me in the right direction. I found one, and what I learned from him played an important role in a later career decision that changed my life.

Peter was a physician who seemed to have it all: beautiful home, high standing in the community, and loving wife and children. The problem? He was deeply unhappy. In fact, he wanted to be just about anywhere except where he was. A financial consultant had advised him to purchase his medical building; eventually it would be paid off, netting a tidy profit for his retirement years. But he was terribly overextended—financially, physically, and emotionally—and his spiritual life was nonexistent. Moreover, he had to work harder and harder to maintain his lifestyle, leaving him no time for relaxation or exercise, and his family life was in shambles.

He confided in me that he felt trapped. "I need to get away for a while, think about what went wrong, and figure out how to get my life back on track." His plan was to earn enough money to take an extended leave of absence from his job and enroll in a spiritual program that helped people find balance in their lives.

The story doesn't have a happy ending. Peter died in his sleep a few years later. He never found the time or the money to change his life.

Who hasn't felt like Peter at some point during his or her life? Overwhelmed by work, school, or responsibilities to family and friends, we'd like to stop our lives, spend the days, months, or years needed to find the answers, and then start over with our newfound wisdom. Our dream might involve a tropical resort, the solitude of a mountain wilderness, or an exotic Himalayan monastery where we'd learn the wisdom of the East. My personal getaway fantasy used to be the "Shikoku Pilgrimage," a 750-mile walk that visits 88 Buddhist temples on the perimeter of the Japanese island of Shikoku. I'd be free to meditate, read, think, help others along the way, and in particular, not carry the burdens that come with life in the modern world.

Henry David Thoreau, one of the first home-grown proponents of Buddhist philosophy in the United States,[4] spent two years watching the grass grow and the seasons change when he wrote *Walden* in 1854. That's not an option for most of us. By the time we acknowledge that a serious life tune-up is needed, most of us have so many work and family commitments that we can't take an extended sabbatical from the real world.

But more importantly, abandoning our current life to find wisdom elsewhere almost certainly won't work. Why would it? Without changing how we deal with people and situations—and more fundamentally, the way that we think—the same problems will always be with us. And even if we did make progress, in all likelihood we'd relapse after leaving the protected, artificial surroundings of the retreat setting, much like people on fad diets who regain their weight when they start eating normal food again.

I treated many patients with physical problems that were analogous to Peter's unrealistic plan for spiritual realignment. The situation would go something like this: A middle-aged man with a heart attack would be told to lose weight, get more exercise, and generally adopt a healthier lifestyle. In the hospital he was a model patient (like the person on a spiritual retreat, isolated from the stresses of real life), in the first few months after discharge he was good (sustained by the residual aura of the retreat experience), and then he'd relapse into the old habits that had gotten him to where he was when I first met him in the intensive care unit. Even a near-death experience wasn't enough to convince him to change.

Peter's beliefs—an amalgamation of his upbringing as a child, a desire to achieve society's idea of success, and his own ambition and experiences—had imprisoned him in an unfulfilling life. Finding a solution would be one of the most important challenges he'd ever face, one that would affect the happiness and welfare of his family and the people around him. He waited too long.

Quitting Medical Practice

Letting Go, Even If a Steep Price Was Already Paid

"We do not receive wisdom, we must discover it for ourselves, after a journey through the wilderness which no one else can make for us, which no one can spare us, for our wisdom is the point of view from which we come at last to regard the world."

—Marcel Proust (1871-1922), France

Between medical school and specialty training in internal medicine, I spent seven grueling years learning to be a physician, including many sleepless years when I was on call at the hospital every three or four nights. Three years after I finished, at the age of 30, I quit medical practice forever. What happened?

Two things. First, my wife, Chris, and I had three children who were then ages five, three and one, and I wanted to be the best possible father for them. I didn't think that I could handle both parenting and the demanding life of a busy internist; something would suffer, and I was fairly sure that it would be my family responsibilities. Second, I wanted a life outside of work—an active, vibrant, multi-faceted life—and this required enough time to pursue interests that ranged far beyond the disciplines of medicine and science. The lesson that I learned from Peter—my overcommitted and deeply unhappy medical school mentor in the prior story—was ingrained in my mind. I was determined not to repeat his mistakes.

So instead of medical practice, I decided to work as a medical director for a life insurance company, an occupation I would not have considered a few years earlier when I was a hard-charging young doctor just out of school. It proved to be a life-changing decision, one that set me on the path to a happier, simpler, and more spiritually rewarding life.

I'm sure many people would think that I made a huge mistake, wasting seven years of my life to learn a profession and then choosing to work in a job where many of my skills would never be used again. However, I didn't see it that way when I compared the pros and cons. Medical practice meant a larger salary and higher status in the community, yet at the price of 60-hour work weeks for the next 30 years. On the other hand, a slower-paced job meant more time with my family, better physical and mental health, and innumerable opportunities to pursue diverse interests that would make me a happier, more well-rounded person. Admittedly, the one aspect of medical practice I truly missed was patient care, but over the years I found a number of volunteer activities that enabled me to help others in ways that would never have been possible for a busy physician.

What troubled me most when choosing between medical practice and a job with an insurance company was the size of my investment. I had worked hard and long to get to where I was, a massive commitment amounting to one-fourth of my life. It was a tough decision, one I pondered for the better part of a year. Once I made it—deciding to work for a company in Fort Wayne, Indiana —I knew it was the right one.

In retrospect, I realize that slowing down at age 30, when most of my medical school classmates were doing just the opposite, was one of the best decisions I ever made. This was also when I began to understand that a person isn't defined by his or her job. True, I was still a physician, but as I developed other aspects of my life, my occupation became less and less important. Being a doctor was just what I did; it was not who I was.

Scores of books have been written about how to reduce stress and simplify life. They all have the same message: shift your priorities to achieve a more balanced lifestyle, and use your newfound time and energy to develop yourself more fully as a person. This involves a combination of more and less:

- More time with friends and family, more time to gain wisdom via lifelong learning, and more time to enjoy life.

- Less work, less commuting, less stuff, and less passive entertainment that steals your time—sometimes all of the free time that you have in a day—but gives you almost nothing in return.

What most of these self-help gurus don't convey so well is the wisdom that Franz Metcalf imparts in his book *What Would Buddha Do?* Not all things are worth the price we pay for them, even when the price is already paid. No matter how strong we grow in carrying our burdens, we are still wise to set some down. [5]

This advice spoke directly to me. I had paid a very high price —seven years of difficult and expensive medical training plus earlier arduous college years during which I struggled with advanced biology and organic chemistry. There was no doubt I had the physical and mental strength to carry on practicing medicine for decades to come. But in the end, what I'd attained wasn't sufficiently worthwhile to me. That was not how I wanted to live my life.

I've seen countless examples of people who were unwilling to change aspects of their lives that clearly needed changing. There was Tom, the engineer who counted the years until he could retire from a stressful job that he hated; the scores of high-powered New York lawyers who wished their parents hadn't pushed them into jobs that paid well but demanded 12-hour workdays; and the secretary who did her best to make everyone miserable by complaining nonstop about her unfortunate life, which wasn't a bit unfortunate—she just had an unbelievably negative outlook on life.

I wanted to tell them what I'd seen when I worked in the hospital emergency room—dozens of people who dropped dead at the kitchen table or at work, or who died in their sleep—and there was no reason that it couldn't happen to them. I wanted to say, "If you're really that unhappy, you'd better think long and hard about making a change while you still can." But I didn't say anything. Self-reflection wasn't high on their list of priorities; they were too busy with other matters and would have scoffed at my advice as too simplistic for the "real" world.

And I would agree. This *is* simple advice, because the best course of action is so apparent: no matter how strong we've grown over the years in carrying our burdens, we'd still be better off if we set them down, even if we've already paid a high price to get to where we are or what we have. This means letting go of things that cost us a lot in terms of time, effort, or money, but that stand squarely between us and a happier, more satisfying life. It's a task that's as difficult as any that we'll encounter in our lives: acknowledging that something important to us no longer works and that a significant change is necessary.

But what do we keep and what do we let go? I found Gandhi's approach to be helpful when making these decisions:

> As long as you derive inner help and comfort from anything, you should keep it. If you were to give it up in a mood of self-sacrifice or out of a stern sense of duty, you would continue to want it back, and that unsatisfied want would make trouble for you. Only give up a thing when you want some other condition so much that the thing no longer has any attraction for you, or when it seems to interfere with that which is more greatly desired.[6]

This advice rings true for me: strive for a simpler life, but know where to draw the line. When I faced my decision at age 30, I had three children to raise and a mortgage to pay. I couldn't just walk away from everything and start over. So I downsized, exchanging the harried life of a busy internist for a more staid career as an insurance medical director. It was clearly the right choice for me. I found a more balanced way of life that nevertheless gave me a good income, an opportunity to improve my physical and mental health, and far more time to be with the people I loved.

This experience taught me that you never know where "letting go" will take you. Instead of spending the rest of my life practicing internal medicine in Omaha, Nebraska, I worked for international insurance companies, traveled the world for 20 years, and made a lot of friends who had different ideas about global politics, religion, and how life should be lived. I had the time to think, learn, relax, and live, and I was there to see our three children grow into wonderful adults who have become my best friends. Choosing less turned into more of what everyone really wants: happiness and a meaningful life.

4

Aunt Olga: A Woman
Who Just Did It

Finding the Time for a Spiritual Life

It is one of the most beautiful compensations of life, that no man can sincerely try to help another without helping himself.

—Ralph Waldo Emerson (1803-1882), USA[7]

My great aunt Olga lived until age 93. She was a fiercely independent woman accustomed to finding her own solutions, which came from living alone for most of her life in the small town of Grand Island, Nebraska. When she was 75, arthritis in her knees began to limit her ability to drive. The problem was that she couldn't move her foot between the gas and brake pedals. Her solution? While driving, she would grasp her right thigh with both hands, lift it, and set it down on the appropriate pedal. She drove like this for more than 10 years without an accident.

The time came when even this wouldn't work, but she wasn't beaten. Wilbur, her boyfriend, had his own health problems although they were quite the opposite of hers: he was in fine physical health but suffered from a failing mind. As Olga would tell it, "Nobody at the senior center dances better, but the poor dear can't even find his way to the bathroom." So they teamed up. Olga drove the short distance to his house, then Wilbur took over as the driver —he had no idea where he was going, but he was good at following directions—and together they got around town just fine. There was one remaining problem with this arrangement: Wilbur was well known to the police because he'd lost his license a year earlier after getting lost while trying to drive home. Olga was truly resourceful. She had Wilbur wear her old blue wig when driving in town so he wouldn't be recognized by the police.

Aunt Olga was a regular guest in our home. She and my mom would visit the local mall, drawn by a shared love of bargains, chocolate, and an inexpensive lunch. The food court was on the second floor, but because of her arthritis, the stairway was out of the question, which left a choice between the elevator and the escalator. "The elevator's for children and old people," Olga would say, and she definitely didn't consider herself old, even though she was in her eighties at the time. So they took their chances on the escalator.

Mom had to make a decision as to where was the best place to be if Olga lost her balance: one step above or below her. As it turned out, Mom was long on planning but short on execution. They got on the up escalator with Mom standing one step below Olga for support. Almost immediately, Olga lost her balance and began to fall. First Olga and then Mom collapsed backwards, both screaming wildly for help and clutching at their hair to avoid being scalped if it got caught in the moving parts of the escalator. They rode like this—feet-first, upside-down, skirts over heads—all the way to the top, where they were deposited into the arms of waiting rescuers. Fearing a lawsuit, the management treated them to a free lunch at the food court. For the last decade of her life, Olga reminisced wistfully about that glorious day at the mall.

Olga was a bit eccentric, one of those unconventional relatives who add so much interest and spice to life. Despite her health problems, she always found a way to do what was important to her.

Most people in the world share two characteristics: (1) they would like to be better people, and (2) they're too busy to add anything else to their already overextended lives. For those of us who are too busy to start or continue a program for personal and spiritual growth, it's worth considering how we spend our free time, including the hours and hours devoted to TV, computer games, text messaging, twittering, and the Internet. The time spent on these activities, which together accounts for most of our day that's not spent working or sleeping, is gone forever. Instead, why not use part of it, maybe just 10 minutes each day, to sit quietly and reflect on how fortunate we are or what we would like to accomplish for ourselves and others? It's simply a matter of priorities.

Aunt Olga has been an inspiration to me as I've gotten older. Like most people, I have regrets for opportunities missed, important goals that were never achieved, and an ever-diminishing number of years to make a difference in the world. I remember the disabled octogenarian who was too busy enjoying life to slow down, who was starting new projects in her nineties, and who refused to take the elevator because it was for "old" people. If she could find time for the important things in life, so could I.

5

Trying Something Else:
The Korean Orphanage, Part 1

Changing Lives—Yours and Others'
—with Hands-On Spirituality

A little knowledge that acts is worth infinitely more than much knowledge that is idle.

—Kahlil Gibran (1883-1931), Lebanon[8]

I looked up from my well-read copy of the *International Herald Tribune* and surveyed the scene around me. The floor-to-ceiling windows of the trendy Cantonese restaurant framed the dazzling beauty of Hong Kong at night: spectacularly lit buildings for as far as the eye could see; container ships, ferries, and junks crossing the short harbor to Kowloon; and an aerial highway paved with the lights of dozens of planes making their final approach to the airport. For me, it was an evening like any other—hundreds of others, in fact—but a turning point in my life.

I was alone in a room of strangers, mostly business people like me, all of us different, yet sharing the loneliness of separation from friends and family. There are time-honored ways that men use to survive endless weeks on the road: sightseeing, television, reading, exercise, nonstop work, heavy drinking, womanizing, and just plain depression. At age 54, I was looking for something else, a significant change in my life, and that night I resolved to find it. Yet I had no idea what I was looking for.

My "something else" came sooner than expected. Some weeks later I received a call from a Korean life insurance company that wanted to hire me. With my love of South Korea (I'd been there many times on business), Buddhism, and Asian culture, the decision was easy. I bid farewell to friends and work associates in Connecticut and began the first of what would be many long-term stays alone in Seoul.

As luck, fate, or karma would have it, I happened to read a single paragraph in a what-to-do-in-Seoul guidebook that suggested visiting an orphanage to play with the children. With the memory of that lonely night in Hong Kong still fresh in my mind—and my resolve to make a significant change in my life—I found my way (after getting hopelessly lost in the labyrinthine streets just a few blocks from my destination) to the orphanage in central Seoul. It was home to about 50 children, ranging in age from newborns to age 10. I walked through the door and was immediately buried under a pile of tiny bodies. The older children wanted to play games, the younger ones just wanted to be held, and some of the four- and five-year-olds grabbed my hands and tried to lead me away from the others so they could have some rare one-on-one time with an adult.

The staff was glad that I had come for playtime, but they really needed more English language instructors who could supplement what the children learned in school. The director asked if I could commit to teaching one class a week. The opportunity was tempting. Was this, I wondered, the change that I was looking for?

Before deciding, I returned later in the week to watch a class taught by a young, bilingual Korean-American woman, and this experience made my decision even more difficult. I watched in envy and amazement as she switched effortlessly between Korean and English, and I mentally listed the reasons why I wasn't qualified for this kind of volunteer work: no formal training, no experience as a teacher, and I didn't know a word of Korean except "*kimchi*."

I had no idea what to do or where to start, but I did know that the children could use all the help they could get. I agreed to return the following Sunday evening for the first lesson. I remember thinking, *Who knows? Maybe learning a bit of English might mean something to them.* Little did I realize how much it would mean to me.

On my first day as a teacher I arrived promptly at 6 p.m. and was shown to the classroom. It was the size of a small bedroom, with a preschool-sized table and chairs, piles of Korean books and toys, and some of the most adorable five-year-olds that you'll ever see. I introduced myself as "Bob" since my long Polish name was unpronounceable for many Koreans, even adults. This was followed by giggles all around. That's when I learned that "Bob" was the Korean word for rice, which was roughly the same as calling yourself "Potato" in an English-speaking country. I then used my poor pantomiming skills to tell the children that I was 54. It took some time for this information to filter through the room, and when it did the children absolutely exploded with laughter. This being an orphanage, many of them had never seen anyone so old.

In Korea most things are very orderly, so I imagined a group of attentive students with beaming smiles all sitting quietly at a table and eager to learn. I was half right. Even at this age the difference between girls and boys was striking: the three girls fought for the best books to color and practice their writing, while the three boys just fought. I finally had to physically drag the boys out from under the table and force them to sit in chairs. To my surprise, everyone learned a thing or two before the session degenerated into utter chaos. We laughed and hugged, and after one lesson I was hooked.

I was absolutely exhausted by the time I headed for home on the subway. Koreans are highly deferential to the elderly, a wonderful tradition that should be emulated worldwide, but this attitude was in short supply that night. I was hoping that someone would give their seat to a middle-aged, white-haired man who'd been confined in a small room for 90 minutes with six hyperactive children, but it wasn't meant to be. The train was full of young people—mostly talking on cell phones, text messaging, or listening to MP3 players—and I went pretty much unnoticed.

Thirty minutes later I dragged myself off the train and walked headlong into a huge bookstore near the subway station exit. Remembering my promise to bring more teaching aids to the orphanage, I found my way to the children's section, where I spent the next hour looking for Korean-English books for my class.

There was no food in my hotel room and I was far too tired to go to a restaurant at nine o'clock on a Sunday night, so I stopped at a convenience store for a three-course meal that I took to my room: beer, canned tuna, and a rice cake wrapped in seaweed. I was as tired as I'd been for a long time... and I couldn't have been happier.

I learned a great deal about myself that day. I wanted to work with the children, but I didn't feel qualified. As it turned out, they weren't interested in perfection. They were happy just to have someone spend time with them, and it was a bonus that I happened to be a native English language speaker. Was the Korean-American woman a better teacher? I'm sure she was, but she only taught one class a week. For my students, it was a choice between me and nobody.

My time with the children was an opportunity for hands-on spirituality. I learned that it's one thing to make weekly visits to a church, mosque, synagogue, or temple (my visits were to Jogyesa, the Buddhist temple behind my hotel), and quite another to put what we learned on these holy days into practice. Because of my long working hours at the company, spending a weekend evening with the children was a real commitment, one that was far more valuable to me than money I could have given to charity.

My work as a volunteer also broadened my perspective for what I could do for others. Once I'd broken the ice, I found a lot more opportunities for kindness and generosity—everyday things like helping people on the street with heavy packages, giving strangers an unexpected cheerful greeting, and having the patience to be a more courteous driver. This was also the time when I started to think seriously about the elements of a meaningful life. For me, it clearly involved awareness of the needs of others who were less fortunate, and doing what I could to help.

I'll never forget the trip back to my hotel after this first class. I felt dead tired when I got off the subway, but was instantly revitalized when I saw the bookstore. This was something that I could do—buy badly needed Korean-English children's books for my class—and if I didn't do it, it wouldn't get done. I'd left behind the "I'm-not-a-good-enough-teacher" attitude; instead, I was busy trying to be a better one. Six eager children would be waiting for me next Sunday evening.

6

Better Late Than Never

Rediscovering Our Dreams for Changing the World

*There is a transcendent power in example. We reform others uncon-
sciously when we walk uprightly.*

—Anne Sophie Swetchine (1782-1857), Russia/France[9]

Most of us are fairly satisfied with what we've accomplished in
life—sometimes because we truly have accomplished a lot, but as
often as not because we've surrounded ourselves with like-thinkers
who don't challenge our beliefs or make too many intellectual or
spiritual demands on us. This was certainly true for me. I'd broken
out of the doldrums of self-involvement, was doing some volunteer
work at the Korean orphanage, and was finally thinking about important issues that I should have gotten to 20 years earlier. I was
feeling pretty good about myself—pride would describe it very well.
That's when I was reminded of how far I still had to go at age 55.

I had just returned from lunch with Paul, my best friend who
still lived in Omaha. We went way back, having met in summer
school prior to our freshman year in high school. He was everything that I wasn't: good looking, athletic, smart, and so mechani-
cally inclined that he could fix anything from a bulldozer to a car
engine, which was a highly desirable skill for young teenage boys
who were eager to find some kind of rattletrap vehicle that would
impress the girls. I don't know what he saw in me, but I've always

considered myself lucky that we became lifelong friends from the day we first met.

After leaving Omaha in 1979, I only saw him about once a year. He became very active in the community—volunteering at his church, serving on the board of directors of three or four organizations that helped disadvantaged people, and using two weeks of his summer vacation to provide free health care for needy people on one of the Caribbean islands. He was even a Big Brother to a neighborhood child who didn't have a father. His many contributions to society were all very much matter-of-fact to him, activities that he did without advertising his good deeds to others. He had reason to be proud, but pride was never a vice for him.

My lunch with Paul was our first meeting since he'd been diagnosed with a rare form of cancer. Once again, I was struck by his unbelievably positive outlook on life. He admitted to being upset for the first few days after hearing the news, but nonetheless he considered himself fortunate because there was a reasonable chance for a cure. Despite the shock of a cancer diagnosis that would have devastated most people, he was back at work one week after finishing treatment and still busy with all of his volunteer activities.

He had his own ideas about God and spirituality, but was always highly tolerant of others' beliefs, lifestyle choices, and religious affiliations. At least part of the reason was that his volunteer work took him into the trenches where poor and disadvantaged people lived, and he saw much more of the real world than most of us ever will. If the world's political, social, and religious leaders could emulate his acceptance of the differences among people, the major global conflicts would grind to a halt in the spirit of reasoned dialogue and a desire for the happiness of everyone on earth.

Paul was a remarkable person in so many ways. He inspired others to lead happy and meaningful lives, and he didn't need the aggressive and often confrontational tactics that are so common among today's political, religious, and social activists. Instead, he did it all by example.

After our lunch, I thought about the legacies that we leave during our brief stay here on earth. Paul practiced the kind of spiritual activism that most people only aspire to, while many of us have almost no interest in what's happening outside of our immediate circle of acquaintances. For some people, their lack of involvement is understandable. For example, mothers who care for young children have little time for themselves, let alone others, and some occupations, such as teaching and health care work, already have strong elements of volunteerism.

But many people have lots of time to spare, and yet they do little or nothing for others. Two retirees that I know are good examples: Karen divides her time between the TV and computer games, while John, who plays golf four or five days a week so he has "something to do," proudly tells his friends that he spends two hours a month—a whopping 24 hours a year—volunteering at the senior center. I know that I'm being judgmental—Buddhist teachings notwithstanding, I'm a long way from perfect—but these seem like selfish, unfulfilling ways to spend the last years of one's life.

In *The Engaged Spiritual Life,* Donald Rothberg explains why many people, even those who consider themselves highly religious or spiritual, don't help others.[10] It's easy to understand some of the reasons: because of the number of social problems that must be addressed, some people become resigned to the inevitability of a world of haves and have-nots, while others find it too unpleasant to cross the boundaries that separate the well-to-do from the less fortunate.

More troubling are those who use intellectual and spiritual rationalizations. In the former, people justify inaction by creating belief structures that explain why haves and have-nots exist, thereby freeing themselves from the need for action. In the latter, which Rothberg calls "spiritual materialism," spirituality is used by those who consider themselves calm, wise, and righteous so they can avoid the challenges of everyday life.[†] We all know people like this who are friends, neighbors, or even respected members of our church, mosque, synagogue, or temple. They're good at talking the talk, but they never seem to get around to walking the walk.

When it came to engaged spirituality, the differences between Paul and me were so extreme that it was uncomfortable to even think about it. But facing the truth helped me learn a few lessons. First, it wasn't too late. With a life expectancy of 75 to 80 years worldwide, there's enough time for everyone to make a difference, even if we get a late start. But the sooner we start, the better—for us and for others.

Second, our efforts grow faster and in more ways than we can imagine. William, a young man who taught English at the orphanage before I arrived in Seoul, was my source of inspiration. When I read about his experiences, I had to follow his lead. After I had been volunteering for eight months, Jennifer, a Korean-American high school student, joined me at the orphanage, and a few months later one of her friends also started to teach English. The following year, a Korean-American businessman from my hotel joined us after I told him about our experiences. Later still, many of my Korean co-workers began to visit the orphanage to play with the children, help with homework, and paint and clean up the building. When I returned to the U.S. between trips to Korea, it was reassuring to know that my wonderful students, all eager to learn English, still had people there to help them. Who knows how their lives were changed owing to our combined efforts? It all started with

---

† Ideally, we want social realities, such as poverty, inequality, and preju- dice, to affect us deeply. Spirituality has gone astray if it leads to a con- trived inner peace that shields us from the need to act.

William, just one man who took the responsibility to do what he could, and the rest of us followed.

Finally, my experiences at the Korean orphanage rekindled ideas that had been long forgotten: my adolescent dreams of changing the world for the better. I was a teenager in the '60s, a time of radical social transformation when everything seemed possible, and I wanted to make a difference. Like a lot of people, I got sidetracked during decades of study, hard work, and raising a family. Thirty-five years later, I got back on track, inspired by Paul, who led by example, and by William, who pointed the way to the orphanage in Seoul.

Most of my teenage contemporaries, now middle-aged men and women, had the same idealism and hope for changing the world, and like me, many of them became so preoccupied with the demands of daily life that they lost their way. With effort, determination, patience, and regular periods of quiet reflection about the nature of a meaningful life, we can all discover that our dreams for changing the world weren't lost at all. They've always been there, just waiting for us to remember them and get started.

7

Tweedledum and Tweedledee

"Little People": My Role Models for a Successful Life

I am only one, but still I am one. I cannot do everything, but still I can do something.

—Edward Everett Hale (1822-1909), USA[11]

Mom was a good 60 pounds overweight, but her siblings still called her "little sister." It wasn't because she was the youngest in the family. All of her brothers and sisters were much larger, a real-life parade of Tweedledums and Tweedledees, with Ken, the biggest of the bunch, topping out at over 400 pounds. Strange things were bound to happen during their family reunion in the desert of southern California.

The kick-off dinner was at one of the many all-you-can-eat restaurants that had sprouted up across the U.S. to meet the growing (literally and figuratively) demand of their customers. It was a no-holds-barred kind of place with dozens of Ken look-alikes, a restaurant where one didn't feel guilty carrying plates overflowing with food. The buffet starting with an enormous salad bar, continued with an even longer entrée section stocked with calorie-laden foods, and ended in an opulent, gut-busting dessert bar. After eating a shocking amount of food, the revelers merrily waddled to their cars. That's when things got a bit dicey.

For most social occasions, spouses travel together, but they were short on cars and there was a delicate logistic issue to resolve —namely, some of the people were so large that planning was needed to find three people who could fit in the back seat at the same time. Mom, the smallest one, was assigned to the car with Ken. They hadn't gone far before he began to complain of "an upset stomach," followed shortly thereafter by a series of audible lower gastrointestinal eruptions that are normally considered taboo in polite society. Packed into the car like sardines, surrounded by clouds of noxious gas (which Ken replenished at regular intervals), all they could do was endure the 30-minute drive to the hotel.

No one slept well that night, perhaps due to jet lag, but more likely due to the fact that each of them had just eaten enough food for two or three people. So when Mom wandered into the lobby after a sleepless night, she had company: her brother Jimmy. He hadn't slept well for a different reason. The men and women shared rooms to save money on accommodations, and Jimmy's unfortunate lot was with Ken. As he discreetly put it, there were "gas issues," and he had to flee the room in the middle of the night.

This being a reunion, they reminisced for hours about happy memories and days long past, until the first light of morning appeared on the horizon. Still dressed in their night clothes, they strolled onto the grounds of the desert resort, ever watchful for the rattlesnakes that often warmed themselves on the sidewalks during the night. They hadn't gone far before the sound of a rattle froze them in their tracks and elicited a rare swear word from my mother, only to find that the noise was not from a surly rattlesnake but from the underground sprinkler system that was timed to start early in the morning.

They finished their morning constitutional at the hotel pool. Mom had been an excellent swimmer in her younger years, and she wasn't about to miss the opportunity. She jumped in, nightgown and all, and did a few laps, all the while maintaining a pleasant banter with her brother, who sat in a nearby lounge chair. When she hoisted herself out of the water, he looked away in embarrassment —his 190-pound sister looked like a contestant in a geriatric wet T-shirt contest. He bid her a hasty goodbye and ran back to the safety of the lobby.

But Mom's morning wasn't quite over. She'd forgotten her room key, so she walked to her ground floor room and tapped on the window for her sister to let her in. Unfortunately, she'd chosen the wrong room. A total stranger opened the window, took one look at the overweight 60-year-old woman in a dripping wet night-gown, and shouted, "Get the hell out of here before I call the police!"

As we get older, it's natural to ask, "Will I be remembered? Did I make a difference?" For my mother, the answer is a resounding "Yes!" She was the real deal. Raised during the Depression, Mom wasn't used to fine things as a child, and marriage didn't improve her situation. She struggled most of her life, often working two low-paying clerical jobs to help make ends meet, later becoming the family's sole provider when my father was disabled. Even as a child I knew her main goal was to raise her two children so they would have a better life. Funny and a bit wacky, especially when she was with her even wackier relatives, she was loved by everyone who knew her as a quiet, self-effacing woman who accepted people for what they were.

One of her jobs—a receptionist during the 11 p.m. to 7 a.m. shift at the busiest hospital emergency room in Omaha—was totally out of character for a conservative Baptist-turned-Catholic woman, but we needed the money. She saw alcoholics, drug abusers, prostitutes, terrible trauma cases, and people who literally dropped dead while talking to her. She often had a tinge of embarrassment in her voice when she related her experiences, such as the time she admitted a fashionably dressed, semi-comatose young woman, only to have the nurses pull off the person's clothes to reveal that she was very much a he.

Like all mothers, she was quick with advice: study hard, go to church (which I did, six days a week for eight years straight), and the one that made the strongest impression on young ears: "Don't get into a car with strangers. They'll cut off your weenie." After hearing this warning as a five-year-old boy, there was no candy in the world that would have lured me into a stranger's car.

On the day I entered medical school, she gave me some of the best advice that I've ever received: "Don't forget the little people." She was reminding me that many people, like my parents and their parents before them, had spent their entire lives working in low-paying, low-profile jobs because they didn't have my advantages—a strong mother who encouraged me to do my best, a good education, and lots and lots of luck—and that the lives of these people were every bit as important to the world as those of a doctor or a well-paid businessman.

It was advice that I've never forgotten. To this day, I have routines that can be traced back to the wisdom I learned that day, like exchanging pleasant "Good mornings" with the friendly cleaning lady in the lobby of my company in Seoul. Her job may have been low paying and low profile, but there was nothing little about her as a person. Like my mother, she was a hard-working, happy woman who was living the best life that she could, and my day was always more pleasant because of our brief encounters each morning.

Was my mother successful? Certainly not if success is defined as fame and fortune. The role models in most modern societies are the actors, rock stars, athletes, and financial titans who grace the pages of newspapers and tabloid magazines. While they may be good at what they do, the example they set for others is often the antithesis of a principled life. The rare superstars of ethical and spiritual behavior—Gandhi, Martin Luther King, Mother Teresa,

Nelson Mandela, and the Dalai Lama—are few and far between. That's why "the little people," those who labor quietly behind the scenes to make the world a better place for everyone, are so important. Mom was one of them. To my way of thinking, she lived a very, very successful life.

Happiness

If an Arab in the desert were suddenly to discover a spring in his tent, and so would always be able to have water in abundance, how fortunate he would consider himself. So too when a man, who as a physical being is always turned toward the outside, thinking that his happiness lies outside him, finally turns inward and discovers that the source is within.

—Søren Kierkegaard (1813-1855), Denmark[12]

8

Hog Tunnels and Catwalks

Laying the Foundation for a Lifetime of Happiness

If you want to be sad, no one in the world can make you happy. But if you make up your mind to be happy, no one and nothing on earth can take that happiness from you.

—Paramahansa Yogananda (1893-1952), India[13]

If we fell we'd break our necks when we splatted on the concrete floor 40 feet below, unless we were lucky and got wedged between the bales during the fall. Then we'd slowly suffocate instead. But for eight- and nine-year-old brothers who spent their days building hay-bale forts in the biggest barn in the world's biggest stockyards, it was a risk we were eager to take. It was the summer of 1960, and that's what we did for fun.

My brother Bill and I were raised in a working-class neighborhood of second- and third-generation Polish immigrants in Omaha. Our family was poor even by the standards of the neighborhood. We lived in a ramshackle house with no hot water (my mother boiled water for cleaning and bathing), there was no bathtub or shower (we bathed in a canvas Army-surplus bathtub that was set up every other night in the kitchen), and the only heat was provided by an oil-burning stove that stood in the middle of the living room. To the best of my knowledge, the house was never painted in the 15 years that we lived there.

Our main claim to fame as kids was that we lived only a five-minute walk from the largest stockyards in the world. (I didn't learn until much later that people didn't want to be near a stockyards, and in fact would pay good money to live elsewhere.) It was breathtakingly massive, and to small boys' eyes, where anything more than two blocks seemed like far away, it was the most spectacular sight we could imagine: mile after mile of animal pens, barns, smoky taverns filled with hard-working, hard-drinking men (my father was one of them), slaughterhouses, and rendering plants that recycled carcasses, heads, guts, and blood, grinding it all into fine sausages and lard for pie crusts that graced the tables of homes across the Midwest. On Sundays, it was the happening place in town when farmers from the tri-state area (Nebraska, Kansas, and Iowa) trucked in cattle, pigs, and sheep for auction later in the week. Once two trucks collided and broke open, releasing a small herd of cattle that ran madly down the street and through our front yard. As we closed our eyes in sleep that night, we were sure that life couldn't get any better.

A stockyards of this size was an anachronism for a modern city, even in the early '60s, and the last of its kind in the United States; today, cattle are slaughtered in small-scale operations in rural areas across the country. Bill and I would roam the maze of wooden catwalks, peering down at scenes that have long since disappeared from most places in the world. Strictly speaking, we didn't belong there because the walkways were reserved for buyers who wanted to view the stock, but the good-natured workers usually let us stroll around to our hearts' content.

Many of our best boyhood adventures took place there. We'd see the blacksmith pound red-hot steel into horseshoes, watch sheep being shorn, or use a pitchfork to dig through mountains of manure to find worms for the next day's fishing trip (manure was a treasure trove of the fat red worms that fish seemed to love). We'd even brave the dimly lit, gag-inducing hog tunnels to spy on the employees when they shot rats in the pig pens. Sometimes we out-lived our welcome and were scolded, or better still, chased by irate cowboys who had other things to do than keep little boys from being trampled underfoot.

The entertainment options available to today's children—hundreds of TV channels (and in color, no less!), computers, elec-tronic games, cell phones, and MP3 players—were unimaginable to us. We were the last generation in America that had to make its own fun. I wouldn't have wanted it any other way.

Like everyone, I've had my ups and downs in life, especially as a teenager and during the frenetic, sleep-deprived years of medical school and specialty training, but when I look back on more than a half-century of life, I realize that I've been happy—truly, deeply happy—almost all of the time. My good fortune has made me ask: *Why me? Why have I had such a happy and fulfilling life?*

The best answer I can find is that I learned early in life that happiness means inner peace, not the outer realm of things. I was fortunate to grow up in a poor family in a conservative Midwestern town, and I was doubly blessed by having a mother who taught me what was really important in life. I learned to appreciate the little that I had as a child, and to be thankful and satisfied when I got more later on. As an adult, my focus shifted to family, so much so that I intentionally chose a slower-paced, lower-paying job in order to have more time with my wife and children. More recently, with the children grown and moved away and my working career wind-ing down, I've spent much of my free time thinking about the meaning of life and trying to make myself a better person.

Yet the perspective of the world we face each morning couldn't be more different from this. Rather than emphasize inter-nal development and the factors that are essential for happiness, conventional wisdom has an external focus, promising happiness when we have everything we want. For most people, this means some combination of more money, better job, nice vacation, more attractive body, sexy partner, new car, or bigger house. But even a brief period of honest self-reflection tells us that deep, lasting happiness can't possibly be attained from pleasurable activities and possessions. We've all read about men and women who seem to have it all—wealth, fame, talent, beauty, and athletic ability—and they're absolutely miserable and lead unfulfilling lives.

As a practical matter, we might as well forget about being happy most of the time—and the sooner we realize it the better—if our focus is on activities or material goals. It won't happen very often (how many "vacations of a lifetime" can someone have?), we'll eventually get bored with what we have and need something more exciting to entertain us (that new car starts to look a bit dated after a year or two), or time will change everything (our wonderful children, perhaps the main source of happiness in our lives, will grow up and move away). Yet the need for joy in our life is so strong that we must have it in one form or another, so our minds, dissatisfied with the lack of happiness in the present, daydream about pleasant memories from the past and imagine good times in the future. In the meantime, we miss the many opportunities for happiness that we have each day.

Saying that real happiness is due to internal factors doesn't imply that we have to live like ascetics and abandon the things that bring joy to our life. That would be both foolish and unnecessary. Rather, it's a matter of balance. Possessions and pleasurable activities aren't obstacles to happiness—they become problematic only when we obsess about them and they keep us from living in the present. But (1) knowing that happiness is internal, and (2) finding the wisdom and determination to change our lives so we can be happier, are much different. These issues, and the solutions that I discovered, are addressed in the remaining pages of this book.

9

The Essence of Happiness

Learning from Those Who Are Always Happy

Just as an arrow smith shapes an arrow to perfection with fire, so does the wise man shape his mind, which is fickle, unsteady, vulnerable, and erratic.

—The Dhammapada[14]

Our younger daughter Elizabeth adopted Jasper and Nala from a dog rescue center, twin mutts that looked like a mixture of Jack Russell terrier and long-haired dachshund. Over the years I spent a lot of time with them, and they loved me for what I was, never seeing my imperfections. They always reminded me of the aphorism, "Someday I hope to be the person that my dogs think I am."

When they were puppies, we took them on overnight backpacking trips in the Appalachian mountains. They wanted be good, but if they smelled a deer they took off running, and it was impossible to hold them back. We tried to be stern when they returned, but they were so happy to see us and so obviously sorry—in a way that only dog lovers can appreciate—that it was impossible to stay angry for long.

The four of us (Elizabeth, Jasper, Nala and me) would sleep in a tent with the screen door unzipped so the dogs could get out to "do their business," plus they were a good early warning system if bears wandered near the campsite. They got into trouble even at night. Once Nala come into the tent and puked up a dead mouse that she'd eaten, and sometimes they'd return from a late-night prowl absolutely reeking of something that they'd rolled in.

The most memorable misadventure was the hike in the Pocono mountains of Pennsylvania. As was their custom, they had disappeared from the trail to follow an interesting scent, usually a squirrel, when we heard unusually wild barking followed by yelps of pain. Both of them emerged from a thicket wearing prickly beards of porcupine quills stuck in their faces and inside their mouths. The hike ended at the veterinarian's office, where each dog was anesthetized so the quills could be removed. Instead of spending a fun night telling ghost stories and toasting marshmallows over a crackling fire, we slept in the car at an interstate rest stop. But the dogs were none the worse for wear.

From time to time, Chris and I would dog-sit when Elizabeth's job took her out of town. It was like watching grandchildren. As soon as we picked up the adorable pooches, our lives were transformed from the peace and quiet of a two-adult household to frenetic days with dogs who were accustomed to being the center of attention. They'd tussle with each other at all hours of the day and night, constantly wanted to go outside, and looked at us with those sad brown eyes that would make you drop whatever you were doing and play with them.

The biggest time commitment was the exercise. Elizabeth took them for two long walks each day, often off-leash in the national forest near her home, and they expected the same treatment at our house. When I lived in Asheville, I would often walk them on the Mountains to Sea Trail, a pristine 900-mile path that winds its way through the mountains of western North Carolina all the way to the Atlantic Ocean. When I removed their leashes they would take off as if shot out of a cannon, thundering down the path in search of adventure.

At first I just thought this was cute, the way that dogs were supposed to act, but after a while I paid closer attention to what was happening. Jasper and Nala saw things for what they were. A tree was a tree, a squirrel was a squirrel, and a friendly man who wanted to pet them was just a friendly man; they were totally satisfied with where they were and what they were doing; and they lived only in the present, never thinking about yesterday or tomorrow.

In a word, Jasper and Nala were happy. If only we could be so happy with so little.

Despite being the force that drives everything we do from morning until night, most people haven't given much thought to the nature of happiness. I certainly didn't, at least not until I grew older and more reflective. For me, happiness is a sense of inner peace. It's based on the same characteristics displayed by Jasper and Nala: wisdom, contentment, and mindfulness.

Wisdom means that we see things as they really are. This requires an understanding of what makes people (1) truly happy—family, friends, helping others, enjoying nature, being creative, and cultivating positive emotions like compassion, generosity, patience, and tolerance; (2) unhappy—preoccupation with possessions, power, and pleasure, and activities that promote negative emotions, such as arrogance, greed, anger, hatred, and envy; and then (3) knowing how to move our lives in the right direction.

Contentment is being satisfied with what we have. Whenever we compare ourselves to others, it's inevitable that we come out lacking in many cases. The solution is to spend less time thinking that our neighbor has a nicer car, that our brother-in-law lives in a bigger house, or that we're not as thin, young, athletic, or attractive as we'd like to be. Instead, we concentrate on the important things that we *do* have, such as friends, reasonably good health, a regular paycheck, and the beauty of each new day.

The third component of happiness is mindfulness, which means paying attention to what's going on now, moment to moment, rather than dwelling on what occurred in the past or what might happen in the future. By doing this, we appreciate the small details of our existence that bring so much joy to life.

There was a YMCA near my home that provided child care while parents exercised in the gym. Most days I would stop for a few minutes after my workout to look into the courtyard filled with frolicking three- and four-year-olds, and I reflected on the simple delights of children. In many ways they reminded me of Jasper and Nala. They saw things for what they were because they hadn't been conditioned by parents, teachers, or life experiences to think otherwise; they were totally satisfied with where they were and what they were doing, and they lived only in the present, constantly in motion until they collapsed from sheer exhaustion.

Simple tenets for happiness, yes, but far from simplistic. Cultivating wisdom, contentment, and mindfulness requires study, practice, and inner discipline. In fact, it takes a lifetime to master these principles, and most people don't even come close. What comes naturally to dogs and young children often seems so difficult for us.

10

My Unhappy Father

The High Personal Price of Unhappiness

Those desiring to escape from suffering hasten right toward suffering. With the very desire for happiness, out of delusion they destroy their happiness as if it were an enemy.

—Santideva (8th century CE), India[15]

As my father got on in years, he became more and more "his own man," which is a polite way of saying "odd." He'd sit on the front porch, which had an unobstructed view to passersby, in just his boxer shorts and a T-shirt. He preferred slippers, not shoes, whenever he left the house, which wasn't often. To his credit, he was on the vanguard of one fashion trend: he usually wore pajamas when he went to the grocery store or a fast food restaurant, a style that wasn't adopted by high school and college students for another 20 years.

Dad was an obsessive TV watcher, but the strange thing was that he didn't like it. Dramas, documentaries, nature programs, even comedies—he hated them all. When cable television became available, it just gave him more channels to complain about. The six o'clock news was his favorite program, and heaven help you if you said even one word during the broadcast. Periods of calm would be punctuated by outbursts of swearing at the appearance of a hated politician or an overrated celebrity. Not even the weather man was safe; his forecasts were greeted with derision and obscene exclamations of disbelief. If money were no object, he'd have put his foot through the TV screen at least once a week.

There was one show that he genuinely liked: the '70s hit *All in the Family*. He never realized that he was remarkably similar to Archie Bunker, the curmudgeon patriarch of the show, except that Dad lacked the softer, more insightful side that Archie showed from time to time.

Dad had remarkably little empathy. Once Mom fainted and he found her on the kitchen floor just as she was regaining consciousness. Instead of the concern that most husbands would display, he eyed her suspiciously from a distance and growled, "What the hell are you doing down there?" And there was the time at age eight when I ran home crying with a chipped front tooth after a bad fall, only to receive a slap in the face from him for being so careless. He was no better with his grandchildren. We'd arrive home for a visit, exhausted after an 850-mile, 17-hour non-stop drive with three young children, and he'd give us a perfunctory welcome, a few minutes of his time, and then turn on the TV.

Even as a child, I knew he was one of the unhappiest people that I'd known in my short life. I'd like to say that he got better when his days were numbered by heart disease and lung cancer, but it wouldn't be true.

We were poor, and my father had a physically demanding, blue-collar job. But he still had plenty of reasons to be happy: friends, good health (at least until alcohol and other excesses sent him to an early grave), a great wife, and two kids who studied hard and didn't get into trouble. Yet he was absolutely miserable.

If happiness is so important to everyone, why didn't he try harder to be happy? I think the main reason was lack of insight ("ignorance" from a Buddhist perspective). He knew that things weren't right, but he had no idea what was wrong or how to fix it.

So he spent the last 30 years of his life doing the same things that hadn't worked in the past.

There was also an element of denial. He wasn't well educated, but one doesn't need education to know that it's better to be happy than not. He set the bar for happiness so low that even the smallest pleasures—TV, a beer (lots of beer!) in the evening, and brief visits with his children and grandchildren—passed for happiness in his world.

Happiness is the focus of a traditional Buddhist story about two monks who were close friends until the day they died. One was reborn in heaven, the other as a worm in a dung pile. The one in heaven visited his old friend and related the wonders of his new life, entreating him to leave the dung pile and join him in heaven, even going so far as to try to pull him out of the pile. But the worm wouldn't budge. The life he knew—the perceived happiness of a warm, steaming pile of dung—was all that he wanted.

We've all known scores of chronically unhappy people like my father. It's so clear that they'd be better off if they woke up and saw what they were missing. But like the dung worm, satisfied with superficial happiness and crippled by ignorance of their situation, they find it easier to stay where they are rather than make the effort to be happier.

11

The Churlish Commuter

The High Social Price of Unhappiness

The angry man will defeat himself in battle as well as in life.

—Samurai maxim[16]

I witnessed a remarkable example of unhappiness early one winter morning while jogging in a large Asian city. I always took a short cut through the subway to avoid a busy intersection on the street above. As I weaved carefully among the homeless people who were sleeping on the concrete floor—it was a terrible place to spend the night, but far better for them than being exposed to the freezing weather at street level—I spotted a well-dressed commuter hurrying to catch a train. He stopped for a moment, looked around in disgust, and then kicked the hat off the head of one of the sleeping men. I thought for a second about putting the man's hat back on, but I didn't speak the local language and was afraid that he might wake up and think that I was stealing his hat. So I just kept running. To this day, I'm still shocked by this random act of unkindness that was directed toward a defenseless countryman.

Unhappiness is profound dissatisfaction that exists even in favorable circumstances. Not many people would admit to long-term unhappiness, perhaps because such an admission would be an acknowledgment of failure in a major part of life. But many people have dysfunctional personal relationships, living closed-minded lives filled with anger, selfishness, envy, and self-righteousness, and the way they treat co-workers and strangers is appalling. These negative emotions show, in a way that could never be captured by words alone, that such people are highly dissatisfied with the person they've become.

In the split second it took to see and reflect on the conduct of the subway passenger, I recognized that he was deeply unhappy with himself and with life in general. The episode reminded me of an Abigail Van Buren adage: "The best index of a person's character is how he treats people who can't do him any good and how he treats people who can't fight back."[17] By this criterion he would score very poorly indeed.

For a long time afterward I thought about the wider implications of this type of behavior. Unhappy people probably believe that they alone bear the burden of their dissatisfaction with life, but as the mean-spirited commuter showed so dramatically, there are far-reaching social consequences of unhappiness. That man would never join a volunteer organization that fed the homeless or provided services for the needy, and it's hard to imagine him engaging in any compassionate endeavor for the less fortunate. His feelings of hostility had blinded him to the broader needs of society. Unhappiness truly casts a wide net, ensnaring those who are unhappy, their loved ones and casual acquaintances, and even strangers.

12

The Zen of Computer Repair

Happiness Is in the Mind of the Beholder

Calmness in quietude is not real calm; when you can be calm in the midst of activity, this is the true state of nature. Happiness in comfort is not real happiness; when you can be happy in the midst of hardship, then you see the true potential of the mind.

—Huanchu Daoren (1572-1620), China[18]

Our son Michael lived in Singapore, 10,000 miles away, so it was cause for a major celebration when he came home for his annual visit. This made it all the more unfortunate when things didn't go as planned. He had a large music collection on his computer and wanted to add some of the songs that I owned. He'd bring my laptop down to the family room every evening so he could be with the family and still monitor the file transfer between our computers. This worked fine until he dropped my computer down the stairs.

At first the damage seemed minor, but the computer wouldn't start properly, so I had to send it to the repair shop in California. Three days later they called me with the bad news: to fix it, the entire hard drive had to be erased. It wasn't a total disaster—most of my files had been saved to an external drive—but it would take me a while to get everything back to normal since I'd have to reinstall and customize many of the programs.

I started the reinstallation as soon as the computer was returned, feeling very Zen and telling myself, "You're busy and don't really have time for this, but it has to be done." As the day wore on, I could see this wouldn't be a quick fix—I didn't finish that day or even the next. It would have helped if I'd had more expertise with computers, but I was doing most things for the first time. I kept getting maddening error messages about missing system files, and I absolutely couldn't reestablish the wireless Internet connection with my router. All told, it took about 15 hours to get things right.

My wife bore the brunt of my frustration. The words I spoke parroted what I'd read in all of the Buddhist books: "Everything's fine. There's no reason to be upset." (I would have loved to see if the ivory-tower philosophers who wrote these books would have thought that "everything was fine" if they were in my place.) But I couldn't hide how I really felt: irritation and borderline anger because Michael had dropped the computer, because I didn't know how to fix it, and mostly because reality was what it was. Chris listened patiently until the second day, and then she bluntly asked, "Aren't you Buddhists supposed to be good at accepting reality?"

I slinked off to my room, embarrassed by my behavior, and later thankful for such an honest assessment from someone I trusted. Clearly, I had a lot of learning and practice ahead of me.

When this episode occurred I had been studying Buddhism for several years, meditating daily, and improving my outlook on life at a rate that I hadn't thought possible. I was feeling a bit smug and thinking, *Hey, this isn't so hard!* But after my wife's gentle rebuke, I was pretty hard on myself for the next few days. A dropped computer was such a trivial event in the grand scheme of things—nobody was hurt and the repairs weren't too expensive—and yet I wasn't able to put it behind me and stay happy all the time. It made me wonder how I'd do when confronted with the truly difficult challenges of life, such as serious illness and the death of loved ones.

As I reflected on what had gone wrong, I remembered a Buddhist story that I found helpful. Three Buddhist monks are looking at a flag blowing in the wind. One says the flag is moving, the other counters that the wind is moving, and the senior monk resolves the disagreement by saying, "No, the mind is moving." All three saw the same thing, but only the senior monk recognized that the mind was putting its own spin on what was happening. It's the same for everything in life—thoughts, conversations, and dropped computers. We label events as good or bad from our own limited and sometimes selfish perspective, and then tell ourselves that we're either happy or sad as a result.

I learned a few lessons from this episode. First, there were different ways to view the situation: (1) "Too bad. The computer's broken and it will take two days to fix it," and (2) "What luck! The computer's broken, but it will be back to normal in two days!" Second, I understood that it was silly to pretend that I wasn't upset after my computer bounced down a flight of stairs. If having a broken computer made me feel good, I could have thrown it down the stairs myself once or twice a week! The problems we face in life are real and often very unpleasant, and to pretend otherwise is to ignore reality. Yet these challenges are almost always manageable, especially if we've already developed the mental discipline to deal with them when they arise.

Finally, I realized how much progress I'd made in the last few years. My old solution for dealing with this type of problem was a long, anger-driven run in the woods to exhaust myself and hopefully forget about reality by the time I got home. Now, however, I stayed relatively calm from start to finish—which would have been unthinkable in the past—even when Michael told me that he'd broken the computer. I remember hearing myself say, "Oh? You dropped the computer? That's OK. I'm sure it won't be hard to fix." My emotional response was also mainly limited to irritation—I didn't follow my usual habit of exploding like a madman and totally losing control—and most importantly, I was mindful of my emotions as they developed from moment to moment. Instead of being a major disaster during Michael's only visit that year, it turned out to be yet another memorable event in the rich history that our family shared.

I wasn't glad that any of this happened, but I learned important lessons without too much pain. For weeks thereafter, I thought about my prior two years of study and effort, and cheerfully said to myself, "Yes, it's working!"

13

Air Sickness Bags and Dancing Tots

Waking Up to the Joy of Each New Day

Someday I'll be a weather-beaten skull resting on a grass pillow, serenaded by a stray bird or two, no more enduring than last night's dream.

—Ryokan (1758-1831), Japan[19]

I may be a physician, but that doesn't mean I can't have crazy ideas about health. Sanitation is one of them. I had an unproven theory that there are only so many germs in the world, and once you've been exposed to lots of them, you'll be immune to most of them. Experience proved me wrong.

My approach was simple—eat the local fare and drink tap water—and it seemed to be working. After 15 years of international travel, I'd had food poisoning only a handful of times—in India, Mexico, South Africa, and Thailand—all relatively mild infections that were more annoying than disabling. An episode in Shanghai made me change my ways.

I had a free day on Saturday, so I spent time visiting museums and parks, bargaining with shopkeepers, and sampling local delicacies from street vendors. (I did have the good judgment to pass on the "bat on a stick" that was sold at one of the food kiosks.) All was well until I reached the airport the following day. It was lunchtime and I should have been hungry after my small breakfast. I wasn't. In fact, I didn't even want to think about food. In the space of 30 minutes, I went from normal to feverish, dead tired, and nauseous.

If I were at home I would have said, "Thank heavens I don't have to go anywhere," and I would have stayed in bed for the rest of the day, attended by loved ones hovering nearby with offers of medicine and chicken soup. Instead, I was about to board a flight from Shanghai to Hong Kong and wondering how I could walk the two blocks to the departure gate. I didn't dare step on the moving walkway; even the thought of motion made me feel worse. I shuffled along, dragging my briefcase behind me, with the young, old, and infirm passing me like I was standing still.

My game plan was to get on board, fall asleep immediately, and ride out the storm, but my condition was worsening by the minute. Waves of nausea flowed through me, each accompanied by hot flashes and profuse sweating. And we were still on the ground. I reached for my air sickness bag, just in case. I wasn't sure how sick I might be, so I turned to the passenger next to me, who was already uneasy after observing my performance thus far, and asked, "Excuse me, but would you mind if I use your air sickness bag? I'm not sure mine will be enough." She nodded, gave me the best smile she could muster, gathered her belongings, and was gone. I had the row to myself, and I needed every bit of it.

I was asleep when we took off, but nausea forced me awake. Breathing deeply, I summoned all the self-control that I had left, but to no avail. I was sick—dreadfully, violently sick—as sick as I'd ever been in my life. I was wrong about the air sickness bags; I needed four of them before I was done. The cabin attendants were angels who earned every penny of their salaries that day. I don't know if any of the nearby passengers demanded refunds, but it would have been justified.

Three hours later we landed. I must have looked terrible because the flight crew asked if I needed a wheelchair to take me off the plane. I thought long and hard about it, but finally refused. The SARS epidemic was very much on everyone's mind at the time, and all the airports had inspection booths to screen arriving passengers. A pale, feverish man in a wheelchair was certain to attract attention —if they didn't stop me, who would they ever stop? So I dragged myself off the plane, through immigration and customs, and finally to my hotel room and bed. After what I'd been through, lying flat on a surface that wasn't moving was all that I wanted in the world. I was so weak and dehydrated that I couldn't get out of bed for 12 hours.

I was in peak health for a middle-aged man, with enviable blood pressure and cholesterol levels, and no significant risk factors for cardiovascular disease, except for an awful family history of heart disease—the Pokorski men had an annoying habit of dropping dead from heart attacks at an early age. Yet I might have died that day from a gastrointestinal bug so small that it was visible only with a high-powered microscope. What a fragile hold I had on life!

This episode was a real spiritual awakening for me. I began a concerted study of Buddhism, reading everything I could find on the subject. I was the embodiment of the adage, "When the student is ready, the teacher will appear." One book that was especially helpful was *1,001 Pearls of Buddhist Wisdom.*[20] It wasn't because of the many insightful observations culled from 2,500 years of Buddhist teachings, although these alone made it worth reading. Rather, it was what I realized when I reached the end: almost all the pearls were written by authors who were long dead. If these people— scholars and ascetics who'd spent their lives teaching, meditating, and practicing their beliefs—were dead, I understood in a very personal way that the same thing would happen to me. This realiza- tion marked the beginning of the end of my fear of aging, illness, and death.

One of the many things that Buddhists do well is to confront the reality of death. This isn't a morbid preoccupation with our eventual demise. Far from it. Buddhists are proponents of many upbeat ideas, such as, "The main goal in life is to be happy." Rather, the intent of their emphasis on the inevitability of death is to remind us of how little time we have on this earth, even if we're alive for 100 years, so we need to live each day as if it were our last. This may sound trite and Pollyannaish, but it's possible and even common in certain situations.

For example, many people achieve their greatest happiness after a serious illness or a traumatic event because they gain an appreciation of the joys of life. There are even books and magazines devoted entirely to this subject, with people believing that a diagnosis of cancer was the best thing that ever happened to them.[21] While the adage "Better late than never" clearly applies in these cases, it's unfortunate that the wake-up call comes late in life or when the time left to us is cut short by illness.

In his book *Ruling Your World*, Sakyong Mipham observes, "It's never too late to change our mind, but when we find ourselves on our deathbed, it's too late to change our life."[22] I found this to be useful advice for the procrastinator in me who planned to deal with the important concerns of life—why we're here, how to be happier, and the certainty of death—but to deal with them tomorrow or the day after, when the kids finished college, the mortgage was paid off, and work slowed down a bit. After my experience in Shanghai, I knew that it was finally time to seriously consider these issues.

Another influential book at this stage of my life was *How to Be Happy All the Time*, by yoga master Paramahansa Yogananda. In addressing the certainty of suffering in the future, he stated, "It is ingratitude to the Giver of all gifts to forget the healthy smiles enjoyed for fifty years just because you have been sick for six months. There is no sense in unbalancing your mind and forgetting years of happiness by taking too seriously the sorrows of a few weeks or a few months."[23]

This is yet another way of saying that life isn't always going to be smooth sailing. When problems arise, we need to keep things in perspective—balance of the mind, as Yogananda puts it—and remember the many happy times that we've already had. It also reaffirmed what I was beginning to understand: aging, illness, and death were not anomalies or reversals of fortune; they were normal, the way that life was supposed to be.

My life got even happier from then on. I was amazed by the many joyful things that could bring a smile to my face if I simply paid attention. There was one special time when I was waiting in the Seoul airport for a flight to Bangkok. The boarding area was crowded, all the seats were taken (in part because some inconsiderate people had put their luggage and duty-free purchases on the seats next to them!), and many people were angry because the flight was delayed. I sat down on the floor and waited.

That's when I observed a scene that made it all worthwhile: a little Thai girl, maybe four years old, her hair braided into pigtails, and wearing the smallest imaginable pair of bellbottom jeans with pink decorative stitching around the cuffs. She was in nonstop motion—running, dancing, and talking to anyone and everyone. I've never had a fear of flying, but I still thought, *If the plane goes down en route to Bangkok, it goes down. Right now, I'm as happy as I can be!*

14

Grapes, Germs, and Good Times: The Korean Orphanage, Part 2

Learning How to Be Happier

When one door to happiness closes, another opens; but often we look so long at the closed door that we do not see the one which has been opened for us.

—Helen Keller (1880-1968), USA[24]

The Korean-English books that I had purchased for my students at the orphanage in Seoul were an instant hit, even with the boys. Nonetheless, it's hard to hold the attention of young children. One little guy quickly became bored. His solution? Put a pair of plastic vampire teeth into his mouth and chase the other kids around the room, and then pass them around to the other kids who were only too happy to wear them, unwashed (yuck!). Order was restored when I confiscated the teeth and set them on a high cabinet, which the same boy tried to scale by using his chair as a ladder.

We were midway through the English lesson when the bell sounded for dinner. It was a reminder of where my educational objectives for the day ranked in five-year-old minds: far below food! Without hesitation they bolted from the room with me in tow, one child pulling on each of my hands. The dining room would have been unrecognizable to most people: a refrigerator and a sink, no chairs, and long rectangular tables with tops about 12 inches off the ground. The children, small and flexible, sat cross-legged on the polished wooden floor. I sat down with them and tried to find a comfortable position. Thankfully, I practiced yoga or it would have killed me.

Everyone was happy to see me, since most volunteers didn't eat with the children. The food was good and plentiful: French toast, soup, and grapes for dessert. I did some table hopping so I could join each group. There were tables for older boys, older girls, and my favorite, the three- to four-year-olds' table. It was a great teaching opportunity. We learned milk/white milk, cup/my cup/your cup… nose picking. Just a joke! A lot of that goes on, but we had more important words to learn during our lesson.

I quickly let go of my concerns about cleanliness and hygiene. These 50 kids shared all of their germs, and no one even thought of washing their hands before dinner—like a lot of adults I've known over the years—and in the rush to take our places around the table, neither did I. One of the toddlers waddled over with a tiny handful of grapes and laughed in joy as he stuffed each one into my mouth. Like the children, I was caught up in the excitement, living totally in the present, with nowhere else to go and nothing else to think about. What an absolutely wonderful experience!

That night I was especially mindful of how my emotions were changing from moment to moment. I was sad to leave the children at the end of the lesson. Dead tired, yes, like a middle-aged man who had just cared for 10 highly spirited grandchildren, and homesick for my wife and children. But the main sensation was one of profound happiness.

I had always been happy, but during the last few years, and particularly after my move to Seoul, my level of happiness and life satisfaction had increased immeasurably. I didn't credit luck, fate, or a good business decision to quit my job in Connecticut and join a

Korean company. Rather, my increased happiness was due to the long hours of study and meditation that I'd spent learning how to be happier.

Most people think that happiness comes naturally without much effort on our part—either we have it or we don't. So when we're not as happy as we'd like to be, it never occurs to us that we're the ones who are responsible for our current situation. Instead, the blame falls on parents, ex-spouses, our jobs, a less-than-perfect body, missed opportunities in life, or just bad luck. As a result, we stay trapped in thought and behavior patterns that guarantee we'll never be as happy as we could be.

The Dalai Lama emphasizes the importance of cultivating happiness in the same way that we'd approach any challenging academic or life-changing endeavor.[25] First, education and learning are needed. This means focused study using a combination of reading, classes, discussion groups, or a spiritual advisor (combined in whatever way works best for us). In my case, when I started this process I didn't know what I didn't know, so I intentionally cast a wide net that included the study of atheism, Buddhism, Christianity, Hinduism, Islam, Judaism, philosophy, and secular humanism. Why the diversity of my search? The old ways weren't working, and I wanted new ideas and different perspectives. Over time, I found that Buddhism was the right path for me.

The second step for cultivating happiness is determination. We resolve to make the changes that are needed to live a happier, more meaningful life. Strong determination will see us through the inevitable periods when we relapse into our old ways of thinking. This kind of inner transformation—we are literally "changing our minds"—calls for sustained effort, and early on I found inspiration from the Buddhist aphorism, "The path is the goal." To achieve my goal—to be a happier, better person—I spent each day trying to be a happier, better person. It didn't happen overnight, but little by little, I moved forward.

Finally, we need to make a concerted effort, both external and internal, to increase our level of happiness. External effort means that we practice what we learned from our studies, such as substituting compassion and tolerance for anger and hatred, reminding ourselves that happiness is a state of mind and not a bank balance, and finding new ways each day to help others. The internal effort involves a regular period of quiet reflection on what's truly important in life. Meditation is one of the best ways to facilitate wisdom and internal growth, because we're alone with just our thoughts.

Other possibilities include religious services and spiritual practices wherein we can think deeply about what it takes to lead a more meaningful life. Less helpful are ceremonies that are heavy on ritual and light on self-reflection—as evidenced by the number of people worldwide who regularly attend these services but are still unhappy.[‡] It's also important to find the right balance between external and internal effort. Without acquiring the wisdom (the internal part) that leads to a happy and meaningful life, we won't know what to do, and without the practical application (the external part), we'll simply be armchair spiritualists. Neither extreme will move us much closer to our goal.

These steps explain how to develop the mental discipline needed to lead a happier life. The approach seems counterintuitive for something that we thought came naturally, and even the choice of words—focused study, strong determination, and concerted effort—conveys the idea that a fair amount of work is required. But just as we resolved earlier in life to spend years or even decades learning to become a skilled carpenter, teacher, engineer, musician, or the best parent that we could be, the decision *Once and for all, I'll*

[‡] For all faiths and secular belief systems, there's a wide spectrum of "lived spirituality." Some people leave the weekly service invigorated anew for living a life of happiness, kindness, and generosity, and others just leave after fulfilling an obligation, like paying the monthly utility bill.

do what it takes to be happier, represents a major turning point in our lives.

Mindfulness

Aware that life is available only in the present moment and that it is possible to live happily in the here and now, I am committed to training myself to live deeply each moment of daily life. I will try not to lose myself in dispersion or be carried away by regrets about the past, worries about the future, or craving, anger or jealousy in the present. I will practice mindful breathing to come back to what is happening in the present moment. I am determined to learn the art of mindful living by touching the wondrous, refreshing, and healing elements that are inside and around me, and by nourishing seeds of joy, peace, love, and understanding in myself, thus facilitating the work of transformation and healing in my consciousness.

—Thich Nhat Hanh[26]

15

Peashooters and Police Cars

Living Life in the Present ... or Not

Having a great time; wish I were here.

—Buddhist proverb

There is no adult equivalent to summer vacation for children, a time in life when one is allowed—even expected—to have fun for months and months at a time, with no deadlines, commutes, alarm clocks, or bills to pay. Your time is your own, and the only challenge each morning is to find ever more inventive ways to spend the day.

It was August 1961, and after 60-plus days of nonstop vacation, we were finally running out of ideas for fun. That's when my brother Bill and I teamed up with Gary, our eleven-year-old cousin and babysitter for the day, on a new scheme: terrorize the neighborhood with peashooters.

We purchased heavy duty plastic straws and three large bags of dried peas from the corner store, and we walked to the end of our street, only half a block away but a distance of some importance for how events unfolded. Our plan was masterful in its simplicity: perch in a partially wooded lot that overlooked L Street, the four-lane road that led to the stockyards, and shoot the passing cars and trucks, using only one pea at a time to avoid detection.

We spent a delightful hour bombarding the unsuspecting motorists, but the novelty started to wear off, and we were ready to move on to something else. The problem was that we still had almost a full bag of peas among the three of us. A unanimous decision was reached immediately: load all of the remaining peas into our mouths and shoot machine gun-style at the same vehicle, then turn tail and run home.

Our target was a car in the fourth lane of the road, outermost from where we sat and moving right to left. It was about to pass a cattle truck in the third lane moving in the same direction. We couldn't see the target very well because it was on the far side of the truck—only its wheels were visible—so our plan was to fire a few seconds early so that our pea fusillade would arrive just as the car emerged from the other side of the truck.

After an hour of practice, we'd perfected our aim. The three of us let fly just as the car appeared, peppering it with dozens of peas. It was the culmination of a wonderful adventure, an event that would live forever in the annals of kiddom—until the targeted vehicle, a police car, fully appeared. The officer stopped in the middle of the road, put on his siren and lights, and started to make a U-turn in our direction. By then we were hoofing it back home, running like our lives depended on it. Actually, our backsides depended on it, because if my dad found out about this I wouldn't be able to sit down for a week.

I wasn't fleet of foot, and Bill was positively slow. Then there was Gary, a good 30 pounds overweight, which was a lot for someone his age. He was still lumbering along as Bill and I disappeared into the house, and even then he might have made it if we hadn't locked the door behind us, leaving him to his own fate. There he stood as the policeman stopped in front of our house, wailing away on the front door with his fat fists, begging us to let him in.

Our adventure had a surprisingly good ending. The policeman must have had young boys of his own, because he went easy on us. We got a stern warning and promised to never do it again, which we didn't, and our parents didn't find out until we were old enough to tell the story without getting the punishment that we deserved.

None of us was aware of the seriousness of the situation, and we never even considered the possibility that we might cause a bad accident. Our only excuse—and it wasn't a very good one—was that we were children at the time. It would be reassuring to think that lack of awareness was confined to the young, and that maturity and mindfulness went hand in hand, but that isn't the case. In all stages of life, we aren't paying attention most of the time.

Mindfulness is one of the most important skills that we need to develop during our lives. It makes us better spouses, parents, and friends; we're more aware of subtle emotions and calls for help that come our way; and from a practical, even selfish perspective, we experience more of the mundane details of each day that make life worth living.

Yet the unspoken plan for many of us goes something like this: When I'm older—after I've paid off the mortgage, put the kids through college, and work slows down a bit—I'll have more time for myself and others, and I'll learn to be more mindful and appreciative of the world around me. And while we're waiting for things to slow down, time marches on, and we miss the countless opportunities that occur each day for us to experience a happier, more fulfilling life.

My wife has the highest natural level of mindfulness of anyone I've ever known, and it's always "on" regardless of how tired she is or how many distractions there are. She seems to experience almost everything. As she puts it, she's constantly "scanning the horizon," finding funky shops, cozy restaurants, and interesting people. She uses all of her senses—seeing the quiver of a lip trying to hide an emotion, hearing the mismatch between what's said and how it's said, or sometimes just feeling that "something's not right." For a while I even thought she was clairvoyant, because she was able to predict what would happen to the people around her.

But after years of marriage I discovered her secret: she always stays in the present, fully engaged with what's happening around her and aware of all the humdrum events that make no impression on me. It was a skill that she used to enrich the lives of family and friends, and on a number of occasions, to turn lives in a better direction because she was "there" when I wasn't.

16

The Purple Raincoat

Not Being There When We're Really Needed

Now has never happened before.

—Buddhist proverb

One of my favorite times with our children was Maple Sugar Day, a Saturday in late February when I'd join other fathers for an outing to a nearby "sugar shack" where we could see how maple syrup was made. The process was amazing even to adults. Metal spigots were pounded into maple trees, buckets were attached, and 12 hours later the workers would return to collect a bucketful of sap that was distilled into some of the finest maple syrup in the world. We'd tour the facility, the children would play in the 19th-century barn, and we'd end the day with fresh pancakes topped with minutes-old hot maple syrup.

This was the first visit for our younger daughter Elizabeth, and she was overjoyed to join an outing that she'd heard so much about from her older brother and sister. She wore her brand new purple raincoat, which she absolutely adored. When she put on the little hood, there wasn't a cuter three-year-old girl on the planet.

We parked the car and headed for the barn, slogging along as best we could. With the warm weather and melting snow, the path was so muddy that we had to struggle to keep our boots from being sucked off with each step. Then disaster struck. Elizabeth slipped and fell face-first, covering her hands, face, and cherished purple raincoat with mud. She lifted herself to her knees, tears in her eyes and arms outstretched for her father to rescue her.

Then I did something very strange. Rather than run over, pick her up, dry her tears, and tell her that everything would be all right, I opened my backpack to get my camera, thinking that it would be an unforgettable memory. I was right. That was her very first memory in life: falling down in her new purple raincoat and having to wait for help until her father took a picture. Like so many of the other dumb things that I've done in life, I've had to live with this mistake. This one has been especially painful.

Well, here I was again, 25 years after the summer vacation of 1961, still with the common sense of a nine-year-old boy shooting peas at police cars. If there was ever a time in life when I needed a big dollop of mindfulness so I could stay fully in the present and recognize what needed to be done—in this case, comfort a crying child, not take a picture—this was it. And I failed. Miserably.

After moving to Asheville, I spent a lot of time in the mountains, where I would take leisurely strolls, long distances hikes, or strenuous trail runs. Without a doubt, the greatest mindfulness always came during the slow-paced strolls. I could see the trees, wildflowers, and rock formations; hear the birds singing and the water flowing; and smell the richness of the earth in the spring and the mustiness of fallen leaves in the fall. I lost some of the appreciation of these things with the long hikes—I was often hungry and tired, or my mind just wandered—and during the trail runs, I experienced almost nothing of what was happening around me because all of my attention was focused on the rocks and tree roots along the trail.

Many people live their lives somewhere between the pace of the long distance hike and the trail run, moving so quickly that they miss the precious details of life: the smiles of children at play, flowers growing between cracks in the sidewalk, and the simple pleasure of idle moments without the need for accomplishment. This need for speed isn't imposed solely by a stressful job or an over-committed family schedule. Rather, it's generated internally as we try to squeeze more and more into each day. The outcome is predictable: exhaustion at the end of another long, frustrating day; anger as we face resistance while trying to shape events and outcomes to suit our needs; and unhappiness as we daydream about a slower, more mindful life that we can imagine but have no real intention to pursue.

There are no "do-overs" in life; if there were, changing the outcome of that day with my daughter in late February would be near the top of my list. I was lucky, though. Of our three children, Elizabeth's the one who most shares my love for the outdoors. During the three decades that followed that regrettable episode, we've camped in the mountains, hiked through torrential rainstorms, and yes, fallen together in the mud. Not really do-overs, but as close as I'll get in this life. And most of the time, I've gotten it right.

17

Three Parks in Seoul:
The Korean Orphanage, Part 3

Being Here Is the Best Place to Be

For everything there is a season, and a time for every matter under heaven.

—Ecclesiastes 3:1 (English Standard Version)

With a heavy heart I entered the courtyard of the Korean orphanage on a warm, sunny afternoon in mid-November. After seeing the children once or twice a week for almost three months, I was returning to the United States. The same three-year-old boy who always met me at the door, arms outstretched for a big hug, was there as usual. I was really going to miss this place. Fortunately, my job at the Korean insurance company required me to spend much of the year in Seoul, so I would be returning fairly soon.

I was one of the gang now, and it felt wonderful. The children really liked me, not because I was a good teacher, but because we laughed and played a lot, and because I was willing to sit on the floor with them—and on occasion, even under the table—if that's what it took for them to learn English. The lessons were so popular that I now taught two classes each week: one for five-year-olds, and another for six-year-olds.

Bittersweet memories were common. There was the nine-year-old boy who sometimes helped me with the younger children because he spoke better English than most of the others. One day he excitedly told me that he was moving to the United States. I couldn't understand when or where, so I asked the director. I'll never forget the sad look on her face as she shook her head. His English was so good because he had been on a trial adoption with an Australian family that lived in a small town outside of Seoul. The prospective parents had returned home, and no one knew if he would be adopted or not—but he didn't know any of this.

More heartbreaking still was the story of Sungbin Park, the wonderful six-year-old boy who loved to learn. He would sit on a tiny chair next to me and we'd pronounce words together from A to Z: apple, boy, cat, and so on. One day he made a picture of two stickmen—a big one (me) and a little one (him)—and then he drew a heart between the two men to show how much he cared for me. I almost cried—and would have if I hadn't been with the children. The picture hangs in my study at home today.

Some weeks later, the director told me that Hyunju Park, a girl in my class for five-year-olds, was his sister. As hard as it was for me to believe, she left the room for a few minutes and then returned with Jinsoo Park, a three-year-old boy who was the youngest child in the family. Three of the most adorable children that you'll ever see, any one of whom most people would love to have as a son or a daughter, and very likely destined to be split up and adopted by three different families.

After the lesson, I walked back to the subway through a middle-class neighborhood of modest homes, outdoor vegetable stands, family-run restaurants, and streets filled with children playing and old people hobnobbing with friends, and all so safe that young women could walk home at all hours of the day or night knowing that they had nothing to fear. I reflected on what represented happiness for so many people in the world: big bank accounts, powerful jobs, oversized homes, imported cars, fancy restaurants, and fashionable clothes. I clearly didn't need any of these things to be happy. A stickman drawing and a hug from an orphaned child meant far more to me.

I hadn't felt like this for a long time. Everyone knows that we're supposed to live in the present, and we can all quote self-help adages along the lines of *The past is only a memory and the future hasn't happened yet. There is only the present.* Which is easy to say when we're sitting quietly at a religious service or reading a book at home. It's a lot harder to follow this advice every second of the day.

For much of my life, I had a habit of mentally chatting with myself instead of paying full attention to the matters at hand. I was good at it. I'd switch into autopilot and think about a pleasant memory from the past, or maybe a regret for something I did or didn't do, and then I'd shift to the future and consider my plans for later in the day. Of course, the present was always there, like a computer program that was running in the background while I thought about something else—always available, but accessed infrequently. It's easy to see why so many people reach the end of their days and wonder, *Where did life go?*

Over the years I've gotten much better. Meditation helps me keep my mind focused: each morning I set an intention for the day, such as practicing patience or humility, and I keep returning to this goal throughout the day. Sometimes I even set my watch to chime on the hour as a reminder to be mindful of the present. It's surprisingly easy when you get into the habit. I used to plan out my entire day while taking a shower, getting dressed, and driving to work. Now, I just pay attention to what I'm doing. Not only do I stay in the present, but my stress level has plummeted. It's hard to feel uptight when all you're thinking about is putting on your socks.

I often count my blessings for the good life that I've had, and among these blessings was being fully present whenever I visited the children at the orphanage. There would be other fun times, but these were once-in-a-lifetime events. Yet when you think about it, isn't everything in life a one-time event, only our minds aren't there to notice it?

18

Mother's Intuition Saves the Day

Listening As a Key Skill for Mindfulness

Aware that lack of communication always brings separation and suffering, I am committed to training myself in the practice of compassionate listening and loving speech. I will learn to listen deeply without judging or reacting and refrain from uttering words that can create discord or cause the community to break. I will make every effort to keep communications open and to reconcile and resolve all conflicts, however small.

—Thich Nhat Hanh[27]

My wife Chris is always seeing things that I miss. There was the time she told me that one of the senior people at my company would be leaving. How did she know? We were talking with the executive's wife at a party when the woman made an innocent comment about remodeling their kitchen, and then she paused, dropped her eyes for a moment, and quickly changed the subject. To my wife, who could talk about kitchen design for hours and hours (and has), it seemed very strange that someone wouldn't follow up on such an interesting topic. Plus, the woman's speech pattern and body language, for just that fraction of a second, suggested that she'd divulged a family secret.

Chris surmised that her husband must be looking for a job in another city. I was highly doubtful of her prediction—as far as I could tell, he was very happy with his current position. Besides, I didn't see anything suspicious about the woman's comments or tone of voice, although I must admit that I wasn't paying much attention during the conversation and had completely zoned out when I heard the words "kitchen" and "remodeling" in the same sentence. But sure enough, six months later he quit the company and moved out of town.

I became a believer in the importance of listening when Chris made an observation that forever changed the life of one of our children. Lisa was attending college in Florida, and everything seemed to be going well. Then one day she called home and asked Chris if she could transfer to a school in the Midwest. If I were the one who was talking with Lisa, I would have done my best to change her mind. After all, we were paying for three children to attend college and our budget would only stretch so far, and I would have reached that conclusion almost immediately with little thought on the matter.

Fortunately, I wasn't the one on the telephone, and it wasn't a coincidence that Lisa raised this issue with her mother and not me. As the two of them talked, Chris was listening to more than just the words. The first thing she said when she hung up the phone was, "Something's wrong. I can feel it." She explained that Lisa was talking a little faster and louder than normal, and there was a subtle sense of urgency in her voice. Chris listed everything that was happening in Lisa's life: her school had a great academic reputation and a fantastic location near the beach, she was getting good grades, she always sounded happy on the phone, and she had a steady boyfriend.

Boyfriend. That was it. She put two and two together—a request to leave an apparently ideal situation plus a voice that conveyed much more than just words. She knew that the boyfriend had to be the problem. Chris talked me into allowing the move. Lisa transferred, fell in love with a young man at the new school, and they were married a few years later. It's no exaggeration to say that

Lisa's life went in a completely different direction because her mother was able to listen with more than just her ears.

Many people are poor, even abysmal listeners. Some of us aren't even listeners at all; we're talkers. Instead of listening, our mind is racing ahead and planning what to say when it's our turn to talk, and we're willing to interrupt if necessary to get our points across. Others are passive listeners. We think about something else as the words of the conversation fade into the background, while our body language says, "I have no interest in what you're talking about."

Then there are people like Chris, who see things that seem to be hidden from the rest of us. This is sometimes called intuition or a sixth sense, but after 38 years of marriage, I've learned that she does it by being mindful of everything that's happening around her. People with this ability experience reality in a way that amazes the rest of us, and it's no exaggeration to say they sometimes know what's going to happen before it happens. Much of this ability starts with being a good listener.

What makes good listeners? First, they're able to concentrate and not let their minds wander away when the conversation turns in a direction that doesn't particularly interest them. Instead, they stay involved, ask questions, and use body language to confirm that they're paying close attention. Second, they hear not only the words, but the choice of words, tone of voice, loudness, and how fast someone is talking. They also listen with their eyes, watching to see if the speaker's gestures, posture, and facial expressions match the verbal communication. Finally, good listeners have a highly developed emotional intelligence that allows them to sense emotions in themselves and others. What amazes me the most is that gifted listeners are able to do all of this—hear, see, and feel—in real time as the events unfold in front of them.

The above definition of what makes a good listener is one you'll find in many self-help books. Personally, I find this overly complicated for day-to-day use. There are just too many things to remember during a conversation: Am I listening carefully? Watching for non-verbal clues? Straining (yes, straining, because it's not a bit natural for me) to sense the emotions of the other person? To make it easier, some books suggest that you divide the task into smaller increments, such as, Devote one day to hearing just the words, the next day to listening carefully to the tone of voice, etc. I find this every bit as difficult; by the end of the first hour, I've forgotten what I'm supposed to be doing, and I'm no better of a listener at the end of the day.

I found some practical advice that's helped me a lot. During a conversation, just remember that the most important person in the world is the one that you're with.[28] The rationale is simple. Since you can communicate with only one person at a time, give that person your full attention. It's really a short cut through all of the overly detailed suggestions for listening, seeing, and feeling. Just imagine how focused you'd be if you were talking to a world-famous politician, religious leader, entertainer, or your husband or wife during the magical first months of your relationship. This one person would get your full and undivided attention, and it would seem effortless.

I'm ashamed to think of the many times when I didn't really pay attention to what my wife was saying, perhaps because I was exhausted or frustrated after a hard day at work, but inexcusable nonetheless. Her exact words, "You're not listening to me," are well known to every husband in the world, and maybe a few wives, too. What she really meant was, "You're not interested in me and what I did today." My paying attention to her stories about the children and her volunteer work at their schools was exactly what she needed to feel respected and worthwhile. One of the unexpected dividends of my interest in Buddhism and meditation has been that I've become a far better listener. Now I sometimes sense that Chris isn't really listening to me, but I have the common sense to just let it go. After the many earlier years of living with the unmindful me, she's earned it.

My main challenge today is trying to listen with my emotions. There wasn't much emphasis on emotional expression in our family when I was a child. In fact, my father would sometimes explode in anger with little or no provocation, so it was best to keep your feelings to yourself. My medical training didn't help either. As a young man in my early twenties, I would see the most horrific accidents and illnesses, things that even now I keep tucked away in a part of my memory where I seldom go. I had to protect myself from getting involved—it was far too much for me to handle at that young age—so I stayed as detached and unemotional as possible. Over the years, I've learned that if we're not careful, emotional detachment can become a habit in other aspects of our lives, including listening.

Chris' intuition, starting with her remarkable listening skills, changed Lisa's life that day. As I look back on this event, I feel both gratitude and uneasiness: gratitude that Lisa's mother was there when she was needed, because clearly her father wasn't, and uneasiness because there were times when it was my turn to be there for someone, to help him or her make difficult choices, and I failed. But I don't dwell on past mistakes, because that would pull me away from the present. Instead, these days I keep it simple. When my mind starts to wander—and it still does—I tell myself, *The most important person in the world is the one I'm with.* It really works.

19

Cherry Pie in the Backseat

The Benefits of Thought Control

*The thought manifests as the word; the word manifests as the deed;
the deed develops into habit; and habit hardens into character; so watch
the thought and its ways with care, and let it spring from love born out of
concern for all beings.*

—Lama Surya Das[29]

Each summer our family would make the 50-mile drive from
Omaha to Nebraska City, the hub of the commercial cherry indus-
try in our part of the country. We'd walk the streets of this picturesque town, munch on popcorn and cotton candy, look in wonder-
ment at museums with antique farm implements, period apparel,
and horse-drawn carriages, and buy cherries, lots and lots of cherries, which would become pies in the following weeks. All in all,
these excursions were some of my fondest childhood memories.

Our annual excursion to buy cherries occurred at the same
time as another important family event. After years of effort, my
mother had finally reached her goal weight in the Weight Watchers
program. She was proud of herself, and she had reason to be. Mom
always had a feast-or-famine approach toward weight loss. Sometimes she ate moderate amounts of healthy foods and exercised
regularly, and at other times she binged on ice cream, bread, and
especially pie. Those days were behind her. Or so she thought.

Although Mom had reached her goal, she still craved the many things that she wasn't supposed to eat, at least not in the quantities she wanted. Baking cherry pies for the family, and then having a small piece when she was accustomed to eating a sixth of a pie at a sitting, plus the requisite amount of vanilla ice cream on the side, was too much for her. She finally surrendered to her craving on the same night as the weekly Weight Watchers meeting.

To avoid suspicion in the family, she invented a story about "doing some extra work for the organization." She left an hour early and drove to the grocery store. Her plan was to buy a cherry pie, eat it, and then go to the Weight Watchers meeting and assume the virtuous role of a dieter who's had an unusually successful week of weight control. But she was in for a surprise. Because it was high season for fresh cherries, all of the cherry pies had been sold. The baker, thinking he was dealing with a normal customer who just wanted a dessert to feed her family, started innocently with, "Oh, don't worry. There are still plenty of pies—apple, berry, and banana cream."

He quickly switched to his dealing-with-upset-customer mode in an attempt to calm this out-of-control woman who was becoming more and more agitated by the minute, which was all the more amazing because my mom is one of the kindest, meekest people on the face of the earth. "What?" she exclaimed. "No cherry pies? I thought this was a grocery store! What kind of business are you running here?" She had planned her week around this event and wasn't about to be denied. Then the baker remembered, "Yes, there is one unsold cherry pie, but it has a broken crust and we were going to throw it away." In a heartbeat Mom replied, "I'll take it," and she dashed to her car with a renewed sense of purpose.

Mom had planned well. Time was short, and no simple eating utensil would do. She'd brought the holiday spoon, the one reserved for family celebrations where a serving spoon was used to ladle massive quantities of gravy and mashed potatoes onto our plates. She got in the backseat, partly because she thought it might (might?) look strange if other shoppers saw a middle-aged woman clutching an oversized spoon and eating an entire cherry pie, but mainly because she was in a hurry and didn't want the steering wheel to get in the way. She methodically ate one quarter at a time, stopping only when there was nothing left but crumbs. Then she composed herself and drove to the meeting, already regretting her loss of willpower and the inevitable weight gain that would occur the following week. No one knew the truth until she told us this story years later.

As Mom's dietary binge demonstrated, the groundwork for what we say and do is laid long before the words are said or the actions are done. This holds for things that are silly (eating a cherry pie in the backseat of a car), virtuous (spending a few hours each week in a volunteer activity), and apparently spontaneous (angry words with a spouse or co-worker). That's why it's so important to spend some time each day—*before* we think, speak, and act—in quiet reflection about how we want to live that day, such as trying to be kinder, more generous, or simply mindful of how we treat others. But many of us would do almost anything imaginable rather than be alone with our thoughts, and as a result, we're at their mercy and we go where they decide to take us.

The fundamental problem underlying Mom's binge eating was the inability to control her thoughts. She simply couldn't rid her mind of the desire to overeat foods that she loved. Lack of thought control is responsible for all of our pleasure vices, such as infidelity in intimate relationships, excessive drug and alcohol use, preoccupation with food, and mental and physical laziness. It's also the cause of most of the stress and unhappiness that we experience in life.

I've had my share of problems with thought control. In fact, I spent the first 50 years of my life believing that thoughts just happened. Uninvited thoughts, hundreds of them, would bounce around in my mind all day long, triggered by random sights, sounds, and conversations. If the thoughts were pleasant, great. If they made me angry, sad, or regretful, too bad, because that's just how life goes. Only later did I learn about a certain kind of thought control that was essential for lasting happiness. With regular practice—meditation was my approach—I found that it is possible to quiet the mind so that both you and your thoughts arrive at the same time, and you, not the randomness of the day's events, are firmly in control of what goes on in your mind.

The benefits are limitless. With practice, it's possible to see our thoughts in real time as they occur and then decide which ones will become words or actions, and which ones will be allowed to fade away. The real payoff is the practical application: we're far happier because we immediately recognize the uninvited thoughts that creep into our minds—thoughts which, if unchecked and left to wander about on their own, would lead to feelings of sadness about the past, apprehension of the future, and dissatisfaction or anger in the present. So we just let these unwanted thoughts disappear, focusing instead on the good things that are happening right now.

There's a Christian adage that reads, "The spirit is willing, but the flesh is weak."[30] This proverb misstates the innate relationship between mind and body. The flesh isn't a bit weak; it's incredibly strong, and we've been on a forced march since birth to find whatever it wants, including food, alcohol, sex, and the creature comforts of modern society, and the more the better. The spirit—really, the mind—may be willing in the sense that it *hopes* to convince the body to do its bidding, but lofty ethical and moral principles alone will never be able to control human behavior.

The solution is mind training. This doesn't mean asceticism whereby we totally eliminate certain pleasurable activities from our lives because we can't control them. That was Mom's "feast or famine" approach. Rather, it means that we (1) train our minds, starting with the wisdom to understand when, where, and how much exposure we want to these activities, and then (2) keep our thoughts focused on the present so that we're not ruminating on pleasures that we'll allow ourselves to have—but not now, not here, or not in the quantities that we may have wanted in the past.

Learning thought control isn't the easiest thing in the world. The easiest thing is giving in to our cravings whenever they occur. But it's not all that difficult either, as evidenced by the many people who stay in long-term monogamous relationships, avoid alcohol and dietary excesses, and find the time for mental and physical development. To slightly modify another adage, you *can* have your cake—or pie, in Mom's case—and eat it too, but not all of it at once.

20

The Chocolate Bunny Incident

Becoming the Person You've Always Wanted to Be

Your worst enemy cannot harm you as much as your own thoughts, unguarded. But once mastered, no one can help you as much.

—The Dhammapada[31]

Lisa, our second child, did everything early. In the late '70s, the fashion craze among 20-month-olds was Star Wars underwear. She'd seen them at the store and desperately wanted to exchange her puffy diaper for the sleek look of real clothes. Her mother, sensing an opportunity, challenged Lisa by saying, "Those are big girls' underwear, and big girls don't wear diapers." The underwear was purchased—Princess Leia was her favorite—and she never had another accident, not one.

Then there was Michael, our firstborn. We knew that boys matured more slowly than girls, but when it came to potty training he sorely tried our patience. A deadline was approaching—preschool for three-year-olds—and training pants were not allowed. The usual things weren't working: an avalanche of praise whenever he wandered into the general vicinity of the toilet, getting him a state-of-the-art potty chair, and seeing Daddy pee in the toilet or a tin can (I'd heard that little boys liked to make the same tinkling noise).

While I was at work, my wife watched him like a hawk. If she could catch him at the right moment, she planned to pick him up, race down the hall to the bathroom, put him on his little chair, and wait for the Ah-ha! moment when he realized what needed to be done in the future. But he was too smart for her. She'd get distracted and he'd sneak behind the sofa and poop in his pants.

Easter was just around the corner, and I had a stroke of genius. I bought the biggest chocolate bunny I could find and set it on the counter in the bathroom, still wrapped in its packaging, but otherwise ready to eat at a moment's notice. I put Michael on the potty and promised, "If you poop in the toilet, you can have this chocolate bunny!" He was thrilled at the prospect, but either he didn't want it that badly or he just wasn't ready. I repeated this drill two or three times a day, each time with the same solemn pledge about the reward that awaited him.

Michael always had a knack for saying just the right thing, and he didn't miss his chance when it came. One night as we started our toilet-training ritual, he sat down on the potty, drew his face into the most serious look he could muster, and promised, "Daddy, if you poop in the toilet, you can have this chocolate bunny!" Chris and I laughed so hard that we thought we'd be sick.

And that was the night. Any three-year-old who was smart enough to tell a joke like that clearly understood the situation. When preschool opened one week later, he was there, hand in hand with his mother, proudly wearing a brand new pair of Star Wars underwear (he liked Yoda), while the last remnants of a chocolate bunny awaited him at home.

In retrospect, I didn't need to worry about whether Michael would meet the deadline. He clearly knew what to do, and when and where to do it. He was just waiting for a good reason—preschool and the chance to wear Star Wars underwear. But I missed all of the signs that he was ready because I wasn't paying close attention to what was really happening. Mindfulness was always difficult for me, and many years would pass before I finally understood the lesson that was taught to me by a pint-sized three-year-old with an oversized sense of humor.

At that time of my life, I could have been a poster boy for the preoccupied, overcommitted businessman who operated on auto-pilot day and night, his mind everywhere but in the present. Most days would go something like this:

- Shower, dress, and drive to work, all the while preoccupied with the upcoming day and giving only passing attention to the many pleasant things that were happening around me, such as the beautiful sunrise, good smells from the kitchen, or courteous drivers who helped ease the stress of my long commute.

- Spend the day hunching over a computer, attending meetings, and above all, being efficient, which often meant blocking out the distractions of friendly co-workers who would have added joy to my life. My specialty was multi-tasking, a highly overrated ability that, if done properly, virtually guarantees that you can never devote your full attention to anything.

- Repeat five or sometimes six times per week.

From this description you'd imagine that my mind was totally focused, if not on the present, then at least on something. No, not at all. Unless I was fully engaged with an issue that required my undivided attention, my thoughts were all over the place. I'd deal with people and situations by using simple, well-honed formulas that grouped things into good, bad, and indifferent, and act accordingly. After all, I reasoned, my free time is limited, so I need to spend it on what's really important to me, not others. I didn't have the inclination or the ability to stop, rest my mind for a moment, observe but not judge, and then think, speak, and act, in that order. And I certainly didn't spend a lot of time imagining a better world and the small part that I might play in helping to achieve it.

All this changed when I learned about meditation and mindfulness training. Everyone knows the value of training the body with exercise, often for one or more hours per day: we lift weights to get stronger, practice yoga to increase our flexibility, and jog to improve our cardiovascular endurance. But most of us never consider a training program for the mind that increases *its* strength, flexibility, and endurance. I certainly didn't. True, I used my mind a lot: working or studying late into the night, creating spreadsheets, memorizing chemical reactions, and learning about the latest developments in internal medicine. But cramming my memory with facts was pretty much useless as a mind training exercise.

Mindfulness training has become mainstream in the United States. It's practiced in hospitals, corporations, professional sports, and prisons, and it's being introduced into public schools to help children and adolescents cultivate "loving kindness" for their classmates.[32] What's also attractive about mindfulness training is that it's nondenominational, so there's nothing that conflicts with other beliefs about God or spirituality; for example, *Zen for Christians* explains how meditation can benefit people of any religion.[33] And it's definitely not a cult movement, a semi-serious concern raised by my 74-year-old mother when I first started meditating.

Meditation has four main benefits. First, it provides a quiet time when we can rest our minds from the nonstop chatter that goes on every waking moment of our lives. While meditating, there's nothing else to think about. We just stay in the present and enjoy peace of mind. Second, it serves as the foundation for mindfulness during the remainder of the day. By focusing on the present moment while meditating, even for short 10-minute periods, we learn how to put our minds on one thing and keep it there, even during the chaos of our days. It doesn't happen overnight, but the progress can be remarkably rapid.

Third, meditation helps us see things more clearly. Most people have a high regard for their ability to experience the world as it really is, but what we actually see is how things appear to us or how we'd like them to be. No one is born with an innate ability to experience reality; rather, this is a learned skill that requires determination, practice, and years of sustained effort. I grossly overestimated my own ability in this regard. My wife and I used to have a recurring argument where I would often unleash my favorite anger-induced idiocy, "You're 100 percent wrong," implying that I alone understood the reality of the situation. After I started meditating, I gave some serious thought to the circumstances that usually initiated the argument, doing a play-by-play analysis of how the events unfolded. I was thunderstruck when I realized that I was the one who had been wrong—for decades! I apologized to Chris, and believe it or not, we've never had another real argument. One of the unexpected benefits of mindfulness training was that I became much better at seeing, hearing, and even sensing the early indications of a conflict. When disagreements occur, I'm able to defuse the situation before it gets out of hand.

Finally, mindfulness training changes our lives from the inside out. We learn how our minds work—always active, rarely focused, quick to judge, and often wrong—and we see aspects of our lives that need fixing: perhaps a bad temper, attachment to things that clearly aren't in our best interest, or an exaggerated opinion of our looks, intelligence, or value in the world. We also start to notice people who have a lot less than us who could use some help, and others who have much more of what we desperately want, namely lasting happiness, contentment, and peace of mind. We get serious about meditation because we see its potential. By concerted effort —thinking deeply and clearly about the important issues in life—we realize that we can become the person we've always wanted to be.

When the chocolate bunny incident occurred, I was only 28 years old, and I had no idea how much better life could be once I freed myself from the self-imposed limitations of an untrained mind. I give much of the credit to meditation. It was during these periods of quiet reflection that I discovered the core insights that would become the focus of my life. When Michael has a child of his own and he's feeling the same pressures that distract him from living in the present, I'll be there, ready to remind him of the lesson in mindfulness that he taught me during an Easter season long ago.

Anger and Patience

Aware that anger blocks communication and creates suffering, I am determined to take care of the energy of anger when it arises, and to recognize and transform the seeds of anger that lie deep in my consciousness. When anger comes up, I am determined not to do or say anything, but to practice mindful breathing or mindful walking, and acknowledge, embrace and look deeply into my anger. I will learn to look with the eyes of compassion on those I think are the cause of my anger.

—Thich Nhat Hanh[34]

21

The Annoying Boyfriend

Learning to Never Be Angry Again

Anger is just a thought that lingers for a few seconds and is gone, like the trackless flight of a bird through the sky.

—Buddhist proverb

One night our daughter Lisa (age 16 at the time) and her boyfriend got into a major argument while talking on the telephone. She hung up, but he was far from finished. He'd call back, she'd ask him not to call, and he'd immediately call again. Lisa finally slammed down the receiver to be sure that he got the message.

After a few minutes of quiet, my wife made a long distance call to her brother in Nebraska—those were the days when telephone calls were expensive and the words "long distance" signaled the need for hushed voices and deferential treatment by the family— only to have the operator interrupt and put through an "emergency" call from the boyfriend. When all else failed, we decided that we wouldn't answer the phone, but he was more determined than we thought. He'd call and the phone would ring and ring—it never stopped.

Finally, I'd had enough. Jumping to my feet, I yelled some obscenity and ran across the room, violently pulling the phone cord from the wall, and then I thundered up and down the stairs of the house to disconnect all of the other phones. It was an unforgettable sight when I reappeared. Barefoot and dressed in my pajamas and robe, I was juggling four telephones in my arms—cords, receivers, and plugs draped around my body and dragging on the floor behind me—all the while shouting incoherently about Lisa's choice in boyfriends. Ten minutes later, I realized what I fool I'd been, and I apologized to the family.

Clearly, I had let things get out of hand. Rather than become angry, I could have stopped the ringing by calmly walking through the house and unplugging the telephones. Why didn't I think of that at the time?

This tirade was a classic example of the dynamics of anger: an annoyance that starts small, builds quickly, and culminates in an explosion of poorly chosen words, actions, and sometimes violence. As I so convincingly demonstrated to my family, angry people are literally "out of their minds."

In my pre-Buddhist days, I would have defended my outlandish behavior in a number of ways. First, I might have said that my anger was warranted because the boyfriend was incredibly rude. True, he was rude, but my reaction was unnecessary and unhelpful, and it set a poor example for my children for how an adult should deal with difficult situations.

Second, I could have invoked the righteous anger excuse, namely, that extreme circumstances justify extreme responses. The problem with this rationale is that "righteous" implies that the rationalizer is right, which may or may not be correct depending on one's point of view. Lisa's boyfriend undoubtedly felt that he had a good reason to call, and maybe he did. From a broader perspective, righteous anger is often used to justify wars, horrible atrocities, and violent retributions of all kinds—actions that are *certainly not* "righteous" to the people on the receiving end.

Finally, I might have claimed that everything happened so fast that I couldn't stop myself. What a lousy excuse! A rational person could have taken all kinds of steps to head off the emotional outburst that occurred, but there was nothing rational about my actions. I simply needed to interrupt the chain reaction of event/first thought/hot thought/anger by putting some space, maybe even a few seconds, between the event and my response. But I didn't, and the result speaks for itself.

As I learned years later, anger is only a thought, one of thousands that we have every day, and if we recognize it as such, it loses its power to control us. It's all about mindfulness and thought control. At the first inkling of a contentious situation, we need to pay attention to what's happening both *outside* (the circumstances that lead to a potential argument, which we often can't control) and *inside* our minds (our thoughts, which we can almost always control).

In my case, the "outside" was clear: the boyfriend wasn't going to stop calling, so I needed to deal with the situation by going to a different room, ignoring the ringing, or calmingly unplugging the telephones. As to the "inside," I could have been mindful of the growing irritation that I was feeling. This alone might have interrupted the chain reaction and allowed me to realize that an already unpleasant situation would be made worse if I lost control. A few deep breaths, asking advice from my wife, or almost any other course of action would have been preferable. Could I have done this? No, not then. Thought control takes practice, and I didn't have the wisdom or the experience at the time to know what to do.

Note that this approach to dealing with conflict isn't about suppressing anger or ignoring an unpleasant situation. Lisa's boyfriend was extremely inconsiderate, and the next day we told him that his behavior was unacceptable. However, he was only 17. I was in my mid-forties. Running around the house like a madman wasn't what was needed at the time.

The only other advice I'll offer is to start now and practice during the relatively quiet times. Maybe you'll be ready when your children become teenagers.

22

Sunday Morning with Ed and Lori

Replacing Anger with Patience, Empathy, and Equanimity

Remember, it rests with you whether you want greed, sense-slavery, anger, hatred, revengefulness, or worries to rule your life, or whether you will let the divine solders of self-control, calmness, love, forgiveness, peace, and harmony rule your mental kingdom.

—Paramahansa Yogananda (1893-1952), India[35]

Ed and Lori, my in-laws, had a textbook dysfunctional relationship that seemed to be the norm for married couples of the 1960s. They had five children—how that happened was a mystery to anyone who knew them—but that was about all they shared, except for time together at their weekly bowling league.

Lori was an accomplished spouse baiter. After 25 years of marriage, she knew exactly how to throw Ed into a rage, and she could do it while discussing the most mundane subjects. Her specialty was Sunday morning breakfast. The script was well rehearsed. There would be good food, boisterous talk as everyone fought to be heard, and all the while Lori would pepper Ed with little jabs about what he'd done wrong the week before.

Ed wasn't gifted when it came to spousal communications, but he was an extremely hard worker who sometimes held three low-paying jobs to make ends meet, and this breakfast was the closest thing to a relaxing morning that he'd have all week. He'd suffer in silence until some seemingly innocent comment from Lori pushed him over the edge, and then he'd leap out of his chair, his face beet-red in anger, turn to his children (never to his wife), shout about their mother's unfairness, and storm out the door under a cloud of obscenities. It would drive us crazy when Lori would ask in her sugary-sweet voice, "Now why is Daddy acting like that?" We all knew why, and her name was Lori. Ed would slink back into the house 20 minutes later, and everyone would pretend that nothing had happened.

Some days they had twofers. Sunday was the only time when my father-in-law shed his work clothes for church and later for a lively evening of bowling at Leisure Lanes. I'm a fast learner for some things, and it took only a few months of marriage for me to develop the habit of asking my wife, "Honey, what should I wear?" Not Ed. His trademark style was stripes and plaids—at the same time. He'd appear in the living room for what should have been a pleasant evening with his wife and be greeted by another of Lori's withering put-downs: "Daddy, you're not going to wear *that*, are you?" Repeat the morning's events, especially the shouting and obscenities, only a bit briefer, or they'd be late for bowling.

Chris and I played a lot of cards with them during our three-year courtship, which was actually fun because they were on their best behavior. (That changed after we married and they could be themselves in front of us.) One night Lori was acting strangely, somewhere between anger and tears. The rest of us asked if everything was OK and we tried to keep the conversation going, but we couldn't change the somber mood that hung over the room.

Finally, after torturing us for most of the evening, Lori stood up, threw her cards on the table, and exclaimed, "I'M PREGNANT! AND I KNOW WHEN IT HAPPENED. NEW YEAR'S EVE!" She stomped out of the room, leaving everyone speechless. Poor Ed looked like a vampire who'd just had a wooden stake driven through his heart. One would think that this type of discussion would be reserved for private moments between husband and wife, but this was the first he'd heard of it. To make matters worse, their New Year's Eve marital tryst must have been pretty special to him, since it was now mid-March and the events of that night apparently had not been repeated.

Lori's last two children were born relatively late in life; now, at age 46, the last thing she wanted was a sixth child. After that evening, she sulked around for three months, an ice queen who made life miserable for everyone around her, until one day she matter-of-factly told Chris that the whole thing had been a mistake. She was just "irregular" due to early menopause. There was never an apology to Ed or the family.

Anger always makes people unhappy. Just ask Ed and Lori if they felt better or worse after an argument. Their Sundays reminded me of the movie *Groundhog Day*, in which Bill Murray relived February 2 over and over, trying to get it right so he could move on with his life. Every Sunday was Groundhog Day at the Wojtalewicz's, and they never broke out of the pattern in all of the years I knew them.

Anger also limits our mental freedom and personal growth by trapping us in repetitive behavior patterns. For instance, what are your current options when a rude driver cuts you off during the morning commute to work? Catch up and do the same to him? (I've used "him" since aggressive driving is more often a male phenomenon.) Wave your fist and shout out the window? Or just fume inwardly until you forget about it 30 minutes later?

None of these choices helps us, our blood pressure, or our outlook on the rest of the day. What if we broadened our perspective and increased the number of ways that we could respond? The driver may have made an honest mistake that he already regrets; he might be young and inexperienced, and not realize that he was being rude; or maybe his judgment was impaired by an unhappy, stress-filled life that didn't leave any room for caring about other people.

Once we consider these possibilities, even for a fraction of a second, everything changes. On a superficial level, we've broken the chain reaction of event/first thought/hot thought/anger and re-placed it with event/first thought/questioning thought (what happened and why?)/understanding. On a deeper level, we've made a spectacular start to the day. Just think about the virtues that we've practiced—patience, empathy, and equanimity—and we're not even at work yet.

One of the other peculiar things about anger is that the apparent cause and the real cause can be much different. Anger often occurs because our idea of self has been threatened or insulted, and we feel the need to rise to its defense. Ed wasn't mad because Lori didn't approve of his choice in clothes or the mistakes that he'd made last week. Rather, he was angry because he was a hard-working man who cared deeply for his wife and family, and his self-image wasn't acknowledged by the most important person in his life.

Think about the last time you were angry. In most cases, the real cause can be traced back to something that threatened you or your view of how things are or ought to be. A few examples are listed below.

Apparent cause of anger	Real cause
Your husband doesn't listen to you.	He doesn't care about your opinion.
You disagree with the views of a well-known politician or religious leader without even considering her perspective.	You're unwilling to admit that you could be wrong or that there might not be a single correct answer.
You wake up angry and take it out on the first person who gets in your way.	Something in your life is making you very unhappy.

One of my pet peeves, and another example of the difference between apparent and real causes of anger, used to be "junk on the kitchen table." This was highly annoying to me during the first few years of our marriage and the cause of a few full-fledged arguments. To be honest, I could have lived with a messy table. The real issue was that Chris seemed to be ignoring something that was important to me. I've gotten wiser and more patient over time, and things have gotten better, although not always cleaner. I just look at the mess and take a few deep breaths. A great wife is entitled to a few eccentricities. Heaven knows I have mine.

23

Lisa and the Facts of Life

Allowing Events to Unfold As They Will

Do you have the patience to wait till your mud settles and the water is clear? Can you remain unmoving till the right action arises by itself?

—Lao Tzu (6th century BCE), China[36]

We were expecting our third child at about the same time that Lisa, our second child, was turning two years old. One evening she asked the question that makes all parents squirm: "Daddy, where do babies come from?" Her mother, the one with better judgment in these matters, was out with friends for the evening. I'd read in parenting books that it was best to answer these questions when first asked, so I did my best. I launched into a toned-down version of the facts of life that I thought was appropriate for a two-year-old. Being a physician, I was comfortable with calling body parts by their proper names, so the description was pretty correct anatomically, although, in retrospect, much more detailed than the situation required.

What I didn't consider at the time was that Lisa had always been special. She learned everything early, including potty training, tying her shoes, dressing herself, eating, and especially talking. She never spoke baby talk; her first words were perfectly fluent, and she would amaze our friends who heard a tiny adult voice coming from a child who could barely walk. That was the problem.

One week later, Lisa had an appointment with the pediatrician. My wife chatted with the other mothers in a crowded waiting room filled with children of all ages, blissfully unaware of the humiliation that was only seconds away. Through the din of the other conversations, Lisa's little voice could be heard repeating a somewhat embellished version of what she'd learned from me: "My father puts his penis in women's vaginas!"

The content may have been lost on the other children, but not on their mothers. Horrified because their children were learning the facts from a two-year-old child, including the anatomically correct names for private body parts, they scooped up their children and ran out the door, leaving my wife alone and mortified. It's funny now, but it sure wasn't when Chris confronted me at home later that day.

This experience taught me two important lessons. First, I learned the meaning of patience: being satisfied with the present and allowing events to unfold at their own pace and in their own way, rather than trying to force the outcome that we want. Lisa wasn't looking for an Anatomy 101 explanation. She was just curious because a new baby brother or sister was on the way. This would have been clear to me if I'd had the patience to relax into the moment and let the conversation take its own course. In 30 seconds she'd have lost interest and switched to a more interesting topic, such as her new Star Wars underwear or the giant toad she'd found that morning in the sandbox behind our house. But I was in a hurry to teach her something important. Instead, she taught me a lesson that I've never forgotten.

Spiritual practitioners advise the following: Be thankful when someone puts you in a situation where you must be patient. They are giving you the gift of an unexpected opportunity for spiritual practice. Good advice, but it will be awhile before I voluntarily seek out my co-workers who have a stamp collection or the smartest grandchildren in the world. I've gotten much better over the years at letting events unfold as they will. To help me slow down and practice patience, I sometimes use a technique from my years of medical training. When talking with patients, and people in general, I often sit down. This more relaxed body position totally changes the dynamics of the situation, showing others that you have time, a willingness to listen, and no place that you'd rather be.

The second lesson from this experience? Whenever possible, leave delicate explanations of bodily functions to my wife, and if forced by unforeseen circumstances to answer similar questions in the future, revert to less descriptive, time-honored anatomical terms. "Bottom" and "wee wee" work just fine at age two.

Reality and Karma

For the great majority of mankind are satisfied with appearance, as though they were realities, and are often more influenced by the things that seem than by those that are.

—Niccolò Machiavelli (1469-1527), Italy[37]

Canned Goods and Meat Slicers

Separating Appearance from Reality

Things pass for what they seem, not for what they are. Few see inside, many get attached to appearances. It is not enough to be right if your actions look false and ill.

—Baltasar Gracián (1601-1658), Spain[38]

Certain characteristics run in families. In mine, it was blue eyes, short stature, and giving bad gifts. On the first Christmas after we were married, my parents gave us a gift that was sure to be the highlight of the holiday: a large, heavy box that probably contained a kitchen appliance, a small TV, or an unaffordable luxury item that we'd cherish for years to come. Even as young adults, we felt a childlike excitement as we waited for the day when we could finally open the package. If we'd lived a million years, we could never have guessed what it contained.

Apparently fearing that the newlyweds would starve to death, my mother gave us an entire box filled with canned fruits and vegetables. Not only that, she removed the labels from every can because she wanted them as a proof of purchase so she could redeem her coupons at the grocery store. For the next year, we'd open a can without knowing if it contained peas, beets, applesauce, or whatever else happened to be on sale when she did her Christmas shopping for us.

As bad as this gift was, I managed to do worse. When I was a child, we often ate bologna sandwiches for dinner, an inexpensive meal for a family on a tight budget. My brother and I would sit in our tiny kitchen with gaudy yellow walls while the delicious aroma of sizzling fatty meat wafted through the air. When the serving platter finally arrived at the table, we paused briefly to savor the moment: thick-cut slices of fried red bologna—the unnatural color was probably due to a carcinogenic food additive that's long been banned for human consumption—with slightly burned edges that curled up and inward. Then we dug in, building oversized sandwiches made with tasteless white bread and slabs of fried bologna, all slathered with bright yellow mustard that perfectly matched the color of the walls. In this one meal, we were able to satisfy an entire day's nutritional requirements for saturated fat, cholesterol, sodium, and chemical additives.

But back to the gift. I often went to the delicatessen with my mother to buy the week's supply of meat. The bologna came in 12-inch-long, five-inch-wide tubes that the butcher cut in front of us with a stainless steel meat slicer. I watched in fascination as the blade whirled and sliced effortlessly through the bologna, each piece falling delicately on waxed butcher paper that was then folded and taped shut for the trip home. I guess this memory of a young boy staring in awe at the marvels of an old-fashioned butcher shop never left me. Unfortunately, it resurfaced at a most inopportune time.

The traditional gift for a first wedding anniversary is made of paper because the couple is young and has little money for extravagant purchases. So a nice romantic card or perhaps a favorite book would be in order, something that expresses the love and happiness of the first year together. Not for me. I bought my wife her very own state-of-the-art meat slicer, beautifully wrapped in the finest paper that I could find, and decorated with ribbon and a pretty pink bow. I still remember the happy look on Chris' face as she held the heavy package on her lap, letting her excitement build before opening what was sure to be a wonderful gift.

Her expression turned to bewilderment as she peeled off the paper and stared at the picture on the box, a 1970s-era woman, dressed in a stylish apron and standing in a cozy kitchen, cheerfully carving a small ham with a commercial meat slicer. Chris thought the box was a joke and that something else must be inside—jewelry, a new blouse, or maybe a gift certificate for a romantic dinner—because no man in his right mind would give his wife a meat slicer as an anniversary gift. She opened the box, starred at the contents in utter amazement, and then turned to me. If I could have slithered away and hidden in a corner, I'd have done it, but there was no escaping the consequences of this monumental blunder. I've spent the rest of my married life apologizing for this stupid gift.

There's often a big difference between appearance and reality. Just think of the times when you misjudged someone based on how he or she looked, or how you scoffed at the advice that your father gave you as a teenager, only to give the same advice to your own children 25 years later. But distinguishing appearance from reality often takes time—sometimes years, decades, or even a lifetime—and in the meantime, we live every day of our lives convinced that we've got it right, and thinking, speaking, and acting accordingly.

That's why I found these two episodes so instructive: in both cases, the appearance of the gifts seemed wonderful—large, nicely wrapped packages that arrived on occasions which called for something special (Christmas and a wedding anniversary)—but it took only a few days, not years or decades, to discover that reality (canned goods and a commercial meat slicer) was not at all what it was thought to be.

It's often not possible to tell the difference between appearance and reality unless we've trained ourselves to view situations without adding the "me" component. Just imagine the rapid-fire judgments, often erroneous, that we make every day based on our own rules and generalizations: the man with a foreign accent who mows my lawn is uneducated; the overweight woman in the grocery store is undisciplined because she's "let herself go"; the nicely dressed person with a fancy car and a big house is happy, probably happier than me; and that woman at my company—the one who's a different race, religion, or sexual orientation—couldn't possibly become one of my closest friends.

These snap judgments classify the people we meet and the experiences we have into broad categories of good and bad, desirable and undesirable, based on highly subjective factors. What's worse, our criteria are often so deeply flawed that they have little or no value for separating appearance from reality. I remember the pleasant, middle-aged taxi driver with an eastern European accent who took me to LaGuardia airport in New York City. He was a Romanian physician who drove a taxi during the day and studied at night so he could pass the certification test to be a doctor in the United States. Not only would the generalization "foreign accent and low paying job = uneducated" have been wrong, but I was absolutely sure that he was much smarter and better educated than I. He spoke English, Romanian, French, and German, and had almost passed the medical certification test on a prior attempt, while I spoke only English and was fortunate to have passed the same test as a young man just out of medical school when everything was still fresh in my mind.

The gap that exists between how things seem and how they are leads to all kinds of personal and societal problems, ranging from simple dislike and envy of people who appear different from us, to intolerance, racism, hatred, conflict and even full-fledged war. Yet it's easier to stick with appearances and not look deeper to find the underlying reality. There would be all kinds of emotional, spiritual, and intellectual repercussions if we discovered that things are *not* as they seem. This realization would challenge some of our long-held beliefs; we'd be in conflict with people in our political, religious, and social networks who still see things the old way; and day in and day out, we'd have to live with the knowledge that significant changes were needed to bring our thoughts and actions into balance with reality. For most of us, it's a lot easier to just stick with the status quo.

Did I become a better gift giver after these experiences? Yes, but it took a while. Later in the same year as the meat slicer fiasco, I gave my wife two pairs of wool socks for Christmas to entice her to join me on a romantic backpacking trip in Colorado. (Note to younger men: there are many ways to romance a wife of 18 months, but a gift of wool socks is not one of them.) The gift proved to be as disastrous as the meat slicer.

But I got much better later in our marriage, and strange as it may sound, I credit my interest in Buddhism because I finally learned how to stay in the present. Instead of zoning out from sheer boredom when shopping with my wife, I now pay attention to what she's looking at, especially what she likes, and later I sneak back to the store, buy the item, and give it to her on the next important occasion. Not very original, but it's earned me immeasurable kudos on birthdays and anniversaries.

Key West—One Way or Another

Accepting Reality as One of the Keys to Happiness

The mind is its own place, and in itself can make a heaven of hell, a hell of heaven.

—John Milton (1608-1674), England[39]

My wife and I planned a mid-February vacation to Florida to escape the harsh Connecticut winter. We were in high spirits during the three-hour flight from New York City to Miami, knowing that it was only a short connecting flight to Key West, one of the few places in the United States where warm weather was guaranteed.

Chris took pride in her ability to arrange all aspects of a trip, especially finding affordable hotels, restaurants, and flights. She'd booked the airline reservation online with a discount carrier, but nobody at the Miami airport knew where we were supposed to check in. As we ran from one airline counter to another, she became more and more agitated because time was running out. We finally identified the problem. Instead of the electronic ticket that was used by virtually all airlines at the time, our carrier required a paper ticket, and we didn't have one. We never determined if it wasn't sent or if it had been misplaced, but the result was the same: we weren't flying to Key West.

Chris was in tears when the gate closed and the flight left without us. I'd managed to stay calm during this time, thinking that one out-of-control person in the family was enough. Just when it looked like our trip was ruined, I said, "OK, so we missed the flight. It's only money. Let's rent a car and drive to Key West." My wife stared at me as if I were from the moon. Truth be told, equanimity during stress wasn't usually my strong point, but I'd recently started meditating and was focusing on "going with the flow" and learning to accept reality—which in this case meant no flight to Key West. We rented a car, thoroughly enjoyed the beautiful scenery en route to our destination—which we wouldn't have seen on the flight—and had a fabulous time. It was a good start to a way of life that I've strived to follow every day thereafter.

One of the most important things that I learned from Buddhism is the importance of accepting reality. We can and should plan for the future, but events will still unfold as they will. I've heard people lament, "My life was going so well and then everything fell apart." Yet no one's life is sketched out for decades in the future with assurances that it will go according to plan. We might win the lottery or lose our job, and neither outcome is a deviation from how our life was supposed to be. It's the way our life is.

Adopting this philosophy is absolutely essential for day-to-day happiness. My lessons in accepting reality are often travel related because I spend so much time shuttling among airports around the world. On one occasion, bad weather delayed my flight to Vancouver and I wasn't sure that I'd make my connecting flight to Seoul. There wasn't anything I could do to affect the outcome—the plane would either arrive in time or not—so I just relaxed, figuring that I'd take the next flight if necessary. In contrast, the passenger beside me also had a tight connection, but she was just about jumping out of her skin from fear of being late. Our situations were identical, but the way we dealt with realty was the difference between an enjoyable and a stressful trip.

Another common event is the "crying child." Air travel is difficult enough these days, given the crowded planes and the absence of traditional amenities—like food. So when the piercing sound of an inconsolable baby is heard, it's enough to throw the passengers into a funk for the duration of the flight. Or not. There are choices to be made that will determine our state of mind for the remainder of the flight. We can (1) be annoyed because the sound is intruding on our space and private time, (2) hear the crying as just a sound without mentally labeling it as good or bad, and get back to our book, work, or conversation, or (3) empathize with what may be a sick child or an exhausted parent and offer to help if we're nearby.

The next time you feel dissatisfied with what's happening around you, ask yourself this question: Is something truly wrong, or is it more a matter that I want reality to be something that it's not? On that February afternoon in Miami, I was able to see reality for what it was. Despite our thorough preparations and the money we had spent on airline tickets, we weren't flying to Key West. The peace of mind that I maintained throughout the ordeal was the reason why we still had a delightful winter getaway together.

26

Don't Touch It!

Karma, the Ageless Principle of Cause and Effect

Whether a dandelion seed or a rock lands on our head, gravity neither laughs nor cries. In the same way, it doesn't matter to karma whether we're moving backward or forward.

—Sakyong Mipham[40]

My parents would often recite a litany of "don'ts" when my brother Bill and I were young. It made these activities all the more attractive. Electricity was my main temptation. I knew that it was dangerous, but I had to find out for myself. At age five, I intentionally stuck a dinner fork into an electric outlet just to see what would happen. I still remember the instantaneous shock, the blackened fork, and the faint smell of burning flesh. I repeated the experiment a few months later with one of the long metal skewers that Dad used to barbecue chicken on the grill. This time I shorted out the electricity in the entire house. In addition to another painful shock, I got a real wailing from my father, who was not amused by my repeated efforts to flaunt his rules, burn down the house, and kill myself in the process.

Two lessons would have been enough for most people, but I needed one more. On Christmas Eve of the same year, Santa Claus gave me a wood burning set, the must-have toy for boys in 1957. (How times have changed. Today's product safety laws would never allow companies to market this "toy" to children.) It consisted of an electric soldering iron that was used to engrave patterns on pieces of cork and wood, much like a paint-by-numbers kit—except that this apparatus was for kids who were too young to hold a paint-brush steady, yet old enough to grasp a glowing metal rod in their chubby fingers. As best as I can remember, my thought process went something like this: If a soldering iron can burn a hole in wood, what would happen if I bored a hole through the electric cord? Sure enough, I got the third (and last, so far) serious shock of my life.

Bill took a different tack. Christmas was always a grand cele-bration at our house, with presents for everyone and a beautifully decorated tree. We had ornaments that would be eye-catching even today, but the downside was that they were based on 1950s tech-nology and the bulbs got incredibly hot. Bill probably knew this at age six, but he had to find out for himself. He reasoned that Dad said we couldn't touch the lights, but he meant with our fingers. So he didn't use a finger. Instead, Bill touched the tip of his penis to the prettiest light that he could find. (Boys really are a strange lot.) The festering red blister that he saw every time he peed for the next three weeks was a good reminder. Hot surfaces never tempted him again.

However, he also needed another lesson. The heat in our house was provided by oil stored outside in 55-gallon drums. We got repeated warnings from our parents to never play on the drums —one of the many don'ts—and for good reason. Besides being covered with dirt and rust, the drums and pipes had lots of jagged edges. It was an accident waiting to happen. One summer day, Bill was climbing on the drums when he lost his footing. He was wear-ing shorts at the time, and as he fell he somehow managed to snag a different but closely related private body part. I can only imagine the chaos that must have ensued when my mother burst into the doctor's office screaming, "We need help, quick! Billy ripped open his scrotum on a rusty oil pipe!"

Karma, the ageless principle of cause and effect, was alive and well when Bill and I were young.[§] These childhood stories are instructive because the outcome was certain and immediate: sticking something metal into an electric outlet or touching a hot surface with a tender body part is bound to cause trouble. Yet the same rule of cause and effect holds true for all of our day-to-day activities and personal relationships, except that years or decades may pass before we reap what we sow. In a very real sense, none of us suddenly woke up this morning to a life that's happy or sad, thoughtful or thoughtless, or kind or unkind. Rather, it's taken a lifetime of individual thoughts, decisions, and actions to get where we are now.

This cause and effect relationship isn't an Eastern superstition or a moralistic judgment; it's just how things work. However, many of us would rather not believe this. Instead, we blame unfavorable situations on a troubled childhood, a broken marriage, a lousy boss, or the bad breaks of life. Karma puts the responsibility, both for good and bad outcomes, squarely on our shoulders.

The good news is that there's always tomorrow, or more correctly, the next moment. Wherever we are in life, we can change course. The key is to acquire greater wisdom so we know what to do, and then stay focused on the present so we can do it. The bad news is that if we don't use today to move in a new direction, it's likely that tomorrow will be more of the same.

Things change for the better once we acknowledge how karma works in our lives. To this day, I have a healthy respect for electricity. And Bill? Well, it's safe to say that he finally learned to keep his private parts well out of harm's way.

[§]   I'm using the term "karma" in a nonsectarian sense to mean simple cause and effect, rather than in the Hindu and Buddhist context where a person's karma determines his or her destiny after reincarnation.

Attachments

Speaking to someone about renunciation is like hitting a pig on the nose with a stick. He doesn't like it at all.

—Matthieu Ricard[41]

27

Transitional Friends

Trading Up, Even If It Costs Us Everything

Nothing is enough for the man to whom enough is too little.

—Epicurus (341-270 BCE), Greece[42]

Rick and Cathy lived in our neighborhood when our children were in grade school together. We'd see them at school and holiday functions, and sometimes they'd join us for pizza on Friday night. We thought we were getting pretty close. As it turned out, we were only transitional friends.

Rick was born into money. His father, a successful real estate developer, brought him into the business at a young age and paid him a generous salary plus a monthly "allowance"—a term that I found amusing since he was a 35-year-old man at the time. They lived in the nicest house in the neighborhood, drove brand new cars, and routinely took vacations that most people would consider once-in-a-lifetime events. When we visited them, I'd park my ten-year-old Buick Skylark at his house—we were saving for college for three children and a new car was unimaginable—and after we left for home Rick would find a large oil leak on the driveway. It would drive him crazy.

Rick's attempts at the common touch were comical. One weekend, he and his son joined my son Michael and me for a father-and-son hike. He prepared for the event by buying a new outfit that he thought gave him a rugged, outdoor appearance, including a $40 leather hat. (In the mid-1980s $40 was real money.) His wife Cathy was nice enough, though we could see that her outlook on life was changing in step with her husband's growing affluence. She never suspected that she and their two children would soon be out of the picture.

After Rick's father died he inherited a fortune in insurance money and controlling interest in the company. In short order, he upgraded everything he had: a palatial home on a large acreage far from our middle-class neighborhood, an Italian sports car, better friends, and a younger wife. He was too embarrassed to cut us off immediately, but the end was inevitable since he only wanted to socialize with like-minded—"like-walleted" would be more accurate—people at his country club. We couldn't keep up with the Joneses; we couldn't even see the Joneses from where we lived.

There's no satisfying end to this story whereby a self-absorbed man gets his comeuppance. In fact, the opposite. Rick would have said that he was perfectly happy and had everything that a man could want. But he also had plenty of things that most people wouldn't want: a broken marriage, children who barely knew their father, friends who wouldn't have looked twice at him if he lived on the "other side of the tracks," little or no self-awareness, and no time for anything or anyone outside of his small circle of interests. If success in life were defined as living a meaningful life, Rick was an utter failure.

I have to admit that I was envious of Rick's lifestyle. He didn't worry about house and car payments, saving for his kids' college education, or a corporate restructuring that might eliminate his job —which is exactly what happened to me 20 years later at an especially vulnerable time in my life. In fact, he was totally insulated from the financial stresses that I faced every day. But he clearly had issues of his own. Who knows what he thought in his heart of hearts, but it looked like he was obsessed with getting as much as he could as fast as he could. In Buddhist vernacular, these obsessions are called attachments.

Attachments are compulsive preoccupations that disrupt our thoughts and sap the emotional, spiritual, and intellectual energy that should be directed elsewhere. These aren't the normal desires that everyone has for a nice home, dinner at a favorite restaurant, and enjoyable work. Attachments grab hold of our mind throughout the day and turn our attention to the objects that we crave, preventing us from living fully in the present.

For example, instead of noticing the elderly man who needs help getting his groceries into the car or listening to our spouse and children tell us about their days, our mind is elsewhere, consumed by what's *really* important to us: an important business deal, the new outfit that we saw at the mall, or how we showed everyone today that we're still the smartest, funniest, richest, most attractive, or holiest person they know (yes, even spiritual devotion can become an attachment).

The principal attachments are well known to everyone: possessions (houses, cars, furniture, clothes), pleasures (food, alcohol, sex, vacations, country club membership), and power (wealth, important jobs). More subtle are the intangible obsessions that have just as much of a grip on our subconscious mind, such as work, time urgency, and views.

Work is unique among the attachments because it used to be considered a drudgery that should be finished and forgotten as soon as possible. With the 21st century's emphasis on speed, productivity, and earning potential, it's been catapulted to near the top of the list. I've seen extreme examples of overwork in every country that I've visited, usually in the context of duty and responsibility: ridiculously long working hours, skipped vacations, sleep deprivation, total disregard for one's health, and nothing even remotely approaching a balance among work, family, lifelong learning, and spiritual growth.

If I mentioned this preoccupation with work I would invariably hear, with a mixture of pride and rationalization but never remorse, something like, "Yes, I know. I work too hard, but there's a lot to do at the office. One of these days I'll slow down." While listening to such unconvincing excuses for why someone willingly trades more of his or her life for an opportunity to work even harder, I would think of the far more likely explanation offered by Michael Carroll in his book *Awake at Work*, namely, that some people use work as an anesthetic to numb themselves to the pain of unfulfilling lives and desires.[43] It takes a wise person to realize that many of the most sublime and ephemeral joys of life, such as reading to young children at night and then tucking them into bed, won't wait for us to finish "just one more thing." If we miss them, they're gone. Forever.

Time urgency—the feeling that there's never enough time to do what needs to be done—is another attachment that has a stranglehold on many of us. I've struggled with this attachment from my earliest memories, probably because my family was poor and my mother encouraged me to work and study hard in order to better my situation in life. It worked, but the constant emphasis on efficiency and productivity took a psychological toll on me. I was always preoccupied with a schedule and a daily routine, and every waking minute had to be spent on something worthwhile. It wasn't until I reached my fifties that I learned how to relax, and even now I sometimes feel the urge to accomplish more than time will allow.

The final attachment that I'll mention is views. I saved this one for last because of its importance. Views are the underlying cause of all of our obsessions—tangible and intangible—and a source of untold personal and societal unhappiness. Views are our beliefs about ourselves, others, and how the world is and ought to be, including our opinions about race, religion, politics, nationalism, social issues, intelligence, and personal appearance. When views become attachments, they do something to us that we'd fight to the death to prevent if imposed by an outside force. They limit what we think, say, and do, and they keep us from learning, changing, and becoming wiser and happier.

For my own part, I find it difficult to tell where normal desires end and attachments begin. It starts innocently enough. We all need and want certain things in life, and everyone has ideas about the world we live in. Over time, we receive direction and reinforcement from society and our peer groups, everything from where to live to what car to drive, what job to hold, what to believe, and how we should live our lives.

And then one day we discover that we absolutely *must* have something to be content, and that we *must* think and act a certain way because it's the "right" thing to do. This power that attachments exert over our conscious and subconscious mind cannot be overstated. Rick could have told you, if he'd had the self-awareness. He traded away the most important things in his life—friends, family, and the chance for true happiness—and received very little in return.

28

Hungry Ghosts of Silicon Valley

Attachment to Possessions, Pleasure, and Power

There is no greater calamity than desire, no greater curse than greed. Know that enough is enough, and you'll always have enough.

—Lao Tzu (6th century BCE), China[44]

There are tens of thousands of "single-digit" millionaires in Silicon Valley, people made rich by the technology boom that they helped create.[45] They're wealthy by anyone's standards, except their own, so they work all-consuming 60- to 80-hour weeks because they don't have enough money to live comfortably in an area where children wear designer clothes, everyone takes fabulous vacations, and most people personally know far wealthier neighbors who drive expensive foreign cars, live in extravagant homes, or own a private jet. Many refuse to leave the area because that would be admitting defeat by acknowledging that others are more successful.

There aren't many better examples of a "hungry ghost." In Buddhism, hungry ghosts live in the realm of intense craving and unfulfilled desires. They're depicted as teardrop-shaped beings with bloated stomachs and thin necks, always wanting to eat but unable to swallow. Their torment is not so much the disappointment of not getting what they want, but rather the craving for things that are thought to bring satisfaction and relief.

Hungry ghosts aren't confined to the ranks of the wealthy. We've all had the experience of getting into bed at the end of a long, stress-filled day, exhausted and frustrated, and wondering, *Was it worth it? Was I happy today?* An interesting exercise is to ask yourself the following question: How much of my free time—the time that I could spend with friends and family, volunteering, or cultivating inner peace—am I willing to exchange for longer working hours so I can buy a better version of what I already have or enjoy a fleeting pleasure that's forgotten almost as soon as it's experienced? If nothing else, this question is a reminder of what's really important in life and what we choose to give up in our quest for more.

I have firsthand experience of the allure of the good life. My wife and I visited Carmel, California, a picturesque town on the Pacific Ocean that is renowned for its beauty, climate, restaurants, and famous citizens. After lunch, we strolled through the park and admired the homes, the views, and the relaxed pace of life. Overcome by the beauty of it all, I suggested that this would be the ideal place for our family to live. Chris was quick to point out the folly of such a plan. We couldn't afford a house in Carmel, I couldn't find a job in a resort community, we weren't going to win the lottery (a possibility that I half-heartedly suggested as a way to deal with her persistent objections), and our three young children would eventually leave us for college, spouses, and careers in other parts of the country.

In other words, for all of this to happen, many highly unlikely events would need to converge, and if by chance everything did come together, we'd need to stop time so that everyone could live happily ever after. Was my idea a dream? Yes, of course, but this is essentially the plan that many of us have for achieving happiness in this life: more of this, less of that, and then try to hold it together as time moves on.

This story about single-digit millionaires in Silicon Valley is a good illustration of the difference between intelligence and wisdom. As a group, they're among the smartest people in the world, but no truly happy person would switch places with them. After working these horrendous hours, the best they could hope for would be a quiet dinner, a few rushed hours with the family—also known as "quality time," the 21st century euphemism for focused time with loved ones to atone for the reality that we're not around very often —and maybe some shopping or a round of golf on the weekend.

Yet I'm sure that most of the hungry ghosts of Silicon Valley would say they were happy. This just shows what passes for happiness in different people. There's happy—fleeting, superficial, self-absorbed. And there's truly happy—lasting, profound, and grounded in a sense of inner peace. If you don't believe it, compare how you feel the next day after (1) a nice dinner at your favorite restaurant, and (2) a volunteer activity that helped others in your community. The sense of happiness is worlds apart.

29

Bob Takes a Walk in the Woods

Attachment to Youth, Health, and Longevity

> *He who understands the true nature of life is the happiest individual, for he is not upset by the fleeting nature of things. He tries to see things as they are, and not as they seem to be.*

> —Piyadassi Thera (1914-1998), Sri Lanka[46]

I've always imagined myself as a tough, independent man, the kind of person who could disappear into the mountains with a heavy pack, a bowie knife, and a good pair of hiking boots, and reappear months later with a full beard and stories of my harrowing adventures in the wilderness. Nothing could be further from the truth.

I'd done a number of overnight hikes, but this would be the big one. My plan was to walk 100 miles along the Appalachian Trail, starting from Manchester, Vermont, a charming town in the heart of the Green Mountains, and ending in southern Massachusetts. I carried only the essentials: a sleeping bag, food for five days, a water purification pump, and an A-frame plastic tarp (which saved me about a pound in weight compared to a tent). I was so excited that I barely slept before starting out just before 5 a.m. on a spectacular July morning. My many years of exercise paid off. I was in my early fifties, but I climbed steadily up one mountain after another, pausing only briefly to admire the many gorgeous views. It was everything that I had hoped it would be.

By the time I stopped for the night I'd walked 26 miles, a respectable distance by anyone's standards. I was too tired to set up the tarp, so I joined another hiker in one of the wooden shelters along the trail. The weather was unseasonably warm, and bugs were everywhere. It was far too hot to get into my sleeping bag, so I planned to lie on top of the bag and cover myself with insect repellant. That's when I discovered that I hadn't refilled the bottle after my last hike. There wasn't enough repellant for a five-day hike; I barely had enough for one night.

After complaining to my fellow hiker about my forgetfulness, he said something that still amazes me to this day: "I know you don't have very much, but could you spare a little of yours? I used the last of my bug spray this morning." Long distance hikers are a strange bunch. How else can you explain the discomfort and isolation that they willingly endure—more correctly, seek out—for days or weeks on end? I handed him what was left. When he passed it back, I shook the bottle in the darkness, listening to the sound of the few sad drops that would have to last four more days.

The next day's hike was more of the same: steep ascents and descents where the elevation would change 1,500 feet in less than a mile, temperatures in the mid-90s, high humidity, and incredibly buggy. I didn't dare use the last of the insect repellant since I needed to save it for nighttime, so I spent much of the day counting the number of mosquitoes that were biting me at any given moment, which was often five or more. I tried to wave them away with my hand, but they sensed a helpless prey and didn't scare easily.

The worst attacks occurred when I stopped to refill my hydration pack at mountain streams, a time-consuming process where a small pump is used to slowly force water through a filter that removes parasites and bacteria. I would wade into a cloud of mosquitoes that hovered over the stream, absolutely defenseless because I needed both hands to work the pump. It reminded me of a commercial that I saw when I was a child. A scientist (he must have been a scientist because he was a handsome man in an official-looking white lab coat) sprayed insect repellant on his forearm, brazenly stuck it into a cage filled with hundreds of mosquitoes, and then withdrew it triumphantly without a single bite, while the announcer exclaimed, "They don't bite. They don't even light!" Only I wasn't the scientist; I was what's known as the "control subject" in the experiment, the guy with no repellant who exposed his unprotected arm to the hoard and then let excited researchers count the number of bites.

As the day wore on, a little voice in my head started to whisper, *You've made a mistake! This isn't going well!* Nonetheless, I trudged on stubbornly, knowing how much time, planning, and ego I'd invested in this trip. By nightfall I finally admitted what I'd been thinking for most of the day. I wanted to go home. But I was on the longest stretch of the Appalachian Trail without intersecting roads, and I needed to walk another 15 miles the next day just to reach a town. I swallowed my pride and phoned my wife. The kind people of Vermont had had the foresight to install cell towers so that exhausted middle-aged men could call home for help. She graciously offered to make the three-hour drive to rescue me the following day.

That last evening in the woods was funny, in retrospect anyway. Once again I waited too long to find a decent campsite, and it was completely dark when I stopped for the night on the side of the trail, totally alone. I set up camp in the dim light of my headlamp, but I'd forgotten to change the battery after my last hike. The light from its single tiny bulb faded to nothing in five minutes. I sat in the dark on my plastic ground cover, as hot, dirty, and sweaty as I'd been in a long time, munching on the tasteless dehydrated food that I'd bought at the outdoors store.

My mind wandered back to the advertisement in *Backpacker Magazine*: happy, sparkling-clean campers relaxing in front of a cozy

133

fire with a fresh cup of coffee in their hands, a state-of-the-art tent (featuring two large screened windows to keep out the mosquitoes) sitting just behind them. A smile came to my face as I brushed a large spider off my bare leg. I was about to lie down on top of a sleeping bag and under a tarp that was open at both ends. If the spider, a skunk, or even a bear or two wanted to come in after I fell asleep, what was I going to do?

As a physician, I'd seen so many patients who abused their bodies, became disabled at a relatively young age, and died long before their time. It wasn't going to happen to me. Exercise was my solution, my prevention, and eventually, my obsession. I paid a steep price for this craziness.

What started at age 19 as an aid to weight loss evolved into a lifelong routine, and its seemingly magical ability to delay aging made it all the more addictive. Within a short period of time, my exercise schedule began to disrupt other aspects of my life. Improvement came quickly at this young age, and I set ever higher goals that required a greater time commitment. I got up at 4:30 each morning to run or lift weights, so I was often too tired to be fully present when I got home from work in the evening. But the real indication of my attachment, what most people miss or ignore, is that thoughts about exercise would often take control of my mind. Instead of staying in the real world, I'd think about yesterday's workout or an upcoming 10K race.

On the surface my attachment was exercise, but there was a lot more going on at a deeper psychological level. My obsession was driven by fear of aging, sickness, and death. Exercise seemed to be a cure-all, a virtual guarantee of youth, health, and longevity. Yet times were changing. I reached an age when my running pace slowed and I wasn't getting any stronger, and I began to notice older people at the gym who had spent the same decades of rigorous training that I had, and they were slower and weaker still. The attachment that I'd clung to for three decades was beginning to fail me. Youth was slipping away, and adding more hours of exercise wasn't going to stop the inevitable.

As so often happens in life, I was given the opportunity to learn an important lesson when I needed it most. Shortly after the Vermont hike, I attended a medical conference where the keynote speaker was an elderly, world-famous personality. His presentation began with comments that sounded more like a eulogy than an inspiration: "It's not a good time of life, limited in body and spirit by the ravages of old age and illness." These words—a negative message conveying his belief that only the young and the healthy can live a happy, meaningful life—made a great impression on me. I resolved to never think or say anything so foolish.

After hearing his speech, I knew that I had to make a decision. I could (1) fight reality tooth and nail by pretending that I could indefinitely postpone the effects of aging, and perhaps grow bitter and angry like the keynote speaker when I failed, or (2) accept the reality that old age, illness, and death were getting closer, and continue to be happy in the time that I had left. With the wisdom that I'd gained from studying Buddhism, my choice was clear. This was how things were supposed to be—birth, aging, sickness, and death —and I was simply entering a new phase of my life.

What a relief it was to put down the burden that I'd carried for 30 years! I felt free, free of the need to run five miles at last year's pace or to lift the same weight that I had when I was 40. It was surprisingly easy to adapt after I made the mental adjustment. I took up yoga at age 52, and my routine now blends equal parts of aerobics, strength training, stretching, and balance exercises. I'm actually a slacker now by my old criteria. (Before accepting the inevitability of aging, I used the word "slacker" to describe people who lacked my obsession for extreme exercise and work. I really did have some crazy ideas.) My current plan is to be one of the fitter late-middle-aged men that I know, but I have no desire to be the fittest. That goal would rekindle my old attachment to exercise, and I'm no longer willing to pay the price.

Would I like to have both the body of a 25-year-old and the wisdom of middle-aged man? Sure, who wouldn't? But that's not reality, and I don't want to spend any more of my time trying to achieve it.

30

Canceling Easter

Attachment to Self

There are those who are aware that they are always facing death.
Knowing this, they put aside all quarrels.

—The Dhammapada[47]

It was the spring of 1997. We were the closest, most loving family that I'd ever known, in the twilight of predictable family get-togethers. Michael was in his third year of college, Lisa was in her first year at a different university, and neither came home very often. So there was plenty to celebrate when they were able to join the rest of the family for the Easter holiday.

We were returning from a pleasant dinner in New Haven, Connecticut, a town about 30 minutes from home, when sibling rivalry broke out. Michael and Lisa had a textbook brother-sister relationship, and we were about to see the dark side. To this day, it amazes me when inconsiderate people that you love very much—often young children, but sometimes adults who should know better—can't see that their petty disagreements jeopardize irreplaceable family memories that are about to be made, and worse, won't stop the behavior when asked in the kindest possible way.

What started as tit-for-tat barbs about the merits of their schools evolved into a full-fledged argument. We had very little time together and didn't want to waste it. I knew from experience that the psychological hangover from these arguments lasted for days, which was about all the time that we had together. My wife did everything she could, imploring them to please stop, but it was no use. We could all see it coming even as it played out in front of us, but Michael and Lisa were both unwilling and unable to stop. Anger had taken control of them; neither could be the bigger or the wiser person, and so they ruined our holiday over something that was never of any real consequence to either of them.

Chris had finally had enough of the bickering. In a stern mother's voice that has never failed to quell dissent in the family—we all still cower in fear when she uses that tone of voice—she proclaimed, "I've had enough of this! Easter is canceled!" By this she meant that one of our traditional celebrations wouldn't happen that year. It had been more than a decade since our youngest child believed in the Easter bunny, but each year Chris would buy marshmallow Peeps, cream-filled eggs, and chocolate bunnies, add a card with a mother's loving message, and put everything in the same little baskets that we'd given each of them since they first learned to walk. But she'd been pushed too far. There would be no Easter celebration that year.

Our idea of self is derived from our life experiences and perceived place in society. For Michael and Lisa, part of their identity and self-esteem was based on the academic reputation of their schools. As this story shows, having to defend one's self-image causes a lot of unhappiness for us and the people around us.

So why do we do it? Because the stakes are so high. Our sense of self was created over an entire lifetime, and it's always been with us, day and night. It's literally who we think we are, and we willingly spend much of each day's emotional, spiritual, and intellectual energy trying to hold it together against the outside world. For example, if we believe that our self-worth depends on being the smartest, most successful, or most expert in our field, then we need to defend this view at all costs because opinions and evidence to the contrary are direct attacks on who we think we are. An average day can be an emotional roller coaster as we feel happy, calm, proud, attractive, smart, and confident when all is going well, followed by sad, angry, envious, unattractive, dumb, or anxious when our self-image receives negative feedback. It gets even harder when the difference between reality and our perception of self becomes too great to ignore.

Buddhists have an interesting perspective: they believe in "selflessness." This means that one's self-image and personal identity exist only as a concept rather than as a tangible, permanent reality. In other words, there is no permanent "I" or "me." At a basic level, it's easy to understand. No one is as young, athletic, or attractive as he or she was earlier in life, and the same is true for all of the other intangible ideas of self that we've cobbled together to represent "me." To base one's self-worth on these characteristics makes no sense whatsoever, and yet this is exactly what many of us do.

We've all met people who can't resist telling us how wonderful they are because of their education, job, or past accomplishments. My wife and I went to a bridge party where we met an older man who managed to tell us in the first five minutes of the conversation that he (1) had attended an Ivy League school, (2) used to be a near-par golfer, and (3) was a retired vice president of a local bank. For heaven's sake! The man was 70 years old! I really wanted to say, "Very interesting. But who are you *now*?" His self-image, totally based on a person that he used to be, was always just below the surface, fighting to get out.

My favorite example of fixation on self was Dr. Morrison, one of my instructors in medical school. He always, and I mean *always*, wore his stethoscope. Once he was spotted in the grocery store with it hanging around his neck. Maybe he tapped on melons and used the stethoscope to determine if they were ripe. More likely, his identity was all about being a doctor, something like, "A stethoscope? Really? I'm so busy, important, and preoccupied with saving lives that I never noticed the awkward medical device that was dangling around my neck while I shopped for tomatoes." I wonder what he'd say if asked, "Suppose you weren't a physician. How would you describe yourself?"

This rigid concept of self restricts—"suffocates" would be a more accurate description—the options for how we allow ourselves to live. For many of us, it would be virtually unthinkable to imagine life if we were a different race, ethnicity, nationality, gender, or sexual orientation; if we were born 10,000 years in the future or the past; or if we had totally different religious or political beliefs. This new person, we might argue, would not be me. Which is *exactly* the point. These superficial characteristics of race, religion, nationality, political ideology, occupation, and social attitudes—so impermanent and changeable depending on life's circumstances—are *not* who we are. Rather, they're labels that create artificial distinctions between people and that keep us from reaching a middle ground of tolerance and acceptance of different beliefs and ways of living.

Recognizing that we're not who we think we are gives us incredible freedom to think, speak, and act without going through a subconscious checklist of self-imposed limitations. The benefits are immense, starting with happiness. If Michael and Lisa had understood that the academic merits of their respective schools had no bearing on how they should interact with each other, the argument would never have occurred and our family could have had a wonderful Easter holiday. Instead, it was a time of regrets, apologies, and the loss of a precious weekend together that would never happen again.

31

Nose Prints on the Glass

Learning to Let Go

Renunciation is not asceticism, celibacy, poverty, obedience, shaving your head, going off somewhere and leaving everything behind, discipline, depriving ourselves of what brings us happiness, turning our backs on family, friends, work, and responsibilities. It's about setting down our heavy load of attachments, about abandoning our intense emotional attachments and compulsive preoccupations.

—Lama Surya Das[48]

My wife has led a charmed life when it comes to accidents. On multiple occasions she's smashed her face into store windows while shopping, leaving nose prints on the glass and throwing herself violently backwards, prompting lawsuit-fearing employees to rush to her aid. And she's always falling down. Maybe it's because she's short and already close to the ground, but she's never been hurt.

Her specialty is the slow-motion fall. She might be on a perfectly level sidewalk, on a cobblestone street, or in an open field, when she catches her foot on a blade of grass or a miniscule irregularity in the surface and suddenly lurches forward. Somehow she throws her body weight into reverse and glides to the ground. The most embarrassing incident was in a crowded upscale coffee shop in Fredericksburg, Maryland. She tripped on a burlap bag of unroasted coffee beans, stumbled wildly for a few steps while trying to regain her balance, and then pitched headlong onto the wooden floor, flinging her purse, packages, and diet soda in all directions. She gathered herself together, joined the other customers in a hearty laugh, and continued on her way.

Some falls are self-induced. On the first day of a family vacation in England, we were returning from a long day of sightseeing at Windsor Castle and found that our way was blocked by a metal fence. Chris, jetlagged after the flight from the U.S., was too tired to walk a half block to the intersection. She scaled the three-foot fence, balanced for an instant at the top, and then fell face-first down the other side. If our daughter Elizabeth hadn't caught her, she'd have smashed her head on the concrete sidewalk.

Once she tried her hand at automobile repair. Elizabeth had a dent in the door of her car that kept it from opening properly. Chris stuck a plunger on the dent and began to pull in the opposite direction. I was certain this was a waste of time, but little by little it was working. The dent was getting smaller and smaller—until the plunger gave way, causing her to hurl backwards into a full somersault and onto the ground. As always, she escaped unscathed.

What's Chris' secret? She doesn't try to fight a losing battle when she knows that a fall is inevitable. Instead, she takes the path of least resistance and eases herself to the ground. Knowing when to let go has saved her from many a serious injury.

Letting go is something that happens naturally every day. We let go of anger after a fight with our spouse, of sadness because we're no longer the most important person in our children's lives, and of dissatisfaction with our aging bodies. But in some cases, letting go is far more difficult, largely because the issues represent a part of "who we are." These situations might be memories, both good and bad; dreams of being rich or famous; regrets that we didn't spend more time with our children or that our father died before we could resolve the differences between us (this regret is one of mine); or our views about religion, politics, and how people should live their lives.

There's a good reason why it's so hard to let go in these situations. We'd prefer reality to be something that it's not. For example, maybe we spend much of our free mental time reliving the carefree years of our youth, obsessing about a past tragedy that's always just below the surface of our conscious thoughts, or agonizing about a bad decision that we've regretted for our entire lives. Letting go would force us to accept the fact that things will never be the way we'd like, and that's not a pleasant thought.

Yet everyone can learn to let go of the memories, dreams, regrets, and views that enter our minds day and night, often uninvited and unwelcome. It requires the wisdom to first acknowledge that a problem exists, followed by the determination and effort to change how our minds work. In the short term, the best approach is to simply stop resisting our lives. By this I mean *think, plan, and do the best that we can*, and then just let go. After that, wherever life goes, it goes, and fighting reality can only make us unhappy and regretful.

Beliefs: The Mother of
All Attachments

Aware of suffering created by attachment to views and wrong percep-
tions, I am determined to avoid being narrow-minded and bound to pre-
sent views. I will learn and practice non-attachment from views in order to
be open to others' insights and experiences. I am aware that the knowledge
I presently possess is not changeless, absolute truth. Truth is found in life
and I will observe life within and around me in every moment, ready to
learn throughout my life.

—*Thich Nhat Hanh*[49]

32

Reincarnation, the Big Bang, and Other Possibilities

Why We Mistake Belief for Truth

So convenient a thing it is to be a reasonable creature, since it enables one to find or make a reason for everything one has a mind to do.

—Benjamin Franklin[50]

I was eight years old when I first realized that belief would be difficult for me throughout life. My ideas were so out of step with those of the other children around me.

Ron, my best friend at the time, and I were walking to school on the Friday before our first Holy Communion, the pivotal event in Catholicism that celebrates the turning of bread and wine into the body and blood of Christ. We'd prepared for this day for most of our young lives by studying the Baltimore Catechism, memorizing prayers, and more recently, purchasing our first real suits and rehearsing the ceremony that would take place in front of friends, family, and just about everyone else that we knew in the world. He was bouncing up and down in excitement as we discussed the event that would take place on the following Sunday. My feelings were much different.

I wasn't convinced. That's not to say that this religious practice might not be true. Hundreds of millions of Catholics received the sacrament of Holy Communion every Sunday. I just didn't believe it—not the idea, not the ceremony, none of it. Nonetheless, I had the common sense to keep my opinions to myself. Life as I knew it would have ended if I'd voiced my reservations, to say nothing of the unimaginable reprimand that I would have received from the monsignor. So I kept quiet and vigorously nodded in agreement with Ron. "Yes, this Sunday will be a really wonderful day!"

This same feeling of uncertainty became a regular feature of my life whenever belief was required. I questioned the truth of Confirmation (another Christian sacrament I received a few years later); my father's strident and uncompromising support of his political party (he was a union man, so he supported the Democrats regardless of their qualifications, and a few of the candidates were abysmal); the rationale for the Vietnam War (a doubt that was later confirmed by U.S. military commanders and historians, and poignantly confirmed by me when I experienced the war from the other side during a 2001 visit to the War Remnants Museum in Ho Chi Minh City, Vietnam); and the assertion by atheists that God doesn't exist (I could accept the theory that the universe started with a cataclysmic "Big Bang," but common sense told me that someone had to pull the trigger—not necessarily any of the gods that are worshipped today, but certainly something far more powerful than us where the designation "God" would fit very well).

My discomfort with certainty has followed me to this day. Although I consider myself to be a Buddhist, I don't "believe" any of the precepts that require a leap of faith, such as reincarnation, nirvana, or the type of karma that determines a person's destiny in the next incarnation. I'm a secular Buddhist who uses meditation and Buddhist ethical principles to find wisdom, happiness, and meaning in life.

My ideas about belief evolved over a lifetime. First dismissive sarcasm ("How can anyone believe something so crazy?"), then indifference ("Who cares if they believe something so crazy?"), and finally, five decades into life, humility, understanding, and acceptance of the differences among people ("Who knows? Maybe their beliefs are true."). My breakthrough came while reading page one of *Autobiography of a Yogi*, the life story of Paramahansa Yogananda, one of the preeminent spiritual figures of the 20th century.

> I find my earliest memories covering the anachronistic features of a previous incarnation. Clear recollections came to me of a distant life in which I had been a yogi amid the Himalayan snows. These glimpses of the past, by some dimensionless link, also afforded me a glimpse of the future.[51]

Was he really able to remember events from an earlier life and have a glimpse of the future? I didn't think it was possible, but even as I was doubting his story, I heard an inner voice cautioning me. He was born at a different time (1893) and in a different place (Uttar Pradesh, India); he followed a different religion (Kriya Yoga, one of the Hindu spiritual paths); and he had had totally different life experiences (my formative years were spent with Catholic nuns and priests, while his were with gurus and Hindu swamis). His beliefs and everything he remembered might very well be true, or not, and it's not possible for me to know for sure. But there was one thing I knew: his faith was a source of great value to him and to the people around him, and he used his beliefs to change the world for the better.

I had come to the realization that my understanding of truth would always be only a partial one. In this case, I had no idea if Yogananda could see past lives or the future, but it didn't matter to me anymore. I had abandoned the ideologies that made me close my mind to new ways of seeing the world. Instead, I embraced what Buddhists call the "Middle Way," a philosophy in which the focus of life is on balance and moderation in all things, especially in one's beliefs. This system encouraged me to continuously reconsider my beliefs about everything—God, religion, politics, international relations, and the difficult social issues that cause so much strife worldwide—and to revise them as I acquired more experience and wisdom over time. It proved to be a life-changing approach that led to happiness, inner peace, and greater awareness and concern for the people around me.

Beliefs are firmly held opinions or feelings that something is true. They govern every aspect of our lives: whom to trust; how to raise our children; our ideas about God, religion, politics, and nationalism; and difficult social issues, including immigration, abortion, and alternative lifestyles, such as communal living, polyamory, and gay and lesbian relationships.

Most of us have strong beliefs, and as a practical matter, it would be impossible to get through the day if we had to constantly re-evaluate our views every time we made a decision. What's more, strong beliefs can be a source of happiness and fulfillment, and the inspiration that we use each day to change the world for the better. Problems arise, however, when we become so sure of our convictions that we mistake belief for truth.** Once we reach this level of certainty, we have the potential to harm others as we try, directly or indirectly, to impose our beliefs on them, and to harm ourselves by limiting our potential to discover a higher truth, a truth that might be much different from what we know today.

Because it's always been difficult for me to accept the beliefs that seem to come so easily to others, I'm fascinated by the feeling of certainty that people have about their own ideas, opinions, and

---

** People with this level of commitment often consider their views about religion, politics, or social issues to be "nonnegotiable truths." This mindset is especially damaging to society and to internal growth. It effectively means, "Right or wrong, I'm going to the grave with my beliefs, and there's no power on heaven or earth that can change my mind."

convictions. In particular, how does one make the transition from the open-minded perspective that (1) "This is what I think, but the issues are complicated and my information is limited, so it's possible that I might be wrong," to the unbending conviction that (2) "I'm right, so you must be wrong"? After years of study and observation, I've learned that it starts with a genetic predisposition[52] toward certain ways of thinking,†† and it continues throughout life as we're subjected to innumerable influences, including our upbringing, culture, traditions, education, experiences, the time in history when we happen to live, and a large measure of chance.

Saying that our beliefs are due to the circumstances of our lives and the times in which we live is simply stating the obvious. After all, if we were born at a time when our current views didn't even exist, if our ancestors had emigrated to a different country, or if we had different influences during our lives, then our beliefs would be totally different today. Yet this notion doesn't sit well with most people. We imagine ourselves gathering the principal ideas from around the world, studying them for months or years, and then sifting through the competing claims to find what's right and wrong. But this isn't how beliefs are formed.

I was a good example. I didn't plan to be a middle-aged Buddhist who spent years in Asia and other places outside of North America. Instead, I expected to live my life as a busy physician in the city where I was born and to continue the Baptist-Catholic faith of my youth. (My mother was raised Baptist and converted to Catholicism when she married my father, but she always retained her Baptist principles—no drinking, smoking, swearing, dancing, or card playing—and my upbringing was based on her conservative way of life.) But I left Omaha at age 27 for three years of military

---

†† Genetic predisposition may partially explain why some people's beliefs are based primarily on logic and reason, i.e., their brains require "hard" evidence to be convinced, while others base their beliefs on "soft" evidence derived from a combination of reason, emotion, and faith.

service, which led to other experiences, and I soon discovered that my traditional American views weren't the only ones in the world. My life went in a totally different, totally unexpected direction.

There's a deeply personal reason for why we hold our views so tightly: if we're not right about the issues that are important to us, then some of the basic tenets of our lives would be in doubt, and most people don't want to live with this uncertainty. So we choose to ignore the obvious, namely, that our most cherished beliefs would be different, maybe even the *exact opposite* of what they are today, if life's circumstances had taken us another way. This doesn't mean that we should change our convictions, but it does mean that we need to acknowledge how easy it would have been for us to have beliefs that are *identical* to those of people whom we now consider to be uneducated, uninformed, evil, or even damned. In so doing, we start down a path that will lead to greater understanding of ourselves and far more tolerance of others.

33

Our Most Wonderful
Family Vacation

The Need to Convince Others,
and Ourselves, That We're Right

Do not hold your views too firmly. Every fool is fully convinced, and everyone fully persuaded is a fool; the more erroneous his judgment the more firmly he holds it. There are some heads of iron most difficult to turn, and add caprice to obstinacy and the sum is a wearisome fool. Steadfastness should be for the will, not the mind.

—Baltasar Gracián (1601-1658), Spain[53]

It was the summer of '68. My future wife Chris and I were both sixteen and madly in love, so we were heartbroken by the thought of spending five days apart while I attended the annual Pokorski family vacation. My parents saved the day by inviting her along.

For as long as I could remember, each summer we'd packed the car with all the conveniences of home and made the two-hour drive north to Ponca State Park. It had everything that a boy needed for a great time: fishing in the mighty Missouri River, swimming in an Olympic-size pool, horseback riding, hiking, and even an old-fashioned ice cream parlor. Unfortunately, with the exception of the ice cream, Chris wasn't even remotely interested in any of these things.

We left in high spirits, but problems developed almost immediately. Our car, a subcompact Ford Falcon, was simply too small for a road trip. There were two adults in the front seat, three almost fully grown teenagers—plus Peppy, our pet Boston terrier—crammed cheek-to-jowl in the back, and the trunk was filled beyond capacity with food, clothing, fishing tackle, a portable TV, and beer for five days. My father, a Marlboro man since his days in the Army, smoked during most of the drive. As far as I was concerned, this was normal, but Chris, who was highly sensitive to odors of any kind, was miserable for the entire trip.

To make matters worse, my mother had fed Peppy a half-pound of turkey just before we left—she ate better than millions of people worldwide—and the dog farted non-stop for a hundred miles. Peppy liked to put her nose out the rear window on car trips, and this pointed her backside directly at Chris, the smallest person who'd been assigned the middle seat in the back. In the tight confines of our car, she couldn't say anything as clouds of smoke and fart gas wafted her way, but she didn't have to. The angry looks on her face made it clear how she felt.

Chris was visualizing an upscale log cabin with three bedrooms, loft, fireplace, multiple bathrooms, air conditioning, and a modern kitchen—the kind of place that advertises "Will sleep six to eight people!" However, tradition required that we stay in the same cabin that had always been sufficient for our four-member family since the days when I was so little that I needed a boost to get onto the bed. There were two knotty pine bedrooms, each so small that it was difficult to walk around the bed without hitting your elbows on the wall; a dilapidated, postage stamp-sized kitchen; a small living room that doubled as an eating area; and a single bathroom where all of the surfaces were stained brown from years of contact with unfiltered well water. As if this wasn't bad enough, there was no air conditioning, it smelled moldy, and spider webs hung from most of the window screens. Chris walked in, took one look at the place and shot another icy stare my way. If it were possible, she'd have turned around and gone home.

The car was unloaded, dinner was prepared, the rabbit ears on the TV were adjusted to allow reception of the same three stations that we received at home, and we took our accustomed places in front of the TV to eat dinner and watch the evening news. Everyone felt right at home. Everyone, that is, except Chris. She probably thought that things couldn't get much worse. My parents weren't leaving anything to chance—no hanky-panky under their roof. At bedtime Chris learned that she and my mother, whom she barely knew at the time, would be sleeping in the same bed!

The rest of the trip was a series of unmet expectations. We saved four dollars per day by staying in a non-air conditioned cabin, a serious mistake in mid-July because it was always hot and humid, even at night. Between my father's loud snoring and the clatter of two old fans that blew hot air point-blank at our beds, Chris barely slept at all. During the day, she and I joined Mom and my brother Bill for spirited card games, which often erupted into laughter and gloating when one of the teams made an especially astute play. The fun ended abruptly when my father, who'd been trying to watch TV the whole time, walked over to the table and threw the cards into the air while shouting, "Is that all you people can do is play with those damn cards?"

This vacation was also the time when I learned that Chris wasn't a fan of horseback riding. It probably didn't help much that the corral was awash in mud after an afternoon downpour, clouds of steam hung over the fresh manure, and gigantic horse flies were swarming everywhere.

Her breaking point came during the hike. This activity was always the high point of our vacation. We'd pack water and a few peanut butter and jelly sandwiches, and walk from mid-morning until dinner time. After much encouragement and tales of the wonders of past adventures, Chris begrudgingly agreed to come along, mainly because the only alternative was to stay behind with Peppy, the ever-flatulent dog, and my father, whose idea of exercise was a walk to the refrigerator to get another beer. So off we went, up and down the steep hills that bordered the river, singing songs from our childhood and generally having a fabulous time.

Or so we thought. Chris was kind enough to point out some of the shortcomings of the outing. It was incredibly hot and humid. We were covered with sweat and being eaten alive by mosquitoes. The sandwiches had congealed into a sodden mass of bread and jelly. We were exhausted. And worst of all, we were lost. We finally had to slide down a muddy cliff to reach the river and then wade along the shore for the better part of an hour until we reached the boat dock near our cabin. For Mom, Bill and me, this was yet another family adventure that we'd happily retell over the next year. For Chris, it was an absolute nightmare. She finally sat down on the trail and cried.

Recognizing the gravity of the situation—this prize of a future daughter-in-law might be lost through our stupidity—we played our ace in the hole. Captain Fudge, the famous ice cream parlor, was located in nearby Ponca, Nebraska. The drive to town got off to a rocky start. It was difficult enough for a sober person to navigate the dark, windy roads of the state park, and my father, who'd already drunk a six-pack of beer—and he was just getting started—somehow managed to high-center the car on a narrow wooden bridge. But fate was smiling on us that night. A bunch of equally inebriated young male campers picked up the front of the Falcon and set it back on the road, and we continued merrily on our way.

After we arrived, Chris agreed that Captain Fudge was everything we had claimed: freshly baked waffle cones filled to overflowing with rich, homemade ice cream and topped with a choice of nuts, candies, and whipped cream. As we drove home, her memories of the many prior disasters were rapidly slipping away when we realized that we'd made yet another mind-boggling error: we'd forgotten to buy a treat for Peppy! Crazed with hunger after the hike, all of us had long since wolfed down our ice cream, except for Chris, who was just reaching the cone, her favorite part. We browbeat her into giving it to "the poor dog who stayed home all day while we had fun hiking." That night marked the low point in our one-year relationship.

After five glorious days, we headed for home. My father, never much for socializing, was tired of vacation and eager to get going so he could watch TV and drink beer in his own house instead of in the cabin. He was in an especially foul mood that day, so we watched him from afar as he repacked the Falcon, afraid that he'd explode if we got too close. He slammed the trunk repeatedly, but it still wouldn't close. Wild-eyed with anger, he searched amid the fans, suitcases, and beer coolers until he found the culprit: a three-inch glass jar of spicy Dijon mustard. He seized the jar, bellowed some imaginative profanity to describe the word "mustard," and flung it down the hill.

For some reason, Chris married me. Forty years later, she still tells this story.

My family looked forward to this trip all year long, and we liked everything about it: the tiny cabin, lack of amenities, and strenuous outdoor activities in the summer heat. In fact, we were certain that it was the perfect vacation. As I would learn over the next four decades, Chris wasn't one to keep her opinions to herself, and she was all too happy to tell us that we were just plain wrong.

Like my boyhood family, we all have our own opinions about what's right and wrong, and we're so sure of ourselves that we think people with different ideas are either uninformed or lack the education and life experiences that led us to our current beliefs.

These rigid and often uncompromising views, which typically involve religion, politics, and social issues, are our emotional, spiritual, and intellectual hot buttons. We fight to defend our positions and try, consciously or subconsciously, to convert others to our way of thinking, as my family tried to convince Chris that she really *was* having the time of her life—but she just didn't know it.

What's unfortunate is that sometimes we're dead wrong about our beliefs, or at least not nearly as correct as we imagine, and we pass through our entire lives without knowing it. I was lucky because I was only sixteen when I discovered that I was wrong. Not everyone enjoys a low-budget vacation with their wacky in-laws. In this case, no real harm was done. But as shown in the next story about my friend Jack, our beliefs can cause serious and sometimes irreparable harm, both to ourselves and to others.

34

Jack, the Perfect Son— Until He Wasn't

Ruining Lives to Make a Point, and Then Changing Our Minds

What man is capable of leaving an edifice on whose construction he has spent all his life, even though that edifice is his own prison? It is difficult to get rid of it in one day.

—Kahlil Gibran (1883-1931), Lebanon[54]

Jack was a friend that I met once or twice a year during business trips to Europe. He lived in a large city, but returned home on a regular basis to see his mother in the village where he was raised. They were very close… until she found out that he was gay. Then she disowned him. His lifestyle was simply incompatible with her religious beliefs.

This story is sad because the bond between a mother and a son is normally strong enough to withstand the differences of opinion that often occur between a parent and an adult child. It's even sadder because Jack's mother changed her mind 20 years later and they reconciled shortly before her death. What did she gain by her inflexible views? On the plus side, she had two decades of going to bed each night knowing that she was "right." On the minus side

159

was the loss of a son for 20 years, a time they could have used to share the joys and trials of each other's life. She spent her last six months regretting a decision that could never be changed.

As shown by Jack's mother, beliefs wield enormous power over our minds by controlling what we think, say, and do, even to the point where we use our beliefs to justify extreme actions that contravene our most basic instincts as parents—in this case, abandoning a child. But what's unnerving about our beliefs is their lability. They seem so important to us at any given moment in time, and then one day, after years or decades of following their lead, we often stop, change our minds and adhere to a new set of beliefs—and regret the decisions of the past.

When viewed over a lifetime, beliefs are like sandcastles. We spend a lot of time and energy to build and guard them against the waves, fight over whose is the best, and then leave them behind at the end of the day when we move on to something else. Everyone has a "sandcastle belief" or two, something that seizes control of one's mind. Maybe it's an obsession about work, money, religion, politics, or our good looks or self-importance. Then one day we wake up to find that it's no longer important to us. Our former beliefs now seem so petty and insignificant, and we ask ourselves, *Why did I spend all of those years fretting about something that was of no consequence?* The tragic thing is that by then we've often caused a great deal of suffering and unhappiness as result of our obsessive behavior and disregard for the beliefs and feelings of others.

Remember Jack's mother the next time your mind is seized by its favorite obsession: I must think/must believe/must have/must do. I'm sure that her decision to disown a gay son was based on airtight religious and ethical beliefs. Yet there are tens of millions of parents in the world who are just as religious and just as ethical as Jack's mother, and they decide differently, choosing instead to accept their children as they are. For them, being right is far less important than being there for the people they love.

35

The Pierced Volunteer:
The Korean Orphanage, Part 4

Crippled by Belief

I don't slow down to avoid the illusory puddles of water that appear on the highway before me in the heat of summer. I can't stop "seeing" them. I can learn that they aren't there.

—Kwame Anthony Appiah[55]

Buddhists observe, "Things are not as they seem; nor are they otherwise." I saw a striking example of this aphorism at the orphanage in Seoul when I joined half a dozen other volunteers to play with the children on a sunny autumn afternoon.

One volunteer, a European man in his late twenties, would have stood out in any crowd. His appearance might be described as 1960s biker. He was dressed in leather from head to toe, colorful tattoos adorned both arms, and his hair was dyed an unearthly red and styled in a three-inch spiky Mohawk. But the most distinctive feature—it was hard not to stare—was his face. Everything was pierced: lips, nose, eyebrows, and ears. At any other time I would have moved nervously away from him, figuring that there could be trouble if actions matched appearances. But I got it wrong, totally wrong! Among the volunteers, he was far and away the children's favorite. He'd pick up as many kids as he could, gallop across the room, and then roll around on the floor with them, buried two or three deep in a pile of laughing boys and girls.

We had a chance to talk later in the day. I immediately realized that despite our outward appearances, which were worlds apart, we were much the same. Both of us shared a love for children and a desire to change things for the better. Humbled by my poor judgment, I resolved not to be fooled by appearances again.

First impressions are often far off the mark. Some people, like the pierced volunteer, are diamonds in the rough—caring, sensitive, and insightful. Others are the just opposite, projecting an attractive physical appearance and carefully chosen words that hide a shallow, self-centered person inside. It's up to us to discover the truth.

Since childhood we've been trained to divide the world into broad groups of good and bad according to criteria learned from parents, friends, and our own experiences. The advantage of this approach is that it's efficient. We don't need to spend time analyzing each situation based on its own merits but can just lump things together, make a decision, and move on. In this case, my rule was: Avoid multi-pierced, leather-garbed men with flaming red Mohawk haircuts. They're probably dangerous (he wasn't), drug users (ditto), and uneducated (he had a master's degree in English and taught at a school in Seoul). The problem is that over time we can become prisoners of beliefs and thought patterns that are habitual, ill-informed, and often wrong. I was certainly guilty of this. I came so close to missing the friendship of this wonderful young man and the lesson that he taught me, simply because he couldn't pass my middle-class American hurdle of outward appearances.

It's all too common to meet people who are emotionally, spiritually, and intellectually crippled by their beliefs, people who live in a small-minded world that is closed to new ideas and who refuse to consider the possibility that they might be wrong about important matters in life. I saw this in my father during every election, when he'd proudly exclaim: "I hate that son of a bitch, but I have to vote for him. He's a Democrat!" (Voting for a Republican, even if clearly the better candidate, was out of the question.) Likewise with religion, where he divided the world into two kinds of people: Catholics, who would generally be saved, and just about everyone else, including many Protestants, who were going straight to hell. (He didn't know much about Muslims or Jews, had probably never heard of Hindus, and would have turned over in his grave if he knew that I became a Buddhist.)

Unsophisticated, untraveled, and poorly educated? Yes, these words would describe my father fairly well, but at least he could use his humble upbringing as an excuse for his ignorance. What's much sadder is when my father's beliefs—that people with different political or religious views were idiots at best, and at worst, idolaters who were doomed to hellfire if they didn't repent—are held by people well-traveled and highly educated. Saddest of all, this latter group sometimes includes the leaders of our communities, churches, mosques, synagogues, or temples.

People like this—dogmatic, judgmental, and self-assured—may be at the extremes, but most of us have a bit of this attitude inside us, carrying beliefs and value systems that are long overdue for a checkup to confirm that they're still true today. Yes, easier said than done. Our views about what's right and how things are supposed to be weren't formed yesterday. They've been with us a very long time, first planted by our parents, later modified by our own experiences as adolescents and adults, and continuously nurtured and reinforced throughout life, until our views and our ideas of self become inseparable.

I wasn't finished learning from the experience at the orphanage. Some months later I met Michael, my untattooed and unpierced adult son, for a weekend in Thailand, where we went on a day trip to the ancient capital of Ayudhya. After taking an elephant ride together, we bought two baskets of bananas and bamboo shoots to feed the animals, hoping that their outstretched trunks could tell the difference between fingers and food. Michael always loved and was loved by children, and he took delight in giving his food to the little children around us so they could help feed the elephants. As I stood there sharing Michael's happiness, my mind flashed back to the pierced volunteer in Seoul, so different in appearance from my son, but so much the same inside.

36

The Wojtalewicz Family Reunion

Ideologues: Mirror Images of Self-Righteous Intolerance

It's better to be unhappy about your own ignorance than to die happily with it.

—Paramahansa Yogananda (1893-1952), India[56]

It was just another sweltering August day in 1973, but it was special for us. My wife and I were driving from Omaha to St. Paul, Nebraska, a town of 2,000 people, mainly farmers, to join upwards of 100 people with unpronounceable Polish names for the Wojtalewicz (my wife's maiden name) family reunion.

St. Paul is near the geographical center of the United States— in other words, in the middle of nowhere. The area is so flat that the locals say you could see Denver 500 miles to the west if your eyes were good enough. The drive had two points of interest: (1) corn fields, hence the state's nickname, "Cornhusker State," and (2) cattle grazing next to corn fields. Periodically one of us would spot something unfamiliar in the distance, point excitedly and exclaim, "Look over there! It's a tree!"

Fortunately the trip was brief. It was the tail end of the muscle car era, and I was flying down the road in a yellow Buick Wildcat with a four-barrel carburetor and a gas-guzzling V8 engine. Stomping on the accelerator would simultaneously slam you back into the seat and make your wife complain about your driving—both great fun for a 21-year-old man. The 120-mile trip used almost an entire tank of gas, but at $0.40 per gallon, nobody cared. Besides, environmental concerns and fears of depleting the world's oil reserves wouldn't surface for decades.

The reunion was held at Sherman Dam, a man-made reservoir surrounded by dozens of rusting mobile homes that the farmers used for weekend getaways to escape the stress of day-to-day life. All that cattle mooing would drive anyone crazy. It was a sad scene: after yet another dry summer, most of the water had been drained away to irrigate the fields, leaving the boat docks landlocked and the nearest water hundreds of feet away. The only ones who hadn't heard about the drought were (1) the mosquitoes—Sherman Dam was the largest body of water for 10 miles in any direction, and it was the destination of every stinging insect in the county, and (2) the flies, who were attracted to the piles of fresh cow dung that adorned the edges of the lake. I probably lost several IQ points that day from all the DEET-laden bug repellant I slathered on.

Everyone tried to stay out of the sun by huddling under beach umbrellas—a misnomer since there was no beach, just a point where dried-out prairie grass met dried-out mud where the lake used to be—but many of us were still badly sunburned by the end of the day. However, in those days, we were blissfully ignorant of more than just oil shortages and environmental concerns. A blistering sunburn was a mark of distinction when people returned to work on Monday, usually signifying a wild outdoor weekend involving sports and alcohol. Today it's viewed as a risk factor for malignant melanoma, a serious skin cancer, and nobody goes out in the summer without layers of sunblock.

The men spent their time drinking beer and arguing about the prospects for the Nebraska Cornhuskers football team, while the women chatted, watched the children, and laid out the spread for dinner. Truth be told, Nebraska farmers' wives, not froufrou chefs in big cities who empty your wallet and leave you half-hungry at the end of a meal, are some of the world's best cooks. Everything was fresh: homemade bread and butter, sweet corn, vegetables, steaks, pork ribs, and heavenly apple and cherry pies with crusts made with pure lard (another 20 years would pass before lard was considered a four-letter word by the health conscious). Even the ice cream was churned on the spot.

The Wojtalewicz clan didn't get together very often, mainly for weddings and funerals, so this was a big occasion, drawing relatives from both coasts and points in between. All families have their characters, and they were no exception. Uncle Joe was a prodigious philanderer, doubly cursed with good looks and no common sense. He was a legend in these parts—there are no secrets in a town of 2,000 people—for his one-night stands and failed relationships that started in his teenage years and showed no signs of slowing down in middle age. His specialty was the balancing act. At the time of the reunion, he was having an affair with woman #1, engaged to woman #2, while in the process of divorcing woman #3 (the mother of his two children). I found it exhausting just to think about.

Tom, a relative by marriage, was a man at war with the rest of the world. Quick with a joke, as long as the punch line was racist or sexist, he was like a hair trigger when it came to anger. He perfected the art of road rage long before it became a chapter in self-help books. When confronted with a real or perceived slight by another driver, he would honk his horn aggressively, roll down the window to swear at the other car, and, as often as not, make an obscene gesture to convey his opinion of the other's driving ability. A real piece of work.

Ellen and Richard were cousins who lived within 50 miles of each other. Their views on life couldn't have been more different. Ellen was an ultraliberal atheist—there was no cause that she wouldn't support as long as it involved unfettered freedom of action. She was highly intolerant of anyone who disagreed with her, particularly people who based their decisions on religious principles, and she looked down her hyper-educated nose at the sad, misguided masses, which included me and almost everyone else at the reunion, who thought otherwise.

Richard, on the other hand, was a rabid patriot, and everyone knew exactly where he stood on the issues. He made sure of that by wearing a T-shirt that featured an oversized eagle, a shield with the United States stars and stripes, and the words, "My Country: Love It or Leave It." It was a strange clothing choice that reflected his ultra-nationalistic views, and even stranger because he'd hardly ever been out of Nebraska, let alone the U.S., so he had no idea how people lived in other parts of the world. He railed nonstop about gays, Catholics, the liberal judicial system, deteriorating moral values, and the influx of immigrants—which was wildly ironic because he was only a third-generation American himself and his grandfather had fought *against* the U.S. during World War I. According to his way of thinking, we were perched on the brink of Armageddon and he expected to be one of the few righteous people left standing when it happened.

Aunt Marie was insufferable; it took all of my patience to spend even a few minutes with her. She complained about her husband, a happy-go-lucky farmer who was missing a few fingers on his right hand after an unfortunate run-in with the blades of a corn picker years earlier (and a lot of brain cells from a lifetime of heavy drinking); her son, who seemed to be following closely in his father's footsteps, given the amount of beer that he drank; and her sad life.

Donna was just as bad, but in a different way. Life had dealt her an enviable hand. Raised in relative affluence compared to the rest of us—her father was a banker in Grand Island, the nearby metropolis of 35,000 people—she had a brilliant mind that helped her land a job at a top accounting firm in Chicago. She was all about success. The nice clothes, the big Cadillac (considered a status symbol in the 1970s; how times have changed!), the upscale friends that matched her lifestyle. And she wasn't about to let the rest of us schmucks forget it.

Then there was Dianne, a breath of fresh air. Her father, a widowed alcoholic pig farmer (he was the alcoholic, not the pigs), had no time for distractions like work and raising children. Dianne was an indentured servant in her own home, up before dawn to feed the animals and make breakfast for her four younger siblings. After school and on weekends, she'd till the fields with the tractor and do other chores, more a man than a 14-year-old girl. Raised with far fewer opportunities than most people, somehow she rose above it all. She became a nurse and moved away to a better life. Open-minded (unlike so many of her relatives), highly spiritual, and beaming with a genuine, through-and-through happiness that's rare in this world, I could have talked with her for days on end.

One of my main recollections of the reunion was the number of unhappy people: Uncle Joe, the practiced adulterer; Tom, the misanthrope; Ellen and Richard, mirror images of each other's self-righteous intolerance; Aunt Marie, poster child for the negative attitude; and Donna, the millionaire-to-be who forgot where she had come from. If I could go back in time and explain my ideas for happiness—a sense of inner peace based on wisdom, contentment, and mindfulness—they probably would have laughed uncomfortably and said, "Well, I guess that means I'll never be happy!"

I don't know about never, but this laissez-faire attitude is more often the rule than the exception. In the hierarchy of life goals, attaining deep and long-lasting happiness is right near the top, but most people give it little thought and no serious effort. Some wake up, perhaps after a battle with cancer, loss of a job, or the death of a loved one, and find happiness in the years they have left. Many others just carry on, setting the bar for happiness so low that they think they've achieved it.

I was also struck by the lack of association between religion and happiness in some of my wife's relatives. Religion usually makes people happier,[57] and these were all church-going people. Why, even Uncle Joe was a regular at Sunday services! Yet many of them were absolutely miserable. I suspect that church was something they just did on Sunday mornings, and they had long since stopped using their faith as an inspiration in their daily lives.

But what most impressed me about the reunion was the number of ideologues, people who had staked out a position at one of the extremes and who were committed to defending it for dear life. Their views were clearly, sometimes painfully visible after only a few minutes' conversation. They had so much invested—emotionally, spiritually, and intellectually—that nothing would ever budge them from their uncompromising beliefs.

Ellen and Richard were especially disturbing. The faces they showed to the world were radically different, but deep down they had many similarities: equally critical of anyone who disagreed with them, quick to anger when defending their opinions, and highly insular in their views of how things ought to be. I didn't agree with Ellen's liberal perspective that "anything goes" and her seeming disdain for any bedrock ethical principles, nor with Richard's sanctimonious, holier-than-thou criticism of people who didn't look, talk, and act like him.

Three decades would pass before I learned about the Buddhist practice of the "Middle Way." It's not a forced, insincere compromise between extremes, like an unhappy married couple that stays together for the children, knowing that a split-up is inevitable in the future. Rather, it's freedom from dogmatic views of all kinds, and a purposeful desire and willingness to learn and to change. This philosophy of life, where we're at peace with ourselves and the world, was in short supply that day.

37

Lobster for Lovers

Separating Good and Evil: Not a Job for the "Experts"

Wisdom frees us from the tyranny of events.

—Buddhist proverb

Bob, my future son-in-law, was head-over-heels in love with our daughter Lisa, so he was spending a week with us during his summer vacation from college. Lisa's birthday happened to occur during his visit, and he wanted to surprise her with a special lunch. The situation was complicated because she was working full time about five miles away in our suburban town of Fairfield, Connecticut, and she didn't have time to come home for lunch, and Bob didn't have a car. We offered to drive him to meet her, but he insisted on handling the operation alone from start to finish. This meant he'd cook the meal and deliver it himself. By bicycle.

Lisa's birthday is in July, and the temperature that day was 95 degrees with high humidity. We didn't have air conditioning—it was a choice between air conditioning the house or paying for the kids' college—so it was even hotter inside the house. Chris and my mom escaped to the back deck in search of shade and a breeze. But weather is of no concern to a love-struck young man, and he planned the meal accordingly: lobster ravioli with broccoli cream sauce, a dish requiring lots of kitchen time.

SAME SAME, BUT DIFFERENT

The meal preparation was disorganized from start to finish because Bob didn't know where anything was in the kitchen, so he kept running out to the deck to ask where we kept the spices, sauce pans, and oven mitts. The last 10 minutes were especially chaotic. As an experienced chef and aficionado of Italian cuisine, he knew that the cooking time was critical for pasta al dente, and near the end he burst onto the deck, totally drenched in sweat from two hours in a steaming kitchen, and demanded to know the location of the pasta strainer. He reappeared five minutes later, still sweating profusely, but now bare-chested and wringing out his shirt. When asked what was going on, Bob replied in his typically understated manner, "I couldn't find the strainer, so I had to use my T-shirt." Chris and Mom looked at each other in absolute silence, trying to decide if they were more inclined to humor or revulsion, and not trusting themselves to express either emotion in front of someone who seemed to have been born and raised on a planet with radically different standards of hygiene.

Undaunted, Bob put on a clean shirt, mounted his bike, and rode to meet the love of his life, a saucepan of lobster ravioli carefully balanced on the handlebars and the tips of a dozen red roses peeking out from the top of his backpack. He related the entire story before they ate, including the part about the improvised strainer. Lisa must have really loved him, because she ate it. I wonder what she would have done if she were her mother's age at the time, and her husband of 35 years had tried to romance her with a similar birthday treat? "Say, honey, I've got a great idea! Let's skip your birthday celebration at that nice French restaurant that we save for special occasions. We'll stay home and I'll cook lobster ravioli, and we can relive the joy of eating pasta strained through a sweaty T-shirt!" I'm pretty sure I know what Lisa would say. In my case, Chris would tell me in no uncertain terms what she thought of the idea.

If there was ever a situation where the difference between right and wrong was so obvious that it was beyond debate, this story fits the bill. Few sane people would knowingly eat food that had been in contact with a sweat-drenched shirt. But people who are young and newly in love often seem a bit insane, and there are a lot of them in the world.

There's a natural tendency to divide things into right and wrong and good and evil. It simplifies life so we don't need to go through a detailed analysis of all the situations that we encounter each day. Part of this process involves deferring to the opinion of "experts"—parents, elders, news analysts, talk show hosts, and political and religious leaders—who, presumably, have done the heavy spiritual and intellectual lifting needed to arrive at the correct decision and thereby make our lives easier by telling us what we should do.

The problems with this approach are obvious. First, simplification stops further analysis. If something is known to be evil because someone older, wiser, or in a position of authority *says* that it's evil, then there's no need for us to ask ourselves, *Why? Am I sure? Did we, or our ancestors, do something to foster the situation that exists today?*

Second, while we're preoccupied with making decisions and judgments in the present, it's easy to forget how often we were wrong in the past, even about important matters. Who hasn't looked back at some of their earlier beliefs and wondered, *What was I thinking? How could I have gotten it so wrong?* This realization alone—that sometimes we're not very good at separating good and evil—should make us cautious, slow to judge, and highly respectful of others' views on life. With the wisdom that will, one hopes, come with age and hindsight, we might see things a lot differently in the future.

Finally, our experts are often wrong, not necessarily willfully so, but because nobody has access to all the information needed to make a correct decision. War is a perfect example. Unless we needed to defend ourselves against some unquestionable and imminent threat, who in their right mind would leave their spouse and children to march off to war, knowing that they might be killed or horribly maimed? And yet civil wars and international conflicts are common. Politicians worldwide are somehow able to convince us to fight for the "greater good," urging us to protect *our* way of life and *our* religious beliefs, with little regard for how others live *their* lives or what *they* believe. The tragedy is that history often proves these leaders wrong.

The next time you find yourself thinking, *These misguided ideas about religion, politics, international affairs, or social issues are wrong, absolutely, unequivocally wrong* ... stop for a moment. Let your mind wander free, before the time of the experts who helped shape your opinions, before you had everything in life figured out, all the way back to your idealistic youth, when you used to think long and hard about what mattered most in life. Picture yourself as a love-struck young man holding roses, a bowl of lobster ravioli, and a sopping wet T-shirt, and ask, *Why not?*

38

Meat Rocks, Stoop, and the Thanksgiving Feast

How Biases and Information Cascades Distort Our Beliefs

I will look at any additional evidence to confirm the opinion to which I have already come.

—Lord Molson, (1903-1991), England[58]

When I was a child, my mother's guiding principle for food preparation could have been summarized in a three-word sentence: Thicker is better. Meatloaf was called "meat rock" because it was heavy, tasteless, and as dry as a bone. This was accomplished by mixing half a dozen eggs with a pound of ground beef, then adding enough bread crumbs to absorb any juice that might have added texture or flavor. Likewise with beef stew, which we labeled "stoop" because, as my mom cheerfully observed, "It's neither stew nor soup!" She started with what promised to be a respectable stew, lots of fresh vegetables and savory beef simmered for hours on the stove, and then she added cornstarch until a fork could stand upright in the pot. Our family would have contests where we'd load a spoon and turn it upside down to see whose stoop would be the last to drop back onto the plate.

Sometimes Mom would experiment with exotic cuisines such as Chinese, Italian, and "seafood." Chinese meant canned chop suey with canned chow mein noodles. Her Italian specialties were canned ravioli; spaghetti with meatballs that were the size and consistency of small baseballs (as with the meatloaf, meatballs were packed with bread crumbs to make them more filling); and hamburger pizza that she topped with semi-solid globs of orange cheese squirted from a pressurized can (the appearance was disturbingly similar to fresh bird droppings).

And seafood. Exotic? This was the 1950s, and Nebraska, a Midwestern state located 1,500 miles from the nearest ocean, was one of the biggest beef producers in the world. (Three decades later, my father-in-law actually became angry when he heard that several of our children were vegetarian.) Mom's idea of seafood was fish sticks: a heavily breaded, tasteless dish made palatable only by covering it with copious amounts of spicy red cocktail sauce and artificial lemon juice that we squeezed from a canary-yellow plastic lemon that sat for years in the door of the refrigerator.

Thanksgiving was her finest hour. Pretty much everything except the turkey was either canned or reconstituted from a store-bought, pre-packaged meal. The boxed stuffing would have been halfway decent if she'd left it alone, but she added giblets (the gizzard, heart, and assorted entrails) and bread crumbs, and then put it through a meat grinder a few times until it assumed the appearance and consistency of mush. Mashed potatoes? From a box. Cranberries, green beans, and yams? Canned. Whipped cream? Squirt can. The gravy was homemade, but Mom managed to put her usual creative spin on things. She didn't waste time simmering the gravy until it reached the perfect consistency; she just drained off some of the turkey drippings and added cornstarch until everything congealed nicely in the pan. For the turkey, she set her alarm for 3 a.m., put it in the oven, and served it 12 hours later. The food was so dry that we had to ladle obscene amounts of gravy over everything except the cranberries. To be honest, it all tasted fantastic.

Finally, to make an already wonderful feast even better, we filled our plates and adjourned to the living room, where we sat on the sofa, our food and drinks carefully balanced on wobbly, overloaded metal TV trays, and watched whatever happened to be on television at the time. Ah, life was good at age 10.

I ate like this every meal of my life until I married and moved away from home. Mom never knew that she was a bad cook, and nobody else in the family knew it either. (I began to have my suspicions as a teenager. The high school cafeteria served the best food that I'd ever eaten, but most of my friends couldn't stand it.) Our little family was isolated in our little house, and this kind of cooking was perfectly normal, so we never even questioned it. In fact, the opposite. In our universe of four people, we thought this was the best way to eat because it tasted good, and our brief forays into ethnic cuisines only convinced us more.

This was our view about cooking, but our beliefs about other issues were just as one-sided. And why wouldn't they be? We lived in a conservative Midwestern town in the United States where most of the people were a lot like us. Of course, we knew there were different ways to do things, but we figured that ours was the best because it worked for us and the people we knew.

This kind of certainty of belief isn't confined to uninformed ideas about food in small-town America. It's also the rule worldwide for the serious concerns in life. Who isn't convinced that they have the correct views on religion, politics, and social issues like abortion, sexual orientation, immigration, and the environment? As with my childhood family, we think our convictions have a rock-solid foundation that is firmly based on evidence for the things that can be known, and on a "higher power" for the things that must be accepted on faith.

This is not the case. Our views about even the most important issues are distorted by the many biases that we've acquired over the course of our lives. These biases—which subconsciously influence our ideas, opinions, beliefs, and even our religious faith—make it difficult, and seemingly impossible in some cases, to tell the difference between how things are and how we think they are.

Some of these thought-bending predispositions are listed below.[59] It's easy to imagine how these biases could influence the beliefs of individuals, families, political and religious groups, and even entire countries. It's much harder to admit that we're personally affected in the same way.

• Family bias. We tend to automatically believe information from family and friends without subjecting it to the same evidence requirements that we require from others.

• Group bias. Preference is given to ideas and opinions from within our group, and we tend to disparage or reject the beliefs of those outside the group.

• Group consensus bias. The more people agree with us, the more we assume that our beliefs are correct. Conversely, the more people disagree with us, the more likely we are to suppress and doubt our own beliefs, even if they're correct.

• Bandwagon bias. This is the tendency to go along with the belief system of our group and to modify our beliefs to fit theirs.

• Cause-and-effect bias. Our brain is predisposed toward making a causal connection between two events, even when none exists.

• Perceptual bias. We automatically assume that our beliefs and opinions reflect objective truths about the world.

• Certainty bias. Our brain doesn't like uncertainty. We prefer to believe or not believe, rather than remain uncertain.

• Confirmation bias. This is the tendency to look for or interpret information that confirms our beliefs, and to avoid, ignore, or undervalue information and interpretations that contradict our existing views.

Confirmation bias is one of the most interesting of these mental predispositions because we experience it every day, often many times per day, and yet never recognize it. For example, when watching a political debate we might be impressed with the articulate, logical, and highly ethical responses from the liberal candidate, and find fault with the opponent. Our next-door neighbor, who supports the conservative, hears the same message and reaches exactly the opposite conclusion. Over time, both of us become more confident that we've made the right choice and that our beliefs have been confirmed by the "evidence" of superior performance in a face-to-face debate.

Sophisticated brain scanning experiments have shed light on what happens in these cases. When listening to information that agrees with existing opinions, people turn off the areas of the brain that are associated with reasoning, but there is a lot of activity in the parts of the brain that deal with emotions, pleasure, and judgments about morality.[60] In other words, when we've already made up our minds on an issue, we feel that we're right, but no longer think about what's being said.

In his book *Predictably Irrational*, Dan Ariely describes an experiment that demonstrates how confirmation bias can limit our ability to make rational choices.[61] The study group, undergraduate students at the Massachusetts Institute of Technology, were asked to evaluate the taste of beer before or after balsamic vinegar was added. Students usually *didn't* like the beer if they knew about the vinegar before they drank it, but they generally liked the beer if they were told about the vinegar *after* drinking it. The preconception that they wouldn't like beer with vinegar overwhelmed their ability to be neutral in evaluating a new situation.

Though humorous in the context of beer preference, which probably isn't on anyone's "Top Ten" list of concerns (except maybe for college students), confirmation bias becomes a much more serious problem when dealing with religion, politics, and the difficult social questions that we face every day. For all of these issues, we're generally not interested in new information if it threatens our current beliefs.

In addition to biases, we make other mental mistakes that can take our beliefs far from reality. One of these mistakes is the "informational cascade," more commonly known as the "herding instinct."[62] The term was first used by economists to describe what happens in financial markets when a surge in selling by a few traders is followed by the entire market because everyone thinks, incorrectly, that the first traders must have had better information. We don't need to visit the stock market to see information cascades in action; they can be found in all aspects of our lives.

The basic problem is that none of us can be experts in everything, so we look to others for guidance. When someone takes a strong position, especially if the person is knowledgeable, confident, and charismatic, it's human nature to defer to him or her. Once a critical mass of people has sided with the "expert," the rest of us make the rational decision to go along because we figure that so many people couldn't possibly be wrong.[63] But they could be and sometimes are wrong.

I've seen plenty of informational cascades in health and medicine. In an article titled "Medical Myths," the *British Journal of Medicine* concluded that there was no proof for any of the following "truisms":[64]

- We should drink at least eight glasses of water a day.
- We use only 10% of our brains.
- Reading in dim light ruins your eyesight.
- Eating turkey makes people especially drowsy.
- Shaving causes hair to grow back faster or coarser.

I found the last myth interesting because I had personal experience with it on two occasions. The first time was when I was 13 and desperate to grow facial hair to look older and, I hoped, increase my appeal to the opposite sex. Each morning I'd borrow my father's razor and sneak into the bathroom to shave the peach fuzz on my face. Not only did it not work, but I still can't grow a decent mustache to this day. The second time was during a visit to Asia when I saw dozens of bald children, often girls. I thought there was an epidemic of leukemia, with scores of unfortunate children receiving chemotherapy. Later I was told that it was common practice for parents to shave the heads of their children to stimulate the growth of thick, luxurious hair. There has been convincing evidence against this idea *for more than a century*, and yet there are hundreds of millions of people worldwide who still hold this belief. One has to wonder how many of our other beliefs, passed down from generation to generation and anointed with the "truth" of time and tradition, are equally flawed.

It would be comforting to think that our biases, flawed judgments, unsubstantiated opinions, and mistaken beliefs would change when we were presented with reliable information which showed the errors that we'd made. But that's not what happens. Research has shown that people's views are extraordinarily persistent in the face of contrary evidence.[65] The reason is that our beliefs form the basis for who we are and how we define ourselves, and we don't want to let them go, even if we're wrong. So we cling to our current views and never become the person we might have been if we'd allowed ourselves the freedom to have a broader, more inclusive outlook on life.

None of us can fully overcome all of the biases that we acquire during life, but we can recognize them and act accordingly. For example, I'm still fond of my mother's cooking (except for the stoop!), but I've learned there are other foods that are different and sometimes better. One of my principal biases today is that the world would be a better place if everyone let go of their strident and often uncompromising beliefs—especially about religion, politics, nationalism, and divisive social concerns—and moved toward the middle on these issues. I recognize that this idea may be wrong, but if it is, the worst result would be a world that is happier, more peaceful, and far more tolerant. It's a bias that I'm glad to acknowledge.

39

Tiger's Milk:
Nature's Wonder Food?

Anchored to Our Views—Right or Wrong

People acknowledge that their own backgrounds have shaped their views, but such experiences are invariably seen as deepening one's insights. But the background of other people is used to explain their biases and covert motivations. It just seems plain as day, to the naïve realist, that everyone is influenced by ideology and self-interest. Except for me. I see things as they are.

—Jonathan Haidt[66]

My mother had a lifelong fascination with nutrition even though she knew next to nothing about it. Her specialty was baked goods. Picture your grandmother's old fashioned kitchen with mouth-watering cookies in all stages of production—some still dough that would be molded into fun shapes and decorated with multi-colored sugars and candies, some browning in the oven, and others cooling on trays while excited children hovered nearby as the wonderful smell of freshly baked cookies wafted through the room.

Now forget it, all of it, because that's not what happened at our house. Cookies weren't for fun; they were a serious source of nutrition. The end result was a cookie in name only. They had a heft to them that instilled both curiosity and caution in first-time eaters, an unworldly red-brown color from high concentrations of molasses and orange juice, and absolutely no smell. But the most remarkable thing was the texture—sort of like a moist, well-used sponge. They'd actually bounce when dropped from shoulder height. My father had a name for them: cookie rocks. Cruel, but a fair description nonetheless.

Here's the recipe. Note the complete absence of sugar, white or wheat flour, butter, and other traditional baking ingredients. Mom was at the forefront of nutritional experimentation: ingredients like soy flour and wheat germ didn't become staples of a healthy diet until three decades later. It's just too bad that she had to experiment on us.

Skim milk powder

Soy flour

Unsweetened gelatin

Orange juice concentrate

Wheat germ

Black strap molasses (the nutritional information on the jar described it as "a thick viscous syrup with a robust bittersweet flavor")

Brewer's yeast (it was marketed as "nature's wonder food"; see the next paragraph for a second opinion).

"Tiger's milk" was her masterpiece, a drink created by a half-crazed, masochistic health food quack who somehow caught the ear of an unsuspecting public in the early 1960s. There were three ingredients: wheat germ, brewer's yeast, and a sweet, orange-flavored powder (which is still sold today, though its appeal faded once people realized that it contained a gut-busting amount of sugar). Copious amounts of each were spooned into an oversized glass of water and stirred vigorously, but particles of undissolved yeast would float to the top, imparting the concoction with a fetid odor and an ominous appearance more fitting for a toxic waste site. The key was to drink it quickly before the wheat germ and yeast settled to the bottom, and before your nose, taste buds, and gag reflex realized what you were up to. The history of tiger's milk was brief at our house. I drank it one day after a particularly large pancake breakfast, retched violently, and vomited everything into the kitchen sink. To this day I can't smell brewer's yeast without nausea-inducing flashbacks to that morning.

Mom's belief that she was an expert at preparing nutritious meals and desserts is typical of how highly we value our own ideas, even if there is strong evidence to the contrary. She was a classic example of how anchoring skews our perspective of the world and fools us into thinking that we know more than we do.

Anchoring is the tendency to rely too heavily or to "anchor" on the limited information that we happen to have. In the original description of this process, Amos Tversky and Daniel Kahneman showed that random suggestions influenced the answers to totally unrelated questions.[67] People simply could not forget what they had heard earlier, and they incorporated this information into later judgments. If random information affects what we think, it's certain that the strongly directed views of parents, teachers, and our social networks would be even more firmly ingrained in our thought patterns. Once we've set our anchors, such as deciding that a person is good or bad, or that a body of belief (religion, politics, sexual orientation, environmental concerns, etc.) is right or wrong, we keep returning to our set point, always seeking evidence to confirm our current opinion. Ironically, the more information we have, the more certain we are of our beliefs, even when we're clearly wrong.

Anchoring is extremely common with political views. For instance, maybe you're liberal when it comes to social issues, with your emotional and intellectual anchors firmly tied to ideas that support your position. You read liberal books and newspapers, listen to liberal talk show programs, and associate with other liberal thinkers—all of which is done subconsciously—while ignoring the many well-thought-out ideas of people who have more conservative views. At a societal level, the effect of this focused, one-sided learning is that people segregate themselves into their own political worlds, surround themselves with reassuring news and companions, and block out opinions that conflict with what they already believe.[68] It's no wonder we're often so self-assured about complicated issues that defy easy solutions.

It's the same with religion. We focus all our energy and attention on one body of knowledge—the Adi Granth (Sikhism), Bhagavad Gita (Hinduism), Bible (Christianity), Dhammapada (Buddhist), Koran (Islam), Torah (Judaism), or texts that advocate atheism or secular humanism—memorize passages and arguments that support our views, and completely disregard other spiritual beliefs that are embraced by hundreds of millions of people worldwide. What is the inevitable result? Over time, we become more and more convinced that we've found the truth.

To demonstrate how anchoring affects our views on spirituality, I've listed some of the most popular religions in the table below.[69,70] What do you think when you see this list? Is your first reaction, "Wow! Look at the diversity of religious beliefs in the world. Isn't it wonderful that there are so many different ways for people to achieve their spiritual goals?" Maybe, but at least one of these belief systems might trigger a negative emotional reaction—skepticism, disbelief, or perhaps even borderline anger. Why? Because we've already set our spiritual anchor at our own chosen faith—or lack of faith—and we keep returning to that point to judge the value and truth of the other beliefs.

Religious movement	Date founded	Members
Unification Church	1954 CE	1,000,000
Scientology	1953 CE	500,000
Wicca (neopaganism)	1939 CE	1,000,000
Rastafarian	1930 CE	600,000
Jehovah's Witnesses	1879 CE	18,000,000
Church of Christ, Scientist	1879 CE	400,000
Seventh Day Adventists	1863 CE	15,000,000
Bahá'í Faith	1844 CE	7,000,000
Mormons	1820 CE	13,000,000
Protestantism	1517 CE	670,000,000
Sikhism	1507 CE	23,000,000
Islam	622 CE	1,500,000,000
Catholicism	30 CE	1,300,000,000
Buddhism	531 BCE	376,000,000
Jainism	900 BCE	4,200,000
Judaism	2000 BCE	14,000,000
Hinduism	3500 BCE	900,000,000
Secular/Nonreligious	--	1,100,000,000

When it comes to our beliefs about religion and other highly personal issues that have the potential to threaten who we are, or who we believe ourselves to be, it's hard to escape the emotional, spiritual, and intellectual restrictions that so tightly limit what we allow our minds to consider. For one thing, we don't often stray from a path that's been well-worn over time. As an example, few would be willing to say, "Although I was raised as a Muslim, I will set aside the beliefs that I have held for the last 40 years and that my ancestors have kept alive for over a thousand years, and seriously consider whether Christianity, Hinduism, or secular humanism might be a better approach." And there's no need to abandon our current beliefs, with the caveat that we need to acknowledge that the circumstances in which we were raised played a major role

in shaping our beliefs, and that if those influences had been different, so would our views on religion and the other so-called certainties of life that are so near and dear to us today.

Another mental limitation that keeps us tethered to our current views is that we don't live long enough—100 years if we're
lucky—to appreciate how the world changes over centuries and
millennia, and how truth can be much different for each generation.
Four of the movements in the table began in the 1900s; for us,
they're new. Five others, represented by tens of millions of believers, were started in the 1800s, and to the people who lived at that
time, they, too, were new. Go back to the 1500s, seemingly a long
time in the past, but only five 100-year lifetimes. When Protestantism (1517 CE) and Sikhism (1507 CE) were started, the established
mainstream religions of their time, Catholicism and Hinduism,
respectively, considered them to be insignificant breakaway movements whose followers were indisputably wrong. The same is true
for the oldest religions. Islam was considered heretical by Christians, Christianity was considered heretical by Jews and followers of
the Roman polytheistic religions, and Jainism and Buddhism were
considered heretical by Hindus.

This kind of thinking—focused on the present and a few generations in the past or future—has been the norm since people first
walked the earth. It's almost impossible for us to imagine that our
descendants will cherish religions and belief systems that may not
even exist until long after we're dead. In turn, these descendants,
perhaps as soon as our children and grandchildren, will look back at
our spiritual beliefs and wonder, "How could they have had such
strange ideas and beliefs?" just as many of us do today when we
look at the religions in the table... except for our own. We think
that religion evolved over eons, always flawed and incomplete, until
it reached our current set of beliefs—or lack of beliefs—and then
everything STOPPED. No more prophets or updated interpretations of sacred scripture, and no possibility for religion to radically

reinvent itself to meet the needs of people who will live a thousand centuries in the future.

So where does this leave us, knowing, or at least beginning to consider the possibility, that what we believe today is far from the certainty that we'd like to have? The Dalai Lama provided some practical advice in this regard: reduce our value system to a few fundamentals and then live life according to these core principles.[71] This advice makes perfect sense. It allows us to choose our own religious and ethical values, while still retaining the flexibility to deal with the innumerable one-off situations that we encounter each day. Most importantly, we free ourselves from the limitations of a rigid belief system—the official position of our political party, religion, or social group that used to tell us what we should think, say, and do.

This approach is easier than you might imagine. With religion, for example, we retain our belief in the main dogmas of our faith, let go of the dozens or even hundreds of non-doctrinal rules and scriptural interpretations, and emphasize the tenets that are common to religions worldwide, such as benevolence, generosity, humility, and tolerance. In this way, there's no need to compromise our fundamental values, and yet we can do what's right at the time, even if it means taking an action that's much different from what we would have done in the past.

My guiding principles are that (1) people are naturally good and will show it if given a chance, (2) true happiness requires wisdom, contentment, and mindfulness, and (3) the world would be a better place if everyone were more accepting of the views of others. Other than that, I'm content to let people believe what they want to believe. To my way of thinking, if you wake up each morning and make a concerted effort to do good throughout the day, you're a good person, and it doesn't matter one bit if you're conservative or liberal; French, Chinese, or Iranian; or if you get your inspiration from Allah, Brahman, Buddha, Jesus, Yahweh, or the spirit of humanity.

40

One-Nighters in the High Country

Lessons Learned About the Formation—
and Errors—of Dogmatic Beliefs

"We only see what we know."

—Goethe

Our passions in life, the activities that bring us so much joy and happiness, are unique to each individual. For this reason, it's usually a mistake to try to convert others to our way of thinking. I learned this lesson twice in the high country of Colorado.

Chris and I were married for only a year when I somehow talked her into going on a three-day backpacking trip in the mountains. In many ways, we've always been polar opposites, even for our ideas of the perfect vacation. Creature comforts were high on her list—she wanted clean sheets, fine dining, a leisurely late-morning breakfast, and the minimum amount of exercise needed to keep body and soul together. In contrast, my dream vacation was a backpacking trip in the mountains, where my main concerns were more like, *How many miles can I hike before the sun goes down? Where should I pitch the tent?* and *How early do I need to get up tomorrow so I can reach the top of that mountain over there?*

We parked at 7,000 feet next to a crystal clear lake, laced up our heavy-duty hiking boots, strapped on our packs, and began a steep climb. Chris started to complain almost immediately. "My pack's too heavy… These shoes hurt my feet… You're going too fast… How much farther is it?"

We stopped for the night at 10,000 feet at a lake surrounded by towering, snow-capped mountains. It was awesome! But there were issues that my wife was kind enough to mention. "There are dozens of people here, but nobody was down at the lake where we parked… The ground's hard [this still ranks as one of her more memorable complaints, and there were many]… It's so cold that the lake is frozen!" All true, and the latter issue was especially problematic because I had to pound through the ice to get water and then boil it for drinking.

My plan was to wake up before sunrise, climb the highest peak we could find, eat dinner, and then relax in front of a cozy campfire with a good book and a night of romance. But by the next morning I knew that I was fighting a losing battle. Chris didn't sleep well—the ground was indeed hard—and she was in no mood for a second strenuous hike in as many days. Seeing me flail away at the ice with a tent stake—we needed more water to make coffee—was too much for her, and she finally exploded in anger. An hour later we were fully packed and walking back to the car. We checked into a charming bed and breakfast inn that provided clean sheets, gourmet meals, and a late breakfast. Our days of backpacking together were officially over.

Chris was a lost cause as a backpacking partner, so I asked my brother Bill. He accepted immediately, and one year later we were hiking up a different peak in the same Colorado mountain range. I had known there'd be trouble, but it surfaced earlier than I'd thought. Whereas Chris was passively fit, Bill was actively unfit (avoiding all types of exercise was one of his guiding principles), a bit on the heavy side (I'm being kind), and a heavy smoker. He huffed and puffed up the mountain, always in good spirits, but constantly stopping for a cigarette break. It took twice as long as I'd planned to get to our base camp, the sun was already setting, and

Bill was totally exhausted—and this was the easiest day of our three-day hike. I resigned myself to our fate. There would be no scaling of mountain peaks the next day; he'd never make it. As with Chris, this trip would be a one-nighter.

We were famished after the day's exertion and decided to splurge, so in one meal we ate most of the food that we'd brought with us. The highlight of our dinner was canned Spam. We fried it until it was burnt black, and made sandwiches with white bread and mustard. Whether it was hunger, high altitude sickness, or good times with my brother, it was a wonderful meal that I've never forgotten.

My dogmatic view—that backpacking in the mountains was so much fun that everyone would love it—was pretty tame in the grand scheme of things. After all, hiking never hurt anyone. (Chris and Bill might disagree. Both could hardly walk the next day!) The problem was that it was no longer just a healthy avocation for me, but an obsession that threw off my mental balance. And of course, I was wrong again—a lot of people didn't like my hobby. Quite a few seemed to hate it.

In Buddhism and many other spiritual traditions, attachment to dogmatic views of any kind is considered a significant problem. Why? Once we've made up our minds about an issue, we're no longer willing to seriously consider other possibilities. At that point, our learning effectively ceases, and we carry on for years, decades, or even a lifetime thinking and acting as we've always done in the past. In contrast, being uncertain or "not knowing" is highly valued. This means letting go of strongly held opinions about how things are or how they should be and opening our minds to the many different ways of seeing the world.

The switch to a belief system that emphasizes "not knowing" is a difficult emotional, spiritual, and intellectual adjustment because our minds have a natural preference for certainty rather than uncertainty (the "certainty bias" mentioned earlier), and if left to its own designs, it will make a choice rather than remain uncommitted—a choice which might be right, wrong, or both, depending on one's perspective. A mindset based on not knowing is also difficult because it forces us to acknowledge that most of what we think we know, including our most tightly held views about God, religion, politics, and social issues, is not truth in any sense of the word, but rather opinion, conjecture, belief, or faith.

In fact, none of our convictions fit well in the truth category. Our understanding of reality, and even our ability to understand reality, is strongly influenced by our genetic makeup and the circumstances of our lives, including when and where we were born, what we learned at an impressionable age, and our education and life experiences.[‡‡] Why else would people in different parts of the world have such locale- and age-specific views? During my travels, I found that Indonesians were mainly Muslim, Indians were generally Hindu, and Italians were Christian; political systems were different in Russia, Argentina, and North Korea; and ideas about social issues sometimes varied dramatically from country to country and in the young compared to the old. For all of these people, their traditions, customs, beliefs, and religious faith were what they knew, and as far as each person could tell, they were right.

The close association between locale, life experience, and belief can be found in the person of Francis Collins, one of the world's most gifted scientists and a strong advocate of the compatibility of religious belief, particularly the creationist view that the earth was created in six days, as described in the Book of Genesis, and scien-

---

[‡‡] This characterization of our ability to "know" doesn't include the metaphysical arguments for why it's impossible to answer questions about God, reality, and the meaning of life. Basically, nothing, not even reason, logic, and the most refined rational thought, can tell us about a world that is beyond our senses. There could be, and almost certainly is, a lot more out there that we simply can't comprehend.

tific evidence, such as the theory of evolution. Raised in a small Virginia town, he attended an Episcopal church as a child, but became an atheist after he left home. He continued to have questions about the faith that he had rejected, so he spoke with a local minister. One thing led to another and he reconverted, becoming an evangelical Christian at age 27.[72]

This example has nothing to do with whether his choice of faiths was right or wrong; these words, which convey a judgmental tone of self-righteousness and religious absolutism, have no place in a discussion of spiritual beliefs. Rather, it shows how and why people make choices. Dr. Collins' early religious experiences were Christian, and even though he rejected these beliefs as a young man, he lived in a place where Christianity was the principal faith. When he felt a renewed interest in religion, he sought advice from a Methodist minister, and the rest is history.

Note that he didn't become a Hindu or a Muslim. Instead, he chose from what was always close at hand. If he were an eminent scientist who had been born, raised, and educated in Egypt, it's all but certain that today he'd be a strong advocate of the ideas espoused in the Koran, not the Bible—which isn't right or wrong, but just different. Likewise with his opinion about the relationship between science and religion, which reconciled both evolution and creationism. How was he able to reach this middle-of-the-road position when many of his fellow scientists were strongly anti-creationist and the majority of evangelical Christians accepted a literal interpretation of the Bible whereby the earth was created in six days? Because his extensive knowledge of both biology and biblical teachings enabled his mind to bridge the gap between these seemingly incompatible ideas, a gap that was insurmountable for many of his scientific and evangelical colleagues.

And I'm another example. After leaving my Baptist-Catholic upbringing, I had no interest in religion for the next 25 years. Then I started to travel regularly to Japan, Thailand, and other Buddhist countries in Asia, and eventually I ended up in Korea, where I lived for months at a time across the street from one of the largest temples in the city. I was attracted to Buddhism by the gentle ways of its followers and by the teachings that encouraged me to question everything, and I learned to be at peace with not knowing. Like Francis Collins, when my time came for a change, I also turned to what I knew best and what was close at hand, which for me was Buddhism. Would I have made a different decision if I'd stayed in my hometown of Omaha, Nebraska, a conservative, overwhelmingly Christian part of the country, where Buddhism was all but unknown at the time? Yes, of course.

Much of my adult life was spent in far-off corners of the world where I was continuously exposed to a series of lessons about differences. I wish that everyone could have a similar chance to be removed from the familiar—to leave childhood homes, families, neighborhoods, schools, jobs, and closely held views about religion, politics, and social affairs, and at a time of life when one's mind is still flexible and open to new ideas—and be set down in the midst of tens of millions of people who believe something different. We'd all come away from this experience, as I did, with a different point of view.

The absolute and unquestioned confidence in our current beliefs, even the deep-rooted, almost visceral sense of faith (or lack of faith) that pervades every fiber of our being, would change in ways we could never predict. We might believe in another God, support a different political party, and hold totally different ideas about abortion, sexual orientation, immigration, the environment, and the other contentious issues that divide people and society. When speaking of truth, conviction, belief, and faith, a large measure of humility is needed: our lives—and our beliefs—could have been so much different.

41

Worm Husbandry and Other Entrepreneurial Ventures

Can We Trust Our Beliefs?
The Answer Surprised Even Me.

The self-justifying mechanisms of memory would be just another charming, and often exasperating, aspect of human nature were it not for the fact that we live our lives, we make decisions about people, we form guiding philosophies, and we construct entire narratives on the basis of memories that are often right but also often dead wrong. It's frustrating enough that things happened that we don't remember; it is scary when we remember things that never happened.

—Carol Tavris and Elliot Aronson[73]

As nine- and ten-year-old entrepreneurs, my brother Bill and I had two get-rich-quick schemes that we hoped would pay off big, which for us meant earning enough money to go to a movie and buy a Coke and an extra-large tub of buttered popcorn. The first idea seemed foolproof because (1) we had access to an inexhaustible supply of the product, (2) it was free, and (3) our only expense was the labor costs of two young boys—again, free. It involved selling worms for fishing bait.

Midwestern summers were so hot that we watered our lawn after the sun went down so the water wouldn't evaporate as quickly.

This forced the worms out of the ground after dark, where they were ripe for the picking. These weren't the skinny little worms that appeared on sidewalks after a hard rain. They were "night crawlers," as big around as a pencil and six to eight inches long. With flashlights and empty coffee cans in hand, we'd creep along the ground looking for worms that had crawled partway out of their holes so they wouldn't drown. We considered ourselves to be unusually adept at the task. Admittedly, there wasn't a steep learning curve, which involved a lightning quick, bare-handed grab for the slimy creature before it could escape underground, followed by gentle traction to ease it out of its hole to avoid snapping it in half. (Worm blood wasn't pleasant, but it was an unavoidable part of the job.)

We collected a full can of fat ones and started to advertise in local shops and bars, and actually sold a few dozen before disaster struck. We knew nothing about worm husbandry, so we kept them in my mother's tin washtub, the old-fashioned kind that had wooden handles at each end so you could carry wet laundry. Or hundreds of squirming worms. There must have been something fundamentally wrong with this approach, because a week later the tub started to emit the most unimaginably foul odor. It was pretty clear that many of the worms had died and were in an advanced stage of putrefaction. We dumped the survivors in the garden, hoping they would make it back home.

The second venture involved selling crawdads, fist-sized crustaceans that were a popular substitute for lobster in Midwestern towns during the 1960s (and they're still the rage in New Orleans in dishes like crayfish étouffée). Catching them was simple. A small piece of meat was tied to a 20-foot string, thrown into the water of a city pond, and slowly dragged back five or ten minutes later. If a crawdad was holding on, we scooped it up with a net and transferred it to a minnow bucket for storage. We caught about 30 over the course of the day and headed home in high spirits, storing them on the back porch in the same tin washtub that we'd used for the ill-fated worm fiasco. (We had to hope Mom never planned to do laundry again!) It was an ideal container because the sides were high, slippery, and pretty much escape-proof.

Bill and I retired for the night, congratulating ourselves for a job well done. It was a classic case of counting your chickens before the eggs are hatched. We were jolted awake at 6 a.m. by the unre-mitting bark of Peppy, our Boston terrier. Crawdads were better climbers than we thought; all of them had scaled the sides of the tub and were on the porch or the steps, heading for imagined safety. Peppy was pawing suspiciously at the intruders, which irritated them to no end. They raised their two formidable front claws in a menacing gesture to show that they meant business. Our dog was a slow learner. More than once she got too close and was grabbed by the whiskers, causing her to shake her head vigorously from side to side to dislodge the multi-legged adversary that was holding on for dear life. So we did what had to be done: took them back to the pond where they belonged. Our childhood money-making schemes were over.

These events occurred so long ago—almost half a century in the past—that I sometimes need to remind myself that they hap-pened to me and not to someone else. In fact, when I think of that nine-year-old boy who found so much joy in the simplest pleasures in life, I wonder, *Where is the person that I used to be?* Is he still hidden deep inside, quick to emerge whenever I display the offbeat sense of humor and perpetual optimism that's been with me since day one? Is he gone forever, a casualty of the many formative experi-ences I've had during a long and eventful life? Or are the Buddhists right when they say that a permanent "I" or "me" has never really existed?

What's more, I've told and retold these stories so often over the years that I'm no longer completely sure what's true and what's not. I know that night crawlers and crawdads were a big part of my life for a while, but I've forgotten many of the details of what I remember. Or at least what I think I remember. Memories are nothing more than beliefs about the past, and like all beliefs, mine are just best guesses of what the truth might be.

This lack of confidence in the accuracy of my childhood memories is yet another example of the uncertainty of many of my beliefs. Even now, well into middle age, I'm still not sure about some of the issues that have long since been answered by most people, including questions about God, religion, complex social and political problems, and the best way to live one's life. *This lifelong sense of uncertainty eventually led me to one of the most fundamental questions of all, and one of the principal topics of this book: Can we trust our beliefs?* As indicated in the next story, which describes my adult relationship with my father, the surprising answer to this question is no. We can't always trust our beliefs, not even those that represent some of the most strongly held convictions that we have in life.

42

Mistakes Were Made—By Me

Why We Need to Be Right,
Even When We're Not

We are all capable of believing things which we know to be untrue, and then, when we are finally proved wrong, impudently twisting the facts so as to show that we were right.

—George Orwell[74]

I wanted to think that my father did the best he could, but I didn't believe it, not for a second. So I scheduled a three-week business trip for a time of the year when the doctors said that his lung cancer might recur. He died the day I landed in New Zealand. I never even said good-bye.

My first memories of Dad were at age three, when I was awakened from sleep by my father's violent shouting. That night was repeated many times during my childhood. As I learned when I got older, he had a habit of stopping at the Grey Eagle after work, one of three back-to-back bars near our home that catered to the manual laborers who worked at the stockyards and packing houses. When he finally got home, there was hell to pay for anyone who got in his way. That person was usually my mom.

Dad was a big man—tall, broad, and so menacing that he was sometimes mistaken for a professional wrestler after he went bald at a young age. He was hard-drinking, hard-swearing, and quick to anger, so we'd tiptoe around the house for fear of upsetting him. During my 20 years at home, I remember eating three evening meals with him. Two were on Thanksgiving. The third was on Christmas Day, the same ill-fated holiday when he got so drunk he fell into the Christmas tree and pretty much ruined what should have been the highlight of a five-year-old's year. The rest of the time, literally thousands of meals, he spent drinking beer in front of the TV, while Mom, by brother and I ate together in the kitchen.

We never had anything even remotely resembling a father-son relationship. No days at the park or trips to the zoo, no fatherly advice, no "Well done!" after the small successes that can be highlights of a child's life. Once I became an adult, he never sat down with me to apologize or to at least tell me why his life had gone so wrong, not even when he finally stopped drinking and his body gave out after decades of abuse. First it was diabetes, then there was heart disease, crippling arthritis, and finally cancer and death at age 62. Maybe he had no regrets. More likely, he was like most men of his generation and just couldn't say the words.

I never knew my father as the man he once was: athletic, strikingly handsome, and filled with idealism and hope for a lifetime of love and happiness. He was sidetracked early in life and could never rise above the challenges. Both of his parents were alcoholics, and they didn't much care what he did. He was lucky just to finish high school. After that, he worked for 20 years as a mechanic in a meat packing plant that slaughtered cattle and made sausages from boiled blood and left-over entrails. No wonder his life went in such a different direction.

Dad clearly had his demons—he couldn't or wouldn't admit that he was responsible for so much suffering in our family—and I had mine. I was stuck in the past, my biased memories fixated on only the bad times, and I missed all of the changes for the better that occurred after he stopped drinking. He may not have been interested in trying to atone for the past, but who knows what might have happened if I'd made more of an effort? As a sober, late middle-aged man, he might have wanted to start over, becoming as a grandfather what he never was as a father. But I didn't give him the chance. I was consumed by anger and resentment, and I wasn't about to let him forget it. Yet I was the educated one, the well-traveled one, the thoughtful one, and it was up to me to be the "bigger person" by trying to build a new relationship.

But I couldn't do it. No, that's not true. I *wouldn't* do it. When his health started to fail, I booked a flight to Auckland. It was one of the biggest mistakes of my life, one that could never be fixed on this side of the grave.

People with strongly held views—our ideas about God, politics, "truth" of all kinds, and in my case, that it was too late to start a new relationship with my father after he stopped drinking—don't fit neatly into a single category. We're rich and poor, religious and nonreligious, liberal and conservative, urban and rural, and educated and uneducated. But there's one thing we do share: we've all traveled so far down the path of belief that it's almost impossible for us to stop, seriously consider other perspectives, including the possibility that we might be wrong, and change course when necessary. Why is this so hard to do? Because we've all made a series of important decisions that have taken our lives in certain directions, and we need to do everything possible to convince ourselves that we did the right thing.

This unrelenting need for self-justification was documented by social psychologist Leon Festinger during an experiment in which he observed the behavior of The Seekers, a cult that believed the world would end on December 21, 1954, when everyone on earth would die, except for the faithful who would be picked up by a flying saucer and taken to safety.[75] They were so sure of the prophesy that many of them made a huge bet on the outcome. They quit their jobs and gave away their homes and possessions.

When the world didn't end, Marian Keech, their charismatic leader, immediately revised her vision, saying that she'd received a telepathic message that the world had been saved because of the faith of her followers. Rather than feeling angry or misled, the group claimed that a miracle had occurred, and they took to the streets to convert others to their beliefs. (A similar episode occurred 43 years later, but with a macabre twist. Believing that the earth was about to be destroyed and that the only chance for survival was to leave it immediately, 39 members of the Heaven's Gate cult committed suicide in 1997, timing their deaths to coincide with the arrival of the Hale-Bopp comet, "which members seemed to regard as a cosmic emissary beckoning them to another world."[76])

Festinger called this behavior "cognitive dissonance," an idea that became one of the 20th century's most influential theories in social psychology. It refers to the mental discomfort caused by holding two conflicting (dissonant) cognitions (ideas, opinions, or beliefs) at the same time. One of the most powerful causes of cognitive dissonance is information that threatens our self-image, such as the belief that "I made the right decision about something that's important to me" or that "I'm a good person."

When confronted with this kind of unsettling information, there are two choices: (1) admit that we made a serious mistake or that we're not as good a person as we thought we were, and then begin the difficult process of changing a deep-seated view or behavior, or (2) ignore or distort the conflicting information so that we can continue our current beliefs and favorable opinion of ourselves. In the vast majority of situations, we take the easy way out, even if we happen to be wrong.

In *Mistakes Were Made (But Not by Me)*, Carol Tavris and Elliot Aronson cite numerous examples when political leaders worldwide made huge, undeniable mistakes, some involving massive loss of life and economic ruin, which they denied to the very end.[77] Underlying their refusal to admit a mistake was the need to reduce the cognitive dissonance caused by making a major decision and then seeing things go terribly wrong. Rather than admit failure, they chose to ignore the outcome and essentially recast events from their own perspective.

To show how this same process works in our day-to-day lives, the authors use the example of two young men, identical in all ways, who are taking an exam that will determine whether or not they're accepted into graduate school. They each have an opportunity to cheat. At this exact moment, they're standing together at the top of a "pyramid of choice," and their decision, and all subsequent decisions, will move them down toward the base of the pyramid to the point of their later beliefs. One cheats and the other doesn't, but their initial choices—cheat or not cheat—were a hair's breadth apart and they could have just as easily gone the other way. After one week, both men have come to grips with their decisions. The cheater justifies his action by saying, "I really needed to pass that test, and besides, everyone does it." Likewise, the non-cheater justifies his action by deciding that cheating is far more unethical than he originally thought and "People who cheat should be expelled from school."

Two things have happened. First, the men are now far apart from one another in their beliefs, and second, they've convinced themselves that they've always felt this way. Both of them have moved from the top of the pyramid where they shared identical views only a short time before, to the bottom where they now stand at opposite corners, each certain that he's done the right thing. (This self-justification after cheating is not speculation. It was reported after measuring children's attitudes toward cheating by putting them in situations where they had an opportunity to cheat, and then interviewing them later to see if their attitudes changed depending on whether they did or didn't cheat.[78])

The need to reduce cognitive dissonance applies to all of the big decisions that we make in life: getting married to our high school sweetheart (or not), going to college (or not), leaving home for a better job in a larger city (or not), smoking cigarettes or taking drugs (or not), drinking more alcohol than we should (or not), cheating on our spouse (or not), and keeping the same religion, political affiliation, and social views as our parents and peer groups (or not). Self-justification is especially important if the decision was irrevocable (deciding to have children) or costly in terms of time (working long hours to get a promotion), money (buying a new car), or effort (getting a professional certification), or if we've made a significant emotional, spiritual, and intellectual investment in the outcome (romantic relationships, religion, and political beliefs).

But here's the important point: our perspective totally changes after we make a decision. The initial ambivalence about a choice—at the time when we were still uncertain, uncommitted, and mentally free to move in different directions—is replaced by certainty, commitment to our decision, and an unwillingness to admit that we'd believe something different if we'd gone the other way. For example, we might be conservative today instead of liberal, Muslim instead of Hindu, or pro-life instead of pro-choice. In fact, our mental health depends on being able to live with the decisions that we make every day. So we overemphasize the reasons for why each choice was a good one, ignore conflicting information, and recruit others who agree with us.

This is exactly what The Seekers did when the world didn't end. Despite being as wrong as they could possibly be, they were energized and redoubled their efforts to convert others to their beliefs. And it's what I did when Dad stopped drinking. I was a casebook example of cognitive dissonance at work. In a sense, we were both starting anew, a middle-aged, reformed alcoholic father and a young adult son with children of his own. I could have tried to build a new father-son relationship, but I chose otherwise.

Like so many of the decisions in life that seem inconsequential at the time, I had no idea where that first step would take me. I didn't even realize that I was taking a first step. Motivated by anger, regret, and guilt—because this time it was me, not my father, who was pushing away—I intentionally passed up opportunities to see him, talk on the telephone, or meet him more than halfway to see what might happen.

I even managed to reshape the past. When my father was still young, before alcohol completely took over his life, we sometimes went fishing together, attended hockey games and wrestling matches, had spirited races with miniature stock cars that Santa Claus gave me for Christmas, and more. But I forced these good memories deep into the recesses of my mind and focused instead on only the bad—and there was a lot of bad to choose from. These distorted memories were exactly what I needed at the time because they helped me make sense of what had happened between us, and they further justified my decision to drift apart. In the end, I made a final, seemingly unthinkable choice not to see a parent before he died. Even then I was confident of the course I'd chosen; otherwise, I couldn't have lived with myself. I was convinced—totally, blindly, and beyond the power of reason or persuasion—that my actions and beliefs were right. And for me, they were.

My father was dead for almost 10 years before I admitted to myself that I'd made a terrible mistake. It wasn't a case of "time heals all wounds"; I could have gone on like this forever. Rather, I finally realized that my beliefs had fooled me, had convinced me that truth was on my side. At the time that Dad stopped drinking, I stood at the top of my own pyramid of choice, side-by-side with other adult children of reformed alcoholics. We were all making the same decision: put the past behind us and try to build a new relationship, or live in the past and forsake any possibility of change. Like the two men who faced the decision to cheat on an exam, we made our choices, followed by other choices as we worked our way down the pyramid, justifying earlier decisions, defending them with selective memories of the past and surrounding ourselves with people who agreed with us.

Note that the issue here isn't about results. Some of the attempts to build new relationships with reformed alcoholic parents would be successful; others would not. Rather, it's about the initial choice to try or not try, how the need to reduce cognitive dissonance makes us view our decisions in a favorable light, and most importantly, how some of our core beliefs might be much different, *maybe even the complete opposite of what they are today*, if we'd made other choices earlier in life.

Switching from a belief that I'd held with unwavering confidence, namely that my father was solely responsible for our failure to have a father-son relationship later in life, to a much fairer and more accurate view by admitting I didn't really make an attempt at something so important, was a shock to my self-image as a thoughtful person who made good decisions. Mistakes were made—by me —and it had been easy to hide them from myself for 10 years.

How did I get to such an extreme position? Even now I'm not sure. Everything happened so gradually, and all of my justifications were behind the scenes in my subconscious mind. It was as though I had simply awoken one day, unable to clearly remember how I had gotten to be where I was, yet all the while remaining convinced that I was right.

This episode marked the time when I first understood that long-forgotten events and choices of the past could have an unbelievably strong influence on what we believe today, and that we'll do everything in our power to convince ourselves that we've gone the right way in life. It was a painful experience, but it taught me that if I was wrong about something this important, then I could be wrong about a lot of other things as well. It was a lesson that changed my life.

43

Breakfast with Christians, Lunch with Buddhists

Stages of Belief: Why It's Hard to Unlearn Later in Life

At 18 our convictions are hills from which we look; at 45 they are caves in which we hide.

—F. Scott Fitzgerald

In Seoul, where I lived on and off for three years when I worked as a consultant, I stayed in a hotel that was across the street from Jogyesa, the main temple of the Jogye Order of Korean Buddhism. From my window I could enjoy the peaceful surroundings of the temple complex, a spiritual oasis in a city of 12 million people. I didn't need an alarm clock. I would wake up at 4:30 a.m. each morning to the gentle tolling of the massive temple bell, the tones hanging in the air and echoing off the surrounding buildings before finally fading just before the next ring. After a few stretches, I'd meditate for 10 or 15 minutes and then head to the hotel gym. By the time I reached the dining room for breakfast, I felt calm, focused, and eager to start another day.

As often as not, I would sit near a young family that I got to know over time—John, an Australian engineer on a three-year assignment to Seoul; Sarah, his wife; and their two young boys, Todd and Isaiah. They would always arrive together, the boys carrying overloaded backpacks for school, John with his briefcase, and Sarah holding the family Bible. It was bound in soft black leather, the pages gilt-edged. Several dozen bookmark tabs protruded from different sections. It was a most inviting book, even if you weren't a Christian.

What always happened next still impresses me to this day. In this crowded room with dozens of people and a TV blaring the latest news from around the world, they would join hands, close their eyes, and one of the family members—even the children on the days when it was their turn—would lead a quiet prayer of thanks. The Bible wasn't opened most of the time; I think it was there as a source of inspiration and a reminder for how they wanted to live the day. They were a happy, close-knit family, and the Christian religion played a major role in their lives. Clearly the world was a better place, undeniably better, because of people like them.

On the weekends I witnessed a similar display of faith, only in a totally different setting and on a much larger scale. Jogyesa would be packed with Buddhist families attending the midday service—bowing, chanting, and listening attentively while the head monk read a passage from the scriptures—and then everyone would adjourn to the temple basement for lunch with their friends. During my travels, I saw the same heartfelt reverence in people who attended religious services in Kuala Lumpur and Jerusalem, only these were Muslim and Jewish families, respectively. The parents' goal was the same in all of these places: instill beliefs and ethical values in their children to set them on the path to a happy and meaningful life. It's too bad that most parents didn't add one final lesson at this most impressionable time of their children's lives, namely, that other people's beliefs were often much different and just as true.

As Todd and Isaiah talk with their parents each morning, dutifully learning about religion, language, science, and the innumerable things they need to know before becoming adults, similar lessons are being taught in tens of millions of homes worldwide. Children assume they're learning facts about the world and, for spiritual matters, the afterworld. They are not. Rather, they're being told what to believe. This early training is essential—it's no exaggeration to say that these lessons keep children alive when they're young—but it makes it difficult to unlearn things later in life when they're exposed to ideas that challenge their beliefs.

In their book *Why We Believe What We Believe*, neuroscientist Andrew Newberg and psychotherapist Mark Waldman address beliefs, especially religious beliefs, from a biological perspective.[79] Part of the discussion focuses on what I call the "chronology of belief": what is learned, when it's learned, and what can or can't—except with considerable effort—be learned and unlearned later in life. I've divided these stages into childhood, adolescence, and young and older adulthood.

Todd and Isaiah are in the childhood stage, where they are being inundated with basic information. Like all parents, John and Sarah are doing whatever it takes—threats, rewards, and punishment—to be sure their children learn what's important for life. At this stage, when young minds are like sponges absorbing everything given to them, the information is highly persuasive, and even more so because it's reinforced by every imaginable authority figure, including older siblings, grandparents, teachers, the family doctor, as well as the local monk, mullah, pastor, priest, or rabbi. Many of these early lessons, the "truths" that we're taught at this impressionable age, form the neurological basis for future beliefs, and they will affect our decisions, experiences, and perceptions for the rest of our lives.[80]

This doesn't mean that we accept everything our parents tell us. We pick and choose from what we've been taught, and eventually we each become our own person with distinct ideas of how the world works, and this evolution of beliefs continues throughout life. But we never escape the influences, positive and negative, from this early stage of development. For example, some of my most important lessons as a child came from my father. If he said, did, or believed something, I generally made it a point to go in the opposite direction. Nonetheless, if I hadn't spent 20 years with a parent whose life included large measures of alcohol, religious hypocrisy, and narrow-minded political ideology, I wouldn't be the person I am today.

Adolescence is next. We begin to think for ourselves, question what we know, and lay the groundwork for future beliefs that will differ from what we were taught by our parents. Group membership and social approval are very important in this stage. However, independent thinking is tempered by the competing influences of our group and what we learned earlier in life. New ideas emerge, but for most things we just revise what we already believe.

By the time we reach the young adult stage, around age 30, we've put some emotional, spiritual, and intellectual distance between us and the tumultuous years of adolescence and our early twenties. We've traveled far down the metaphorical pyramid of choice, and our beliefs have taken shape. We may or may not be liberal on social issues, strongly nationalistic, or convinced that God —especially our God—absolutely exists. Regardless of which choices were made, we've long forgotten the time when our views were neutral and when we would have gone a different way if life's influences had nudged us in another direction. Our beliefs have become the embodiment of self, who we are—or at least, who we think we are—and this is the face we show to others and the prism through which we see the world.

In the fourth stage, as older adults, we continue to refine our views, but major changes are increasingly uncommon as we age. One of the main reasons for why it's difficult to accept new beliefs later in life, or to even consider the possibility that we might be wrong about something that's important to us, is that the aging brain loses some of its plasticity—the flexibility to change in response to new ideas.[81] Our neural pathways, the physical connections between different parts of the brain responsible for memories, beliefs, and thought patterns, have been created and reinforced over many decades of use, and like a path well-worn by frequent travel, it's hard to stray far from what we've come to know and trust. This is why it takes decades for social and moral values to evolve. It's difficult for older people to update their beliefs, so significant changes are generally made by younger generations who are more open to new ideas.

Two thoughts occurred to me as I read about the chronology of belief. The first is how easily things could have been different for all of us. In my case, I could have had a different family, a different education, or a different job, or I could have been born and raised in Israel, India, or Ghana. If even one of these events had happened, my life and some of my most fundamental views would be totally different. Instead of being a social and political centrist today, I might be a staunch liberal or conservative, or if I were born in one of the countries above I might be an orthodox Jew, a Hindu, or a follower of one of the African traditional religions—and be totally convinced of the truth of my beliefs.

It's the same for everyone. For example, if you're a deeply religious person at heart, but had been born elsewhere or had different life experiences, your new self might still have the same zeal for the spiritual life, except that you would now be a respected champion of a *different* faith, and thankful that you found the path to the one true religion. In fact, how do you know this *didn't* happen? Maybe your formerly Christian father accepted a job transfer to Malaysia where he converted to Islam, and today you're a Muslim, as are your wife and children. Or perhaps he turned down the transfer and stayed home, and so you and your family are still Christians today.

Impossible that a parent's choice or a random event might have led us to our current beliefs? A one in a million chance? No, not at all. In fact, this is a common occurrence. I saw numerous examples of this exact chain of events when I lived in Seoul. Families were Buddhist for a thousand years until a parent converted to Christianity after the Korean War. Now the children are Christians who attend church on Sunday, when just a generation ago they would have joined me at the Jogyesa temple for a Buddhist prayer service.§§

The second thought regarding the chronology of belief is more unsettling. Rather than be impressed with the countless influences and random events that were responsible for our current beliefs, and thereby decide to hold our views more loosely, we generally move in the *opposite* direction. Our beliefs become unequivocal truth for us and we cling to them for dear life, and over time they become more and more resistant to change.

Newberg and Waldman explain why we have so much confidence in our beliefs.[82] They performed brain scans on people with different views on religion—Franciscan nuns as they prayed and Buddhist monks while they meditated. Each group reported totally different feelings about the experience. The nuns felt the presence of God, and the monks experienced pure consciousness. Yet scans showed identical areas of the brain (the frontal lobes) lighting up with activity during prayer and meditation. What was happening? The brain was providing a sense of reality that was custom-made

---

§§ I'm personally uncomfortable with the explanation that an unseen force—God, fate, or a universal spirit—gives us the opportunity to encounter, and if we so choose, to accept a certain faith. It begs the question, "Why ever would someone think or feel that he or she, *rather than others who believe something else*, received the 'true' guidance?"

for their *existing* beliefs, which over time had become more and more real to them.

This same neurological process occurs in all of us. As the final arbiter of truth and reality, we believe what our minds tell us, regardless of whether it's right, wrong, or even outrageously wrong, such as with The Seekers, the Heaven's Gate cult, and their present-day equivalents. This "reconstructed reality," whereby perceptions (information brought to the brain by our senses), emotions (the feeling that our beliefs must be right), and reason are distorted to fit what we *already* think, is the foundation of all beliefs.

To say that our core beliefs depend on life's circumstances and that the brain does everything it can to make these beliefs seem real is merely stating the obvious. The problem is that such an admission opens the door to doubt and uncertainty, and this makes people very uncomfortable. It reminds us that a belief, even one that is highly cherished, is only one of many possible beliefs that we might have had. If we could turn back time and retrace our steps on the pyramid of choice to the neutral point where we could have just as easily gone another way—and this time make a *different* choice —then our ideas about God, country, and everything else would be much different today.

None of this means that our beliefs are wrong, although they could be and we might never know it. But it does mean that our views are just best guesses that are highly dependent on the circumstances of our lives. This realization changes everything. Rather than dismiss others' ideas as the misguided views of people who lack our intelligence, education, insight, or divine revelation, we begin to understand how easily their ways of seeing the world could have been ours. We become more comfortable with doubt and uncertainty because we realize that there's no one right answer for the complicated issues in life, and less comfortable with zealots who ferment discord by advocating extreme political, religious, or social positions. We seek the company of people who share our moderate views of tolerance and acceptance. In effect, we move to the center, or from a Buddhist perspective, toward the Middle Way.

44

Election Day: My Difficult Decisions about Guns, Gays, and God

How Clusters of Belief Rob Us of the Power to Think and Feel

Voters with strong partisan affiliations are a case study in how not to form opinions: their brains are stubborn and impermeable, since they already know what they believe. No amount of persuasion or new information is going to change the outcome of their mental debates.

—Jonah Lehrer[83]

The election was approaching, and I needed to take stock of my positions on the important issues. None of the decisions were easy, and on a few of the issues I could have voted either way. When I was unsure, my guiding principle was to vote in a way that would allow people to make their own choices rather than have the government tell us what to do.

Gun ownership

As a physician, I've treated many gunshot wounds in the emergency room, and I've seen how much harm guns can do. For this reason, gun ownership would be restricted if my opinion was the only one that mattered. But there are convincing reasons to think otherwise. First, the United States Constitution specifically gives Americans the right to bear arms. Second, I've known plenty of law-abiding citizens who have guns for hunting and self-defense. Third, I've spent a lot of time in two countries that represent the extremes of gun ownership—Switzerland, one of the most heavily armed countries in the world, where most men between the ages of 20 and 48 keep an assault rifle at home since they're in the militia; and Japan, where no one has a gun—and the violent crime rate in both countries is among the lowest in the world. But I don't think that the average citizen should be allowed to own military-style weapons; except for collectors, there is no good reason to have them.

Separation of church and state

This issue concerns the role of religion in secular institutions, such as school prayer and faith-based programs that address social problems. I favored the continued separation of church and state. One reason was that this was the intent of the United States Constitution. During the run-up to the election, it was disheartening to see the flimsy and contradictory arguments offered by both political parties. Democrats invoked the Constitution as a reason to separate church and state, while conveniently forgetting that the same Constitution specifically gave citizens the right to bear arms (a right which they hoped to severely restrict). The Republicans took the opposite approach—invoking (for gun ownership) and forgetting (for separation of church and state) the Constitution when it fit their agenda. Total victory, rather than a reasoned compromise that tried to be fair to most people, was clearly the primary objective on both sides.

But there was a more practical basis for my position on the separation of church and state: the United States was becoming far more diverse in its religious beliefs. The 2008 Pew Forum on Religion and Public Life reported that only three-fourths of Americans were Christian, and the remaining one-fourth followed other religions or were unaffiliated.[84] And more demographic changes were just ahead. Americans of European descent (who are more likely to be Christians) will be the new minority by 2042,[85] supplanted by growing numbers of immigrants from Africa, the Middle East, and Asia (who are more likely to have non-Christian religious beliefs). This meant that faith-based programs within the public sector would not be appreciated by many of our fellow citizens.

However, despite my support for the separation of church and state, I recognized the other side to this issue. It is impossible to overstate the good that religious organizations do in the U.S., and I thought that it would be foolish to prohibit all faith-based initiatives. I didn't know where to draw the line, but religious organizations had an important role to play in this regard.

Same-sex marriage

With the exception of a handful of liberal states, most voters weren't ready to approve same-sex marriage. Maybe in the future—it wasn't that long ago that women couldn't vote and interracial marriage was illegal—but not today. As a compromise, I thought that all states should pass laws allowing same-sex civil unions that gave gays and lesbians the same legal rights that are granted to married people. How did I reach this decision? I've known too many gays and lesbians who were in long-term relationships, too many who were upstanding citizens of the U.S., and too many who were deeply religious people, to think otherwise. If I ever wavered in my view on this issue, I only needed to think of Ed and John, my neighbors and good friends in Connecticut. They adopted Aaron, an inner-city child who had languished in foster care for years because nobody wanted him. His life was turned around by the intervention of this wonderful couple.

Abortion

I think that life begins at conception. That's why this issue was so difficult for me. Mistakes have already been made if abortion is even considered: insufficient sex education, inadequate use of or access to contraception, loss of self-control (easy to say for a middle-aged man who is far removed from his youth), and depending on one's personal beliefs, moral failings as well. I didn't want to add to this list of mistakes by imposing my personal views on a woman who was making one of the hardest decisions of her life. Mothers, not the government, know what's best for themselves and their children, born or unborn, and this most private of decisions should be left to them.

Nonetheless, I had concerns about late-term abortions, except where conception was due to rape or incest, or if the mother's life was in danger. I cared for many premature babies when I was in medical school, and I knew that they really were "little people." So on this issue, as with all the others to be decided by the electorate, there was only one option for well-intended people who disagreed: find a way to meet in the middle.

I knew that none of the candidates would agree with all of my positions. The social, moral, and economic questions being addressed were far too diverse and unique to each individual to expect point-by-point agreement among voters and candidates. So I planned to vote for the people who shared my concerns on the issues that were most important to me. What I discovered was a different kind of problem altogether. While none of the candidates shared all of my views, they did share one another's views, by political party, on almost everything. I was witnessing the end-result of a country-wide segregation of American society that began in the 1960s when people fled the tolerance and understanding of the political center for the extremes of the left and right.

In their book *The Big Sort*, Bill Bishop and Robert Cushing describe how Americans had formed homogeneous "tribes" in their neighborhoods, volunteer groups, and churches, filled with people who looked and thought just like them.[86] Most people lived in a giant feedback loop where they heard their own ideas bounced back to them by the news programs they watched, the talk shows they listened to, the newspapers and books they read, the Internet sites they visited, and even the sermons they heard at the weekly worship service.

Historically, old disagreements between political parties would disappear as new issues developed. Not now. Both parties kept the old issues and added new ones, forming tight "clusters of belief" on economics, the environment, health care, stem cell research, abortion, gay rights, and separation of church and state. The voters responded by realigning their own beliefs, even on highly personal, incredibly complex subjects that defied categorization into right and wrong, with what it meant to be a liberal or a conservative. As Bishop and Cushing observed, "When party leaders, candidates, and platforms take distinct stands on these issues, it signals to citizens which views on these issues go with each party. This creates pressure for citizens to bring their party identification and views on these issues closer together."[87]

In effect, tens of millions of people were saying, "If my political party supports (or doesn't) gun ownership, separation of church and state, same-sex marriage, abortion rights, immigration reform, new health care initiatives, and changes to the current environmental policy, then so do I!" The process reached its low point when the candidates realized that they couldn't be elected unless they espoused the same extreme views as their constituents, and thus the narrow-minded ideology of voters was transferred onto the local, national, and international stage.

Like-mindedness even spread to the spiritual realm, where parishioners worshiped with people who had identical beliefs, and if necessary, changed churches to find congregations that were like them. What a change this was from the time when churches were gathering places for exchanging ideas with others who had somewhat different beliefs about God, politics, and social issues, and where tolerance was a part of each lesson because these were your friends and neighbors. With today's boutique churches customized to the pre-existing views of the congregation, we attend services that tell us just what we want to hear. One result is that many people, even some who are deeply religious, have become more extreme in their views and less understanding of those who believe something different.

This clustering of beliefs into ever more extreme and polarized positions clearly isn't good for individuals or society. For one thing, it encourages an us-and-them philosophy that makes us forget we all have the same basic goal, namely, to lead a safe, happy, and fulfilling life. Our differences lie in ideas about how to get there. But what I most regretted about the Big Sort was the lost human potential, both intellectual and spiritual, that occurs when we accept our party's cluster of beliefs as our beliefs. At this point, we stop using our minds to think and our hearts to feel what is right and wrong about each individual issue, and we effectively close the door to new ideas that may have given us a far wiser view of the world and the people in it.

Religion and Secular Belief Systems

Aware of the suffering created by fanaticism and intolerance, I am determined not to be idolatrous about or bound to any doctrine, theory or ideology, even Buddhist ones. Buddhist teachings are guiding means to help me learn to look deeply and to develop my understanding and compassion. They are not doctrines to fight, kill or die for.

—Thich Nhat Hanh[88]

45

Pan-Fried Slug and Wart Hog Stroganoff: It's What's for Dinner

Different Strokes for Different Folks, Especially When It Comes to Religion

Wise ones do not grasp at any views. For them there is no conflict with the views held by others.

—The Buddha[89]

All countries have local delicacies that are unappealing to people from different cultures. I've had the good fortune to try more than my share, such as haggis (Scotland), pig knuckles (Germany), black pudding (England), tripe (France), lung (Switzerland), vegemite (Australia), and wart hog stroganoff (South Africa).

The most imaginative dishes were from Asia. On my first visit to Japan, my flight was delayed because the plane blew out two tires when we landed in Anchorage to refuel. My host, a true gentleman, met me at the Osaka airport at 11:00 p.m. on a Saturday night and insisted on taking me to dinner (after a 24-hour trip, what I really wanted was to go straight to bed). One of the items he ordered had a vaguely familiar appearance, something I recognized from my years in medical school, but I couldn't quite place it. He paged through his Japanese-English dictionary until he found the translation, and then matter-of-factly told me that it was "raw fish testicles."

On the same trip I was introduced to *uni*, or sea urchin sushi, a mushy, pumpkin-colored creature that's scooped out of its shell and squished atop a bite-sized piece of sticky rice. I actually gagged when I first tasted it and came dangerously close to retching it into the beaming face of my host, who was daintily eating his *uni* in small bites in order to savor the exquisite taste. I was saved by chugging half a bottle of beer to wash it down and out of harm's way, which greatly impressed my all-male lunch companions.

Then there was a seaweed soup, intensely green in color and the most viscous food that I'll ever eat. When I swallowed a spoonful it was so gooey the first half of the 18-inch strand reached my stomach while the rest of it was still in the bowl. I started to panic, facing a choice between slurping up the entire bowl in one continuous seaweed strand or grabbing it in my bare hand and dragging it back out. I finally managed to bite it in two, swallowing the first part and letting the other half slither back into the bowl. Other Asian delicacies I've eaten include fish entrails; pig tendons; "rotted" fish ("fermented" would have been a more accurate translation for the menu, but "rotted" was a far better description of the taste); 100-year-old eggs; ox intestine stew; "bones of the four legs of a cow rice cake soup"; fish balls in savory broth (for the sake of my mental health at the time, I assumed that "balls" was a culinary rather than an anatomic term, but who knows?); and the aptly named "outhouse meal."

Slugs are found worldwide. In most countries they're pests killed by leaving a bowl of beer in the garden at night, leaving the slugs to literally drink themselves to death. In Asia, they're eaten. More correctly, Asians eat sea cucumbers, an ocean-dwelling, lookalike cousin of the garden slug that is valued by epicures for its gelatinous quality and rubbery texture. I've seen them undulating in aquariums outside of trendy restaurants in Seoul, apparently to entice diners who are thinking, "I have a taste for slug, but it has to be fresh!" Here are some of the ways that I've enjoyed sea slug:

- shark skin and slug soup
- pan-fried slug garnished with jellied octopus
- slug-stuffed shrimp
- tripe and slug soup (also known as "Monk jumps over the wall soup," named for a Buddhist monk who, smelling the mouth-watering aroma of slug simmering in its own juices, broke his vegetarian vows and jumped over the temple wall to get a bowl of soup)
- in large chunks ("chunk-o-slug")
- diced squid and slug salad (I couldn't tell where the squid ended and the slug began)
- sliced fatty pork with equally thick sliced slimy slug, all covered with a brown, gelatinous gravy.

For my money, you can't top the combined visual, olfactory, and gag-inducing effect of silkworm pupae sautéed in garlic and herbs. As we walked past the street vendor in Insadong, an upscale shopping district near my hotel in Seoul, my host told me that pupae were a tasty treat, high in minerals and protein, and greatly coveted by the locals young and old. I'd heard that deep-fried grasshoppers and scorpions tasted like French fries, so I thought, *Why not? How bad could they be?* It was among the worst culinary mistakes of my life. They looked like bugs—I think they were dead, but I wasn't fully sure—with a slimy consistency and a taste and smell as vile as anything I've ever put into my mouth. For a nanosecond I worried about offending my host and the vendor, and then I vigorously spat everything into the gutter. I could never again walk down that street without feeling nauseated.

Sea slugs are a delicacy in the East, so much so that people will pay top dollar, or the equivalent in their local currencies, for a single slimy bowl of them. Yet they're not appreciated in the West, and in fact are avoided whenever possible. How can this be?

Most of us spend our entire lives in a single culture, surrounded since birth by people with fairly similar views. The advantage is that contact with "sameness" provides us with security and a sense of belonging; the disadvantage is that like-thinkers, by definition, think pretty much alike. It's only when we're exposed to different influences that we begin to re-examine what our social network considers to be normal and right. These influences might be more education, moving to a different city, or contact with good people who have totally different views on world affairs, politics, religion, and social issues.

I've been fortunate during my life to see the religious side of people in their home countries in a way that most people will never experience, including visits to churches, mosques, synagogues, and temples on five continents. If there was a clearly "superior" spiritual path where the followers were kinder, more generous, happier, more peaceful, or more favored in the afterlife (I'm guessing on this one), I would have seen it. But I didn't see anything even remotely like it. After all my years of travel, I'm still amazed at how similar people are, with the same concern for family, friends, happiness, and a love of their own beliefs and traditions.

It's common to view others' lives from our own perspective and to judge the merits of their beliefs and actions according to criteria that work for us. This is a mistake. If you worry about forgetting this lesson in the future, just remember that while your idea of a good meal might be a thick, juicy steak, others would prefer pig knuckles, tripe and slug soup, or raw fish testicles. It's a reminder that there are as many ways to do things—and most of them right —as there are people in the world.

46

Pluralism in Bukhansan

Why We Want to Hear that Our Faith Is Right

> *I am a believer in the truth of all the great religions of the world.
> There will be no lasting peace on earth unless we learn not merely to tole-
> rate but even to respect the other faiths as our own.*

—Mahatma Gandhi[90]

On one of my first weekends in Seoul after taking a job with a
Korean company, I took a short taxi ride from my hotel to Bukhansan National Park. Hiking is one of the national pastimes, and
they cater to trekkers in a way that I haven't seen anywhere else in
the world. The approach to the park was lined with all manner of
shops that sold mountaineering clothes and equipment, fresh fruit
and vegetables, healthy precooked meals, and dried squid and
boiled pig knuckles for those who preferred the local fare for lunch.

Koreans are among the friendliest people in the world, especially when they lace up their hiking boots, leave the crowded cities
behind, and join family, friends, and co-workers for a walk in the
woods. I was staring at the sign for the trailhead, already lost before
taking my first step because everything was written in Korean,
when I was befriended by a group of six hikers who asked where I
was going. In the best Korean I could muster, I repeated what I'd
read earlier that morning in my travel book, "Baegundae," while
simultaneously entertaining them with a comical pantomime of a

really big mountain. There were excited whispers and expressions of surprise—this was the highest peak in Seoul—followed by approving smiles, as if to say, "Ah, the elderly Westerner must really like our mountains, or be a fool!" I soon learned why they were impressed with my choice. They asked if they could join me, and we started off together. It was a real stroke of luck because they were all well-traveled and spoke English.

At first I was disappointed that they chose the shortest trail to the top, but a 2,000-foot increase in elevation in only three miles made for a tough climb. The last half-mile was almost straight up, and we inched our way forward via rock climbing and 45-degree stairways chiseled out of solid granite. At the summit we were rewarded with fabulous views. Seoul stretched far beyond the horizon to the south, North Korea was a mere 30 miles north, and the trees were ablaze in their peak autumn colors on this perfect October day.

I'm not fastidious when it comes to food, especially when hiking—my meals usually consisted of whatever I found in the pantry on the morning when I packed for the trip—so I was flabbergasted by the lunch that appeared from their packs. They spread a tablecloth (on my solo hikes, I usually ate a quick lunch while sitting in the dirt in the middle of the trail), added plastic cups and plates, and finally brought out fruit, vegetables, meat, crackers, juice, and plenty of alcohol. We were all tired and a bit dehydrated after a three-hour trek over difficult terrain, but otherwise in high spirits. The alcohol went straight to our heads as we toasted each other with long drinks of soju, the traditional Korean beverage.

Then the culinary theme of our all-male group, and the unprintable jokes and innuendos that cross any cultural barrier, shifted to lunch selections that were reputed to enhance "men's health": Chinese deer antler wine, pickled ginseng, and kimchi made from "bachelor radish"—so named because of the decidedly obscene shape of the uncut vegetable. I didn't have the heart to tell them that this was the start of a two-month solo trip to Korea—my wife planned to visit me at the end of the year—and so the purported benefits of the aphrodisiacs would be lost on me.

What did I contribute to the feast? My cold instant coffee and unsalted nuts were a surprising hit, no one wanted any of the soybean bread that I had purchased earlier that day from the hotel's convenience store (Korea is a rice society, plus the bread was horribly deformed after being smashed into my pack all morning), and I was too embarrassed to bring out my can of tuna.

During the descent, we stopped to refill our water bottles at one of many temples hidden deep in the remote valleys. It was an unforgettable experience: a beautiful wooden temple carved out of the dense forest, smiling monks strolling about with the sun glistening off their shaven heads, and the soothing sounds of Buddhist chants wafting through the air. I closed my eyes and simultaneously thanked God, karma, and my good fortune for allowing me to be in such a wonderful place.

After we finished our walk, I was reminded again of the remarkable hospitality of the Korean people. No outing was complete without a post-hike meal together. We stopped at one of the dozens of restaurants located just beyond the park gates and feasted on potato pancakes, stewed chicken, four kinds of vegetables (including the ubiquitous kimchi), savory rice, and ice cold beer.

Over dinner we got to know each other even better. In Korea, asking about one's personal life isn't considered rude, including questions about age, marital status, hobbies, and religion. This being Asia, I had some preconceived notions about which faiths would be popular, but I was surprised to hear of their diverse religious backgrounds: two were Buddhists, one was a Confucianist, and one each a Presbyterian, a Methodist, and a "nothing special." Even more interesting was the fact that their spiritual beliefs (or lack of them) were relatively new—four of my companions were either first- or second-generation converts.

What a difference a day can make! I started the morning as a serious solo hiker, intent on distance and speed, and finished the day as a social walker who was far more concerned with good food, drink, and pleasant conversation with my new friends. It was a wonderful introduction to Korea.

I had spent a delightful day with six nice people who followed five different spiritual paths, and they were still close friends. Too bad much of the world doesn't live like this. If a global poll asked the question, "What are the most divisive issues in the world?" it's likely that religion would be at the top of everyone's list as the number-one cause of hatred, violence, racism, war, and genocide. How can it be that something that should promote peace and happiness is the source of so much suffering? There are a lot of reasons.

First, religions have different beliefs, and this alone is enough to cause animosity. Our spiritual views are a major part of our concept of self, and they strongly influence how we deal with the world on a day-to-day basis and what we hope will occur in the hereafter. Affirming our convictions, and rebuffing the beliefs of others, reassures us that we're on the right track.

I heard a radio report to this effect in which the commentator described a big upswing in the purchase of religious books in the United States after the 2001 terrorist attack in New York City. The reason? People were buying more spiritual books because they "want to hear why their faith is right, who the bad guys are, who the good guys are, and why the worldview that they're comfortable with is the one they should stay with and is better than all the others."[91] This gets right to the heart of why other faiths make us feel so uncomfortable: different beliefs about God, even if we're staunch atheists, challenge our conviction that what we think, say, and do is right. The report also noted that, given the demographics of the United States, Christian books were the dominant sellers. I imagined the likely book-buying patterns in other countries at this time. Surely there would be a similar rush for books on Buddhism, Hinduism, Islam, Judaism, and secular humanism, as others sought the same confirmation of their beliefs.

The second reason why religion causes so much strife is that people who follow different religions may come from different cultures, look different, and sometimes speak different languages, and this makes some people uneasy. I've always been impressed with the religious diversity in international meeting places, like Changi airport in Singapore, where it's common to see fully veiled Muslim women, saffron-robed Buddhist monks, Hindu women wearing a bindi (red spot) on their foreheads, and Christians with crosses around their necks. Any of these people, except for the Christians, would attract attention in my small town of Asheville, North Carolina, but in Singapore it's normal and not worth a second glance. When it comes to religion, familiarity clearly breeds understanding and friendship.

Third, religious differences are often used by politicians to garner support for domestic or nationalistic agendas. There's no doubt that it's a lot easier to demonize an opposing faction or even an entire country if religion can be used to unite people to defeat the "nonbelievers," figuratively in an election or literally via warfare. Just consider the misinformation and unfair generalizations that are the regular fare of newspapers and the evening news. I know these reports are wrong because I've been in many of these countries and have seen how people really live.

Finally, the world's major religions have themselves been guilty of perpetuating, and in some cases encouraging, centuries-old conflicts among different faiths. It's a mystery to me why religious leaders, the people who are most familiar with the strengths and weaknesses of their own faiths (no religion is perfect) would foster discord by claiming the moral high ground and the inside track to what God is thinking. Yet spiritual leaders worldwide sometimes use religious differences to fan the flames of intolerance, hatred, and nationalism. It may be an official pronouncement that certain people, groups, or even countries have committed a transgression worthy of punishment according to their holy scriptures, or claims of doctrinal superiority that allegedly prove their beliefs are correct.

Most of us speak with a "higher power" on a regular basis—Allah, Brahman, Buddha (who is respected by Buddhists as a great teacher, but is not God), Jesus, Yahweh, the cosmos, or the spirit of humanity—and we're very capable of making up our own minds about how to interact with others who think differently about spiritual matters. Without the interference of religious leaders who continuously emphasize the indisputable truth of their faiths and tell followers what they're supposed to believe, most of us would be like the six Korean hikers and say, "Other spiritual beliefs? Sure, that's just fine with me."

As I've gotten older and a bit wiser, I've found my own way to be at peace with conflicting religious beliefs. I remember the Zen image of a finger pointing to the moon. The moon is the spiritual goal, and the finger represents the many ways—different teachers, scriptures, and religions—to reach that goal. The great religious leaders in history, such as Buddha, Jesus, Mohammed, and Moses, did not want us to concentrate on the finger, but rather to see the moon. My personal opinion is that these spiritual leaders would be quite satisfied with the tenets of one another's religions—if they could only convince people to actually live by the principles of whichever religion they chose.

I also think that too much time and effort is spent discussing the differences among religions and trying to convert others to our points of view. Questions about whether God exists or not, and if so, which religion has the "right" God, can never be answered to our satisfaction. In the meantime, there are important issues that can't wait, including war, poverty, racism, global trafficking of women and children, and disadvantaged people in our own cities who need all kinds of help. The world would be far better off if we all spent more time focused on the moon and not the finger.

47

Tuan, My Friend…
As Long As I Believed Like Him

Individual and Societal Harm
Caused by Exclusivism

When we come across a religious enthusiast causing strife with his beliefs, it is incorrect to blame the religion. It is just that the novice has yet to learn his religion well. When we come across a saint, a maestro of her religion, it is such a sweet encounter that it inspires us for many years, whatever her beliefs.

—Ajahn Brahm[92]

I knew what Tuan was going to say even before he knew that he was going to say anything. I'd heard it many times before.

We met at a hotel in Japan that I reached in a roundabout way. My month-long business trip to Asia coincided with the first major outbreak of SARS (Severe Acute Respiratory Syndrome) in March 2003. After reaching Beijing, I learned that my seminars in Hong Kong and Taiwan had been cancelled because the disease was spreading so quickly that people were afraid to meet in large groups. So I was fortunate to spend more than a week in Tokyo at the height of cherry blossom season, a time when the parks were stunningly beautiful and the entire populace had one goal in mind:

spread a blanket on the grass and enjoy the four "F's": food, family, friends, and foliage (plus a fair amount of sake).

Tuan and I would see each other at the gym, two of the crazies waiting for the attendant to open the door at 5 a.m., and later we'd have breakfast together. He knew I was interested in spirituality because each morning I'd read a few pages from an inspirational book to set the tone for the day. After several days he asked me, "Where do you worship?" The question seemed innocent enough, but there was nothing innocent about it. I told him that I was a Buddhist, and he immediately launched into a well-rehearsed explanation for why I'd made a mistake.

He was raised as a Buddhist in China, but was never serious about his religion. For him, Buddhism was purely social, something to do with the family on holidays and a way to observe major events, especially deaths. So it wasn't surprising that he made a change later in life. Here's the interesting thing: his choice was about as random and uninformed as you could imagine. For something as important as one's spiritual beliefs that will serve as an ethical guide for life and perhaps be passed on to children and grandchildren, changing religions would seem to require the utmost care. But he didn't investigate, not even briefly, the most popular or fastest growing religions and then choose the one that best fit his emotional, spiritual, and intellectual needs. In fact, he knew almost nothing about the world's religions. He didn't even know much about Buddhism. And yet he was supremely confident that he'd "found the truth." How was this all-important life decision made? He'd switched faiths five years earlier after talking with a stranger he met at a coffee shop in Hong Kong.

When I observed that there were a lot of good people in the world who believed something else, he was quick to agree, but countered with, "Yes, but their beliefs are misguided, and they won't be saved." I was dumbstruck. I had thought that we were friends, but in a matter-of-fact way he'd just written off me and most of the human race when it came to prospects for the hereafter. And write me off he did. Our morning breakfasts together were over once he realized I was happy with my current beliefs.

Tuan ended our morning chat, which was really more a recruitment speech, by giving me some literature that explained his faith in more detail. He meant well, so I read the pamphlet and kept it for a few months as a bookmark. It was a good reminder to practice humility when I was tempted to be overly confident about my own views on life.

Some religious enthusiasts champion their beliefs to the detriment of others. They know everything about their faith; it's too bad that's all they know. These zealots simply can't imagine that other people—good people, happy people, people who lead meaningful lives—have different ideas about spirituality, and they aren't at all worried about going to the grave and the hereafter with their own beliefs. So, like Tuan, they point out the error of your ways, seeking to substitute their path for your path, and their truth for your truth.

While I admired Tuan's willingness to question his childhood beliefs, I couldn't shake the uneasiness that I felt as he told his story. At first I thought it was because he had effectively ended the spiritual traditions his ancestors had followed for centuries, and he did so without even understanding the basic tenets of their beliefs. But that wasn't it. Tuan didn't subscribe to the live-and-let-live philosophy that "truth has many faces" depending on the myriad influences that shape one's worldview. Rather, he was an exclusivist, someone who felt that "If I'm right, you must be wrong." This attitude causes all kinds of trouble in the world, whether we're talking about religion, politics, social issues, or the mundane aspects of daily life.

Exclusivism harms both individuals and society. For individuals, it forces us into a false dichotomy—right or wrong—that fails to recognize how truth can vary depending on one's perception. I witnessed this approach in my business career whenever an autocratic boss would end meetings with the simplistic pronouncement, "Well, you're either part of the solution or part of the problem," as if there were no other possibilities. An exclusivist approach, with its total, uncompromising commitment to a belief, also stops learning because we're no longer willing to look further once we've found the single "right" answer.

Worse still, it limits our freedom to think, speak, and act differently. Tuan was a perfect example. He was right, that was that, and the door was closed to any possibility of learning something new that might change his mind. The final problem for individuals is the very real possibility that *we're* the ones who are, as Tuan put it, "misguided," as I've found time and again when I looked back on some of the things I thought when I was younger... only to later realize I was dead wrong.

It's tempting to say, "Who cares if some people are so self-righteous that they refuse to acknowledge different points of view? They're only hurting themselves." That's where the societal perspective comes into play. Narrow-minded people don't just hurt themselves; to the contrary, their dogmatic views creep into everything they think, say, and do. With some exclusivists, it's limited to pride mixed with arrogance because of their perceived superior insight. For example, some atheists (who can be as strident in their disbelief as the Tuans of this world are in their belief) have a condescending attitude that implies anyone who believes in God is either uneducated or naïve, which is echoed by the mirror-image sanctimoniousness of religious zealots who maintain they are the only ones who really know God and what he (or she) wants. For other exclusivists, their absolutist views might be manifest as an active dislike or even hatred of those who think differently, or as an effort to "save" people who have other points of view—which often causes resentment and anger in people who are the targets of this unwanted proselytizing because they feel that their own faith is being challenged.

To this day, I struggle to grasp the magnitude of Tuan's claim. He was convinced that everyone with different spiritual beliefs was wrong, including the billions of people who lived before him and the untold billions who would live after him. I would have felt better if he were an extremist in a fringe religious cult. But he had company, lots of company. There are hundreds of millions of people worldwide who are unwilling or unable to step back from their spiritual beliefs (or in the case of agnostics and atheists, their lack of beliefs), rest comfortably in the uncertainty of not knowing, and acknowledge that some things simply aren't within our power to comprehend. Instead, living here on earth for maybe 100 years, we convince ourselves we know truth as it exists now and will exist for thousands of generations and tens of thousands of years in the future. With this certainty comes all the harmful side effects of these extreme views—everything from intolerance and hatred to genocide, religion-inspired wars, murder in the name of God, and political wars that use religious differences as their justification.

When it comes to religion, I don't spend much time wondering if I'm right or thinking that others must be wrong; the former is a waste of time since we can never know for sure, and the latter invariably hurts other people because it affects how we interact with them. Was it divine revelation that finally led me to Buddhism (which is what Tuan claimed when I asked how he could trust his decision, given that he knew very little about the other religions in the world)? No, not at all. I arrived here as a result of the innumerable influences of a lifetime: being raised in a working-class neighborhood in the United States, a Baptist-Catholic upbringing, years of medical training, the person I married, what I read, who I met, and where I traveled.

Would I have different ideas about spirituality if I'd been born elsewhere or had different life experiences? Yes, absolutely. And the same is true for everyone on the face of the earth. For all of us, a few small changes in our lives would have made a world of difference in our beliefs, and this understanding should give us a profound sense of humility about the truth of even our deepest convictions.

My breakfasts with Tuan often come to mind when I hear about incidents in which religious strife causes hatred and violence among people of different faiths. In a world that desperately needs open-minded people who can accept different ideas about religion, politics, and complex social questions, it was unsettling to see how his mind became inflexible in such a short period of time. What will happen in another generation or two when none of Tuan's descendants remember their kind and gentle Chinese ancestors who had different ideas about religion? Will they be told that a chance meeting in a coffee shop was the reason for their current beliefs, and that perhaps they're no closer to the truth than their relatives were before?

48

Same Same, but Different:
Gay Clergy in Waynesville

How Life Experiences Shape Our Beliefs

One half of the world laughs at the other, and fools are they all. Everything is good or everything is bad according to who you ask. What one pursues another persecutes. He is an insufferable ass who would regulate everything according to his ideas.

—Baltasar Gracián (1601-1658), Spain[93]

It's amazing where life can take you. Shortly after I started a new job in Seoul, my son Michael was transferred to his firm's office in Singapore. We decided to meet for the weekend in Bangkok. On our first evening together, we were strolling through one of the night markets when I happened upon a shop that had a large number of Oriental wall hangings. I've always loved decorative Asian scrolls, especially landscapes and traditional rural scenes that depict how people used to live before the big cities of the world all started to look the same. Over the years I've collected quite a few—to the consternation of my wife, who insists that I display them in my office, the only room in the house that's mine to decorate. None of them was expensive, and even my treasures cost only a few hundred dollars. In the shop, I sorted through the items until I found two scrolls meeting my criteria—peaceful and inexpensive—and I asked the vendor for the prices. His reply, "Same same, but different," caught me off guard.

This shorthand expression is used throughout Southeast Asia for anything that involves a choice between things that are similar, but not quite the same. In this case, the prices were the same, but one of the scrolls was mass-produced in another country, while the other was hand-painted by Thai artists. The vendor wanted to support the local economy, and I agreed, so after some good-natured haggling, I left with a beautiful picture of a village in northern Thailand.

Some months later I returned to the United States, and one morning I saw a headline in our local paper that caught my attention: "Split Leads to New Congregation."[94] The article described a split in the First Presbyterian Church in Waynesville, a town of 10,000 people in western North Carolina, when half of its 170 members left to form a new church. The reason for the split was a disagreement over the interpretation of scripture, particularly, ordination of gay clergy.

This story was interesting for a number of reasons. First, similar splits over the issue of sexual orientation had also occurred in Baptist, Lutheran, Methodist, and other Presbyterian denominations.[95] Second, it reminded me of the many schisms that had taken place over centuries and millennia within Christianity (Catholic, Eastern Orthodox, Protestant), Judaism (Conservative, Orthodox, Reformed), and Islam (Shia, Sufi, Sunni), often because of disagreements that would seem minor to outside observers. Finally, I had a *déjà vu* experience as my mind flashed back to the night market in Bangkok: two decorative scrolls that were almost identical except for the countries where they were painted, and two congregations whose beliefs were almost identical except for a different interpretation of scripture. It really was same same, but different all over again.

The parishioners of the First Presbyterian Church were remarkably homogeneous compared to the differences that exist within congregations in larger cities. In Waynesville, close friends often attend the same church; some of them grew up together, played sports together, and maybe even married people they knew from their childhood or high school. They stood arm-in-arm for years and decades in their shared beliefs about God, moral principles, and the afterlife. And then one day they parted ways.

I thought, *How can this be? What kind of faith-inspired decision making process did each member of the congregation use to make his or her choice?* Remember, the parishioners had fairly similar backgrounds and they saw eye to eye on most spiritual issues, so it wasn't a matter of superior intelligence, greater life experience, or deeper insight. Of course, they could always rely on the advice of church elders or the inner voice that tells us when something is right or wrong, but so could those on the other side of the argument. So while each person could make a decision, how certain could each one be that it was right?

Confidence in this kind of spiritual judgment call decreases even more when a few things change. What if everyone in the congregation had grown up in a slightly more liberal or conservative family, or instead of being Presbyterian, maybe had belonged to one of the other Christian denominations in the United States, of which there are more than 1,000 to choose from, most formed by groups who had different ideas about how to interpret the Bible?[96] Or maybe they married a high school classmate who had different views about religion compared to their current spouse's ideas.

Thomas, a friend of mine in Asheville, was one such example. I once asked him why he had become a Baptist and he replied, "My wife wouldn't marry me if I didn't!" Instead of a Baptist, what would have happened if he'd fallen in love with a Jewish or Muslim woman and converted to *her* religion? Thomas' children were also strict Baptists, and they were so committed to their faith that they'd done missionary work in Africa when they were teenagers. Yet chances are good—more than half of American children retain the religious affiliation of their parents[97]—that they'd be Jewish or Muslim today if their father had converted to either of these religions when he married.

All of this is fine. If being Presbyterian, Baptist, Jewish, or Muslim helps us be better and happier people, it's the right choice for us. But if the decision of a parent can have such a strong influence on what we believe today, what does this say about the inherent truth of our convictions?

I also wondered, *Would their scriptural interpretations, either supporting or opposing ordination of gay clergy, have been different if they had lived at another time?* I was thinking of two relatively recent disagreements that divided churches and congregations in the United States, only to be resolved later by a 180-degree reversal in the official position of the church and its followers. The first was in the late 20th century when Protestant denominations struggled with the issue of women's ordination. Female ministers, considered a sacrilege for most of the five-hundred-year history of Protestantism, are now common worldwide.[98]

A more extreme example was the 19th century disagreement over the morality of slavery in the United States. Baptists, Methodists, Presbyterians, and other denominations split North and South over whether the Bible condoned or condemned slavery. One faction argued that the scriptures sanctioned slavery (basing their arguments on a literal interpretation of the Bible), while those opposed to slavery (including most Canadian and European Protestants) insisted that it did not.[99] When they finally reunited, the seceding southern churches acknowledged that they and their members had been wrong... for more than a century.

Why do people who are alive today have such different views about slavery compared to their ancestors who lived just a few hundred years ago? Because of the influence of time. While our selves of the past would probably have supported both slavery (if we lived in the South) and a male-dominated religious hierarchy, these beliefs are anathema to our selves of the present. In both cases (slavery and women's ordination), the change of heart and the total reversal of opinion closely mirrored changes in a world that had taken a strong stand against slavery and gender discrimination. People in the 21ˢᵗ century, and in every century, for that matter, have different beliefs than people who lived in the past or who will live in the future, and this should give us pause whenever we're tempted to think that our time-specific ideas represent truth.

The broader issue raised by these disputes is whether it's ever possible to be totally certain of our beliefs. Our decisions on important matters are wrong all the time. We trust politicians who mislead us; marry "the love of our lives" and yet half the marriages end in divorce; accept scientific and medical discoveries that are later debunked; and make major mistakes when choosing investments, jobs, and places to live.

Because of my education, I'm familiar with many of the medical certainties that were abandoned after decades of unchallenged belief. For example, the use of hormone replacement therapy (estrogen), formerly a virtual fountain of youth for older women, has been drastically curtailed because it increases the risk of heart disease and breast cancer; stomach ulcers, treated for centuries by drinking large amounts of chalky, unpalatable antacids, aren't usually caused by gastric acid but by a bacterial infection that is now treated with antibiotics; and in the second half of the 20ᵗʰ century, Americans were advised to severely limit their consumption of nuts, olive oil, and chocolate because of the high fat content, and today we're told that these are health foods that should be eaten on a regular basis!

We're often wrong about religion, too. Those of us who have changed to a different faith (or to no faith) are compelling examples of the frailty of spiritual belief. For much of our lives we remain committed to one religion—or to no religion—we change to a different set of beliefs, and then we insist that our earlier views, which we might have held for decades or most of a lifetime, were mistaken.

Given the inherent uncertainty of our beliefs, where a small change here or there can dramatically alter our views, along with the incredibly powerful historical component of our convictions—our past, present, and future "selves" would often having opposing views on the same issue simply because they lived at a different times—I've grown much less trusting of my beliefs. Statements such as "I know that I'm right" and "I'm as sure about this as anything in my life" are just shorthand ways of saying, "Based on what's happened to this point in life—my genetic predispositions; when, where, and how I was raised; and my limited exposure to different ideas, cultures, religions, and political structures—this is what I think today." I'd add one final qualifier to this statement: *And because of my admittedly limited perspective, I might very well be wrong.*

Whenever possible, I recommend that people take a deliberate, centrist position on contentious issues, including religion, politics, abortion, sexual orientation, immigration, and the environment, especially if the decisions that we make today have the potential to harm others. We might be certain that we're right—as certain as our ancestors were when they supported slavery and practiced religious discrimination against women—and just as wrong.

49

Different, but Same Same: Rama's Monkey Bridge

Turning Our Beliefs Upside Down

Do not believe in anything simply because you have heard it. Do not believe in traditions because they have been handed down for many generations. Do not believe in anything simply because it is spoken and rumored by many. Do not believe in anything simply because it is found written in your religious books. Do not believe in anything merely on the authority of your teachers and elders. But after observation and analysis, when you find that anything agrees with reason and is conducive to the good and benefit of one and all, then accept it and live up to it.

—The Buddha[100]

The following headline from New Delhi appeared in the newspaper a few weeks after I read the story about the split in the First Presbyterian Church in Waynesville over the issue of ordination of gay clergy: "Hindu Hard-Liners Protest Planned Sea Channel That Could Damage Bridge Created by God Rama."[101] The article described protests by thousands of Hindus against plans to dredge a new shipping channel off India's south coast because it would damage Rama's Bridge, a chain of shoals and reefs between India and Sri Lanka.

In Hindu mythology, the god Rama built the bridge with the aid of the monkey god Hanuman and his army in order to rescue Rama's wife Sita, who had been abducted by the demon king Ravana. Nationwide protests were planned if the government went ahead with the project. Another Hindu group disagreed with this interpretation, claiming instead that the story about Rama's bridge was never meant to be a historical account of actual events, but rather a spiritual lesson for the Hindu faithful who lived more than 2,000 years earlier. I asked myself the same question that had occurred to me after I read the Waynesville story: It's fine for both conservative and liberal Hindus to believe whatever they want, but how certain could anyone be that his or her opinion was right on this issue?

These stories from Waynesville and New Delhi are real-life examples of how prior experiences play a major role in shaping our beliefs. If you're not convinced, try this simple experiment. Ask the Hindu faithful if they believe the stories in the Bible, and then ask the Waynesville congregation if they believe the story about Rama's bridge. In almost all cases, the answer from both groups would be an unequivocal and resounding No! But I'd bet a week's salary that most people, Hindus and Christians alike, would say Yes if they'd been born and raised in each other's environment. If this happened —if the Christians awoke the next day as Hindus, and the Hindus as Christians—then the beliefs that are now so important to them (scripture for the current Christians and Hindu mythology for the current Hindus) would be of little or no concern in their new lives.

The different perspectives of people in Waynesville and New Delhi are also reminders of the role that chance plays in shaping our beliefs. In *The Drunkard's Walk*, Leonard Mlodinow relates, "I have Hitler to thank for my existence, for the Germans had killed my father's wife and two young children, erasing his prior life."[102]

This tragedy led to his father's emigration to the United States, a new family, and the birth of a child who would later become a successful teacher and author.

All of us can tell similar stories about random events that led to who we are today. In my case, the events included a rigorous Jesuit education where thinking outside the box, even the Christian box, was highly encouraged; a chance meeting in a bowling alley with a wonderful 16-year-old girl who later became my wife (39 years and counting!); and 20 years of global travel that showed me both the similarities and the differences among people.***

In *Experiments in Ethics*, Kwame Anthony Appiah further develops this idea of how life's circumstances determine our fundamental beliefs. As he observes, "Human behavioral possibilities are, in part, the result of what concepts are available to people.... It's only because of an institutional and conceptual background that one can be, say, a Republican or a Democrat, a Catholic or a Muslim."[103] In other words, we wouldn't be a Catholic or a Muslim today if we hadn't had significant exposure to these religions during our lives. This idea also largely explains why there aren't many Muslims in Ireland or Catholics in Saudi Arabia, and why most people worldwide who have a religious epiphany usually choose a faith that was fairly well known to them before their conversion.

Once we acknowledge that chance events greatly affect what we believe today, and that a different self would have much different ideas about the important issues in life, our perspective on certainty, belief, and faith changes dramatically. It's no longer possible to say, "Fortunately, I was lucky to be born here and now with my current beliefs, which are the correct beliefs." Why? Because all of our other selves—who might have been born in Brazil, Kenya, or just down the street but in a different family, or who might have

---

*** This idea has been popularized as "the butterfly effect," the phenomenon whereby a small change in a complex system, such as our life, can have large effects elsewhere, including the formation of our core beliefs.

lived a hundred years earlier or later—would say the same thing. They, too, would be certain of their convictions and thankful for living in a time and a place where they were able to find the right answers about religion, politics, and social concerns.

This doesn't mean that our beliefs are wrong; I support the "principle of credulity," which holds that if something seems right to us, we're entitled to believe it. However, it does mean that we need to be honest with ourselves and thereby open the door to our emotional, spiritual, and intellectual minds, first to doubt, and eventually to tolerance of other ideas that might be just as true as, or even more so than, ours.

These stories from Waynesville and New Delhi reaffirm the reasons for my discomfort with literal interpretations of anything, be it medicine, science, politics, religion, economics, or experts of any kind. There are too many conflicting opinions from equally well-informed and well-intended people, too many reinterpretations that occur over time, too many subtle nuances of interpretation that seem crafted to fit the current situation, too many cases where interpretations are manipulated to advance a political, religious, or social agenda, and too many times when observations are taken literally without considering the historical context. When it comes to the really complicated issues, especially where religion is involved, I prefer the practical advice found in the Talmud:

> Thus, Moses pleaded with the Lord, "Master of the Universe, reveal unto me the final truth in each problem of doctrine and law." To which the Lord replied, "There are no pre-existent final truths in doctrine or law; the truth is the considered judgment of the majority of authoritative interpreters in every generation."[104]

In other words, the ultimate guide, including for issues like gay ordination and Rama's monkey bridge, doesn't rest with the Bible or Hindu mythology, but instead rests on the living interpretation of these texts by each new generation. When it comes to religious scriptures and all other strongly held convictions that we have in life, I've learned that inflexible belief and inflexible disbelief are equally short-sighted positions.

To my way of thinking, the views of Hindus who believe or don't believe in Rama's bridge are within an eyelash of being the same, as are the views of Christians who believe or don't believe in the ordination of gay clergy. For that matter, so are the fundamental goals of atheists, Buddhists, Christians, Jews, Hindus, Muslims, and secular humanists, namely, to live a happy, meaningful life and to prepare for the afterlife (if that is one's belief) in the best way possible.

With the insight I've gained from visiting dozens of countries, experiencing scores of different cultures and traditions, and meeting countless numbers of good people across the globe, I would like to suggest a slight rewording of the expression I first heard at the night market in Bangkok. When it comes to the religious beliefs of people worldwide, rather than "Same same, but different," I would say, "Different, yes, in outward appearances, but for the bedrock issues that concern all of us, it's definitely *same same*."

50

Churches, Mosques, and Temples

21ˢᵗ Century Beliefs:
A Snapshot in the Eons of Time

A God who is good knows of no segregation amongst words or names, and were a God to deny His blessings to those who pursue a different path to eternity, then there is no human who should offer worship.

—Kahlil Gibran (1883-1931), Lebanon[105]

After we moved to the East Coast, I almost never returned to Omaha because my mother, who still lived there, spent about half the year with us in Connecticut. This changed in 2006 when she had a stroke and couldn't travel, so I tried to return home every three or four months. It was on one of these visits that I saw something I'd never noticed in the 27 years I lived in Omaha: there are a lot of churches. In fact, the same is true for most cities of the United States, where a church can be found by driving only a few minutes in any direction.

What made this observation so noteworthy was what I *didn't* see during a recent business trip to Asia: churches. My first stop during this trip was Jakarta, Indonesia. From my hotel room I could see the majestic minarets scattered among the skyscrapers, and each morning I would awaken to the beautiful Islamic call to prayer wafting through the city, the first of five daily times of prayer. On the last day of my visit, I saw a devout Muslim stop his taxi, take out his prayer rug, and pray by the side of the road. The next week I was fortunate to have a free weekend in Kyoto, the ancient capital of Japan and home to some of the world's oldest Buddhist temples. I marveled at the beauty of the architecture, the tranquil gardens, and the tens of thousands of people who came there each day to pray. I finished my trip in New Delhi, India, birthplace of the Hindu religion. The temples were abuzz with exotic music and worshipers chanting millennia-old mantras and prayers, and some of them were so large they resembled self-contained cities, providing space for worship, education, and community gatherings.

On the last day of the visit with my mother in Omaha, I had dinner with five of my best friends from high school and college who still lived in town. We talked about the good old days, our children, and the new riverfront development in an area that was just abandoned factories when I lived there. Eventually the conversation turned to national and international politics, and that's when I realized how much people change, or don't change, depending on their environment and life experiences. Four of my five friends had viewpoints that were similar to what they might have been 30 years earlier. The ideas of the fifth, who was far more involved with diverse groups of people because of his volunteer work, especially with the poor and disadvantaged, had changed a lot, and we both shared remarkably similar perspectives on world events even though he hadn't traveled much outside of the U.S.

The six of us were raised in working-class neighborhoods, attended the same Catholic schools, and started our adult lives with very similar ideas about the world. Thirty years later the friendships remained, but many of our ideas were much different. Not right or wrong, just different. As I flew home the next day, the churches receded in the distance, just as the mosques and temples had faded from sight when I left Asia. I felt a deep appreciation for how life's circumstances mold our beliefs, even when we start from almost the same place. It's no wonder that people worldwide, who start from far different perspectives compared to my small group of friends in Omaha, also have much different beliefs, and again, not right or wrong, just different.

Omaha, a mid-sized town in the center of the United States, is almost exclusively Christian. That's all I knew as a child and a young adult. I never met a Jew until medical school (half of the students were from New York or California, and many of them were Jewish), a Muslim until I was 35 (an Iraqi who worked out at my gym in Fort Wayne, Indiana), a Buddhist until age 41(my first trip to Japan), and a Hindu until age 49 (my first trip to India). Most people are a lot like this. They live in a country or a part of the country where there's one dominant religion, they don't know much about other faiths—except for the extremes often reported on television and in newspapers—and they don't have neighbors who are exactly, and I mean *exactly*, like them, except that they have much different religious beliefs.

Whenever I meet people who are highly certain of their beliefs about religion, politics, nationalism, and difficult social issues, I think of the three Parks I met at the orphanage in Seoul—Sungbin (age 7), Hyunju (age 5), and Jinsoo (age 3). Innocent, friendly, and eager to learn, these siblings will spend their formative years with 50 other homeless children, and their lives will take a much different direction compared to how things would have been if they'd grown up with their natural parents. They'll probably be adopted by different families, move to different towns, and have totally different and separate lives.

Then I imagine them 30 years in the future when they're adults with families of their own. How will their views have changed because of their different life experiences? Perhaps they'll meet one sunny afternoon at a tea house in Seoul and share stories of the orphanage and their lives after being adopted. Eventually the talk turns to religion, and in unison they might say: "Wow! A lot's happened in my life. I'm so lucky to have been raised in an environment where I could find the true faith. I'm a Muslim (Sungbin), a Buddhist (Hyunju), and a Christian (Jinsoo)!" Given the countless experiences that would have shaped their beliefs about religion, and everything else as well, how could they be so certain they'd found the "true" faith? Each of the siblings might credit divine revelation for steering him or her in the right direction, starting with life in an orphanage that took each of them far from the traditional path of a Korean child. But instead of validating their choices, this merely adds another layer of complexity. "Which of us," they would ask each other, "received the true divine revelation?"

The good news for the three Parks is that none of them will go wrong regardless of which faith they choose. Beneath the dogma and traditions adopted over the centuries or millennia, most forms of spirituality—including secular humanism, which emphasizes universal moral values rather than religious beliefs—have a similar focus: fostering friendship and community; teaching ethical principles; and helping people live happy, meaningful lives.

What about the hereafter? I won't presume to speak for God by citing the beliefs of any of today's principal religions. Our current concepts of the afterlife are only a snapshot in the eons of time, and our ideas may very well change in the future. For these three wonderful children who will take different paths in life, any higher power in the universe that is worthy of the name "God" will assuredly say, "All good people are welcome here."

51

Sunday Afternoon
with Ali and Bob

A Sane World Made by Sane Individuals,
One Person at a Time

Ignorant people see everything in black and white—they rely heavily
on the myth of pure evil—and they are strongly influenced by their own
self-interest. The wise are able to see things from others' points of view,
appreciate shades of gray, and then choose or advise a course of action that
works out best for everyone in the long run.

—Jonathan Haidt[106]

During the years when I worked in Korea, I stayed at a hotel popular with expatriates from around the world. Each morning the lounge felt like the United Nations as busy workers, some wearing the distinctive garb of their native countries and speaking languages from Asia, Europe, and Africa, ate a quick breakfast before hurrying off to jobs in Seoul. That's where I first met Ali, a quiet, slightly built man from Saudi Arabia. He always ate by himself and looked a bit lonely, a look that I had had when I first started international travel 15 years earlier. He needed a friend, so I introduced myself and asked if he'd like to join me for a weekend hike in the mountains. He agreed immediately.

When Sunday arrived, we took a taxi to Bukhansan National Park, where we joined hundreds of other hikers for a well-deserved break from the hectic pace of life in a large city. We spent the first 30 minutes of the hike in a steep ascent, struggling to catch our breath as we exchanged the kind of generalities that are typical of strangers. He was 28, unmarried, one of seven siblings, and a member of a much larger extended family. He told me about his life at home, surrounded by friends and family, and his long years of study to earn an engineering degree and become fluent in English. I rounded out the exchange of information by telling him about my work, family, and life in the United States.

With our newfound sense of mutual trust and respect, the conversation turned to more serious matters. Five years had passed since the terrorist attack on the World Trade Center, and the war in Iraq was entering its fourth year. Both of us had things we wanted to say.

Ali started first, telling me he was terribly saddened by the tragedy that occurred in New York City on September 11. I'll never forget the sincerity in his voice when he told me that Saudis and Muslims were deeply religious people with the same life goals of people worldwide: family, friends, satisfying work, and happiness. In his closely knit family, hospitality to strangers was of the utmost importance, even rising to the level of a duty, and he finished by inviting me to visit him if my travels ever took me to the Middle East. He meant it.

I, too, felt a need to clear the air. I had been a globetrotter since the early 1990s, and it was impossible to overstate the immense change in global politics that occurred after the World Trade Center attack. I explained that America was a land of immigrants where newcomers had opportunities that would have been unimaginable in their home countries. Like Saudi Arabia, the United States was a deeply religious country and most people were highly tolerant of others' beliefs, a tolerance that reflected their diverse racial, ethnic, and cultural backgrounds. And like Ali, I expressed remorse for things that had gone badly in recent years as events on all sides sometimes spiraled out of control.

After reaching the summit, we joined other hikers for lunch. From our vantage point we could see the vast metropolitan area of Seoul and the mountains of North Korea. We were from two different cultures, but shared remarkably similar perspectives on the long-standing conflict between North and South Korea. Both of us expressed the conviction that reunification was likely if diplomats would be guided by patience and respect for different points of view.

During our descent, I surprised Ali by stopping at Seungsa, a Buddhist temple established in the eighth century and one of dozens of ancient temples scattered throughout the mountains of Korea. We were so preoccupied with our earlier conversation that I hadn't told him I was a Buddhist and that a visit to a mountain temple was a regular part of my weekly hikes. We entered the Main Hall together—an American Buddhist and a Saudi Muslim—and sat in silent contemplation with an unspoken bond of friendship, trust, and hope for a world that had much more in common than it realized.

Ali and I started small from our many commonalities and built on from there. Both of us were alone, we worked killer hours during the week, we had spent long, difficult years in school earning advanced degrees, and we had a love for family, hiking, and reading. After establishing a base of trust and acceptance, we also discovered that we had similar views on more complex issues.

Given the stereotypes of the West and the Middle East and the incendiary political situation early in the 21st century, we could have found plenty of reasons to disagree, such as Saudi versus American and Muslim versus Buddhist. But neither of us consi-

dered these differences to be causes for disagreement. I was fascinated to learn how he lived, what he did, and what he believed. He
and his family had been Muslims for more than a thousand years—
more than 40 generations. I remember thinking, *If I'd been born in
Saudi Arabia, I'd be much like him, and that would make me very happy.*

There were two reasons we hit it off so well. First, both of us
listened to each other. We listened as hard as we could, each sensing
that there were important stories to tell and lessons to be learned.
Second, there was never an us-and-them situation where we needed
to take a stand on the divisive issues that often alienate people from
each other. Instead, we were just two men talking about our lives.

Buddhists have a term for the us-and-them point of view:
duality. It refers to situations in which we position ourselves as
separate and distinct from others on issues such as age, gender,
race, religion, politics, and even things as basic as the schools we
attended and the neighborhoods where we live. These perceived
differences fuel the negative emotions of dislike, anger, fear, intolerance, greed, discrimination, arrogance, pride, and envy, and they
are responsible for much of the world's suffering.

The word "enemy" vividly conveys the idea of us and them. It
evokes a feeling of fear, hatred, and anger, and it blinds us to alter-
nate courses of action because it's so evocative that there's no mental distance between hearing the word and immediately rising to the
defense of our beliefs, our faith, and ourselves. But who is the
enemy? Profound ethical dilemmas arise when we judge individuals
based on the behavior of their groups (religion, politics, country,
etc.), and likewise when we judge groups based on the behavior of
individuals (race, ethnicity, etc.). And there's also the issue of
change. Once branded an enemy, is someone always an enemy? Or
will we allow the possibility that people change—for better or
worse—just as we've changed during our lives?

Finally, why is someone an enemy? When I attended medical
school in Omaha, I had a neighbor across the street who never

liked me. Once he intentionally backed his pickup truck into my car while it was parked on the street in front of our house. Why? He was a meticulous gardener with a manicured lawn, while I was a harried student who didn't bother to cut the grass for weeks at a time, and that was his way of telling me that I wasn't a very good neighbor. After quiet reflection, which certainly wasn't when I saw him back into my car, I realized that I was the one who was responsible for the situation. If he was an enemy, it was mostly my fault.

On a global scale, things are a lot more complicated than un-cut grass and peevish neighbors. Yet even the most complicated and seemingly intractable disputes are based on a series of individual tit-for-tat retributions that perpetuate distrust and hate, and underlying each link in the chain of atrocities is an unwavering belief in us and them.

As Ali and I discovered, there are a lot more similarities than differences among people, even people from different cultures, religions, and political systems. After our hike, everything became clearer to me when I watched the world's leaders on the evening news. They were acting in accordance with the wishes of their constituencies—millions of individual citizens with an us-and-them point of view—and their leaders were putting this narrow-minded perspective into motion at a global level, sometimes with disastrous results. If a sane world is made by sane individuals, the responsibility falls on each of us to understand why people are different, how they got that way, and what we can do as individuals to find common ground.

I left Seoul soon after our hike. By the time I returned to Korea four months later, Ali had returned home. This time I was the lonely new arrival who was befriended. One of his co-workers, also from Saudi Arabia, introduced himself at breakfast. Ali had not only told his friends about me, but he'd even led a hike for his fellow Saudis along the same trail that the two of us had walked together. It was weeks before the happiness from this conversation began to fade. The goodwill that Ali and I had generated—just two people doing their best to be friends during troubled times—had been transferred to others. It was a good start.

52

Vengeful God, Light-Emitting Moon, and Other Apocryphal Beliefs

Fooling Ourselves with the Myth of the Autonomous Rational Mind

Nothing is easier than self-deceit. For what each man wishes, he also believes to be true.

—Demosthenes (384-322 BCE), Greece[107]

All faiths, including organized religions and secular belief systems, can help us find the ethical values and guiding principles we need to live a happy, peaceful, and meaningful life. However, problems arise if we become so committed to our views that we confuse belief and faith with certainty and truth, and act accordingly. The two stories below show how people deal with situations in which their convictions collide head-on with reality.

Lily was a client whom I visited a few times a year during business trips to Asia. She was way "over the top" when it came to religion, always turning the discussion to the evils of the world and how things would be better if everyone shared her beliefs. It's too bad I wasn't a Buddhist at the time; I could have gotten a week's worth of practice on the virtue of patience during a 30-minute conversation. During one meeting, we were discussing a famine in Africa that was causing thousands of deaths, many of them infants and children, when she made a real conversation stopper: "This tragedy would never have occurred if they believed in the true God!" I was too shocked to reply—and I didn't trust myself to say anything because I might have said what I really thought—so I changed the subject as quickly as possible and made a mental note to steer clear of similar topics during future visits.

The second story was told by the Dalai Lama prior to his speech at the annual meeting of the Society for Neuroscience.[108]

> Science has always fascinated me. As a child in Tibet, I was keenly curious about how things worked. When I got a toy I would play with it a bit, then take it apart to see how it was put together. As I became older, I applied the same scrutiny to a movie projector and an antique automobile.
>
> At one point I became particularly intrigued by an old telescope, with which I would study the heavens. One night while looking at the moon I realized that there were shadows on its surface. I corralled my two main tutors to show them, because this was contrary to the ancient version of cosmology I had been taught, which held that the moon was a heavenly body that emitted its own light. But through my telescope the moon was clearly just a barren rock, pocked with craters. If the author of that fourth-century treatise were writing today, I'm sure he would write the chapter on cosmology differently.
>
> If science proves some belief of Buddhism wrong, then Buddhism will have to change. In my view, science and Buddhism share a search for the truth and for understanding reality. By learning from science about aspects of reality where its understanding may be more advanced, I believe that Buddhism enriches its own worldview.

Certainty is an alluring idea, and one that is highly reassuring to the emotional, spiritual, and intellectual parts of our minds. Over a lifetime, we selectively input countless thoughts, ideas, and experiences that appear to confirm our beliefs, and carefully filter out the contradictions in order to avoid the angst of contrary information that might make us question our convictions. The end result is that we become so sure of ourselves we find it difficult to change.

These two stories reveal striking differences in certainty of belief and how people use their views to determine what's real in the world. For Lily, her beliefs were cast in stone, and everything had to conform with her ironclad rules for what happens when one doesn't choose the right God—in this case, the deaths of thousands of innocent people whose crime was living in the wrong place and the wrong time.

In contrast, the Dalai Lama had highly flexible views that were not irrevocably tethered to scripture, tradition, or the words of long-dead Buddhist writers and saints. One of the traditional Buddhist beliefs was wrong: the moon did not emit its own light. He acknowledged it as an error due to the historical times when the story was written, and he moved on. (The Dalai Lama's willingness to change his beliefs wasn't confined to inconsequential teachings in obscure scriptural texts. On another occasion, he was asked what he would do if an important tenet of Buddhism, such as belief in reincarnation, was disproved by science. He replied, "If science found a serious error in Tibetan Buddhism, of course we would change Tibetan Buddhism."[109])

When it comes to the many different beliefs about the world and our place in it, religion is a special case. Philosophers tell us that we don't have the intellectual ability to know for certain if our faith in God—or our lack of faith—is true or not.[110] However, we do have the mental capacity to understand that *we might very well be wrong*, and that our ideas about God and religion would be much different if our lives had gone in another direction. Yet very few of us are willing to seriously consider other possibilities. Why? Because we overestimate the ability of our minds to find truth. Whereas we're quick to admit the limitations of our bodies—none of us thinks we can fly or breathe under water, and with each passing year we're reminded of our increasing physical limits—we don't acknowledge the same limitations of our minds. Instead, we imagine that ultimate truth and reality are attainable via logic, scientific evidence, study of sacred scriptures, or divine revelation.

This disconnect between *what we think we know* and *what we actually know*, or can ever hope to know, is largely explained by the "myth of the autonomous rational mind." This idea was advanced by neurologist Robert Burton after years of studying how people develop their beliefs and the many times when we're not only wrong, but flagrantly and indisputably wrong, and never know it.[111] His underlying premise is that certainty is not possible—not with the most sophisticated "cognitive knowledge" characteristic of fact-based beliefs that can be tested with reason and science, nor with the most persuasive "felt knowledge" typical of faith-based beliefs where we experience truth as an overwhelming and emotionally convincing "feeling of knowing." As described by Burton, the basic problem is, "There is no isolated circuitry within the brain that can engage itself in thought free from involuntary and undetectable influences."[112] In other words, none of us can fully escape the biases and distortions of perception that have been with us since the day we were born.

Existing at either of these two extremes of how beliefs are formed—(1) overemphasis on cognitive knowledge acquired through logic and science with disregard for the "irrational" need people have for ideas that are beyond what reason can tell us, and (2) overemphasis on felt knowledge acquired via faith, religion, and scripture with disregard for credible contrary evidence—is not a healthy way to live. And to my way of thinking, neither approach is entirely correct.

The world has profited immensely from scientific discoveries, and further advances are essential for dealing with environmental concerns, a crowded earth, poverty, and a host of other problems. Yet science is not the ultimate arbiter of truth. As sociologist Deborah Lupton has observed, "Scientific knowledge, or any other knowledge, is never value-free, but rather is always the product of a way of seeing."[113] This means that a scientist's belief system influences the design and interpretation of a study, just as a theologian's views influence his or her perception of God. Both are biased by what they already believe, and this affects how they see the world.

Nonetheless, I think we need to acknowledge that scientific discoveries generally point in the direction of reality, or at least as close to reality as we're going to get in this life. It would be unwise to summarily discount scientific findings simply because they disagreed with our worldview. Besides, it's not necessary to reject convincing scientific evidence simply to affirm our faith—science, faith, and religion are not mutually exclusive ideas. If we took this approach, we'd need to bend ourselves into all sorts of mental contortions to explain why some things in the world are *exactly* as they seem because they agree with our spiritual beliefs, and yet other things are *totally different* than they appear because they're at odds with our views.

If Buddhists did this, they'd have to ignore a scientific finding that is as likely to be true as most things that we'll ever know in life —namely, the moon is a rock, not a star. This doesn't mean that Buddhists need to abandon all of their scriptural and historical references to the moon; rather, these sacred texts are reinterpreted in the context of what's known today. When one sees the famous Zen image of a finger pointing to the moon, it's still true that our spiritual goal is the moon, not the finger, and it doesn't matter in the least that the moon isn't emitting its own light.

The world has also benefited immensely from the contributions that religion has made to personal happiness and to the development of civilization, including architecture, music, the arts, and science. The spiritual beliefs themselves may or may not be right, but it doesn't matter—they still have real value by giving us a sense of hope, purpose, and comfort. And, of course, if they are true, those of us who are believers may have an advantage when we pass into the afterlife!

However, religion, including Buddhism, is not the ultimate arbiter of truth either. The scriptures of all religions have similar shortcomings: concerns about the accuracy, perspective, and biases of the writers; revisions of original texts over time that changed the events; stories that allow multiple interpretations that change with each generation (which to my way of thinking should be actively encouraged); failure to consider the historical context when the events took place; and how the stories and the messages would be much different if they were written today. What's more, there's a vast emotional, spiritual, and intellectual chasm between accepting the *fundamental tenets of a faith* and accepting the myriad other spiritual and social beliefs *that are peripheral to the faith* itself, but which have become part of a religion's dogma over time.

For instance, when one reads about the creation of the world in the Book of Genesis, the principal message (analogous to the moon as our spiritual goal in the Zen image) is crystal clear—God exists, he or she is all powerful, and he or she cares about us. Today's dueling interpretations—whether the earth was created in six days or over billions of years, and whether it was done immediately or via eons of evolution—represent the finger pointing to the moon. They're totally peripheral to the message itself and only serve to distract us from achieving our spiritual goals, to say nothing of the considerable time and effort that is lost by arguing about these questions.

As with all of the contentious issues in life about which well-intended people endeavor to reach common ground, the solution is to find a way *within our belief system* that allows us to become more accepting and tolerant of people who think differently. Those of us who are more influenced by cognitive knowledge (logic, reason, and proof) must acknowledge the tremendous personal and societal benefits of faith-based beliefs, and that our scientific findings, while highly convincing, do not and can never represent absolute truth about metaphysical questions. Likewise, those of us who are more influenced by felt knowledge (emotions, religion, and faith) need to acknowledge the possibility that there could be natural, rather than supernatural, explanations for the events that underlie our beliefs, and that our holy scriptures, while of unquestionable value as a guide to a happy and meaningful life, may not be literally true. Above all, it means that everyone needs to understand that our beliefs, even those that are most important to us, may not be true.

A survey of religious beliefs in the United States suggests that there is already greater understanding, acceptance, and tolerance than we might imagine.[114] Two of the groups in the survey—Evangelical Christians, and agnostics and atheists—represent what are often considered to be the opposite ends of the religious, political, and social spectrum. Almost half (47%) of evangelical Christians thought that many religions can lead to eternal life. Significant percentages of this group also said that eternal life was possible for Muslims, Hindus, and atheists.

At the other end of the spectrum, more than half of agnostics (55%) and a fifth of atheists (21%) said they believed in God or a universal spirit. This apparent paradox—agnostics and atheists who believe in God or a universal spirit—probably reflects the common belief among most people, regardless of their religious affiliation, that there is a higher power somewhere in the universe. The organized religions call it God—and sometimes even one specific God —while agnostics and atheists think that this higher power is better represented as a universal spirit or cosmic energy, rather than by an anthropomorphic God who intervenes in human affairs and is concerned with our day-to-day struggles. When considered from this perspective, the majority of agnostics and many atheists are not nonbelievers, but "other-believers." These findings aren't as surprising as they appear. Research has shown that when it comes to God, there are few true believers—even the most religious people express doubts about the validity of their faith—and the same is true for atheists, who are often less certain of their disbelief than the label "atheist" suggests.[115]

On the surface, this survey demonstrates once again that things are not as they seem. There is a surprising degree of overlap among people who are often considered to be at the extremes of faith: about half of evangelicals and agnostics, and one in five atheists, accept an idea of God that is broad and inclusive. At a deeper level, it shows that many of us are indeed able to have strong core beliefs —evangelical Christians believe in the Christian idea of God, while many agnostics and atheists are other-believers—but we can still acknowledge and accept other viewpoints about religion. In effect, we are able to focus on our own spiritual goal (the moon in the Zen metaphor) without being distracted, angered, or dismissive of the many other ways of reaching it (the finger pointing to the moon).

Note that this willingness to seriously consider other ideas about God doesn't indicate a lack of commitment to our own beliefs, convictions, and faith. Rather, it means we acknowledge that there are unanswerable questions and uncertain answers; that our current views are due to the combined influences of our temperament, upbringing, time in history, and chance; and that a good person is a good person regardless of his or her spiritual beliefs. It also means that evangelical Christians, agnostics, and atheists are much closer in their opinions about God—as broadly defined—than they appear, and the same is true for people worldwide.

Finding the Middle Way

Aware of the suffering brought about when I impose my views on others, I am committed not to force others, even my children, by any means whatsoever — such as authority, threat, money, propaganda or indoctrination — to adopt my views. I will respect the right of others to be different and to choose what to believe and how to decide. I will, however, help others renounce fanaticism and narrowness through compassionate dialogue.

—Thich Nhat Hanh[116]

53

My (Short) Life as
a Buddhist Monk

How Our Worldview Changes When
Seen Through the Eyes of Non-Self

The beginning of wisdom is found in doubting; by doubting we come to the question, and by seeking we may come upon the truth.

—Pierre Abelard (1079-1142)[117]

On one of my many weekends alone in Seoul, I traveled to the Lotus Lantern International Meditation Center on Ganghwa Island to participate in a temple-stay program to learn about Korean Buddhism. It turned out to be a lot more valuable than I had expected.

After my arrival on Friday afternoon, I donned grey, loose-fitting monk clothes—I looked like a comical Western version of Kim Jong-il, the pudgy North Korean ruler—and toured the grounds of what would be my home for the next three days. The scene, traditional Korea at its best, could have been taken directly from a travel brochure. It was a sunny mid-October day with the trees about half-turned in their autumn colors, birds chirping, innumerable ladybugs warming themselves on the exterior of the buildings, and the temple bells tolling softly in the gentle wind.

The complex was located in the countryside and nestled in a small forest, with a view of rice paddies stretching on and on until blending with the distant mountains. I walked past a gurgling brook that fed a small pond containing lotus flowers and koi, and up a stone stairway to the brightly colored Main Hall. Inside was a large statue of Buddha. I sat on one of the meditation cushions and spent the next few hours thinking about life.

As I left the temple I met An, a delightful young Vietnamese monk who was maybe 4'10" and 100 pounds. The remarkable thing about him was his ever-present smile. I liked him immediately. I'd heard about people who continuously exude happiness and kindness and thereby inspire others to do the same, and he was as close to such a person as I'd ever met. He made tea in the outdoor gazebo, where we sat at a wooden picnic table and thoroughly enjoyed each other's company with smiles, pantomimes of the ideas we were trying to convey (he spoke almost no English), and tea toasts to our health and peace in the world.

I thought things couldn't get any better, but then he offered me a bag of treats while simultaneously over-pronouncing the word "cookie." I thought, *How delightful, tea and cookies.* They were the strangest cookies I had ever seen: round, very small, with a slightly pungent smell. I had no idea how cookies should look and taste to meet the simple needs of Buddhist monks. Not wanting to lose the magic of the moment, I grabbed a handful of the treats and was about to pop them into my mouth, when An gestured for me to come over to the pond. By way of more pantomimes, I realized I was holding a bag of fish food—*koi ki* in Korean—and he wanted me to feed the fish. I gracefully recovered my composure and threw the food into the water.

I was hungry when dinnertime arrived because I'd missed lunch while en route to the temple, so I was quick to answer the bell that summoned everyone to the dining room. We sat cross-legged on the floor in absolute silence for the entire meal, but before eating we gave thanks to everyone involved in growing, harvesting, and preparing the food, and then we prayed for compassion for all sentient (self-aware) beings, including people, animals, and even insects. Monks spend most of their energy, including their digestive energy, in the contemplation of virtue, enlightenment, and other lofty ideals. Thus eating was part of their religious practice.

The food was vegetarian and quite good, but a bit on the bland side because they avoided vegetables that were high in calories, strongly flavored, or aphrodisiacs. (I made a mental note to investigate the latter food group for possible future use.) It's surprising how fast meals go when there's no talking; we started eating at 5:30 p.m. and were finished 20 minutes later. I helped clear the tables and then joined the four monks and two lay assistants for 30 minutes of chanting.

All organized activities were finished by 7 p.m., and I retired to my simple dormitory room to wash up in the austere communal bathroom. I would be alone the first night, or so I thought. While brushing my teeth I cause a glimpse of my roommate: the largest, fattest centipede that I'd ever seen, inching its way under the bathroom door and into my bedroom. It was comforting to know it would be at the temple until it died of old age. Monks don't harm any living creature, not even bugs, and after my brief exposure to monastic Buddhism, I wasn't about to bother it either.

The wooden floor of the bedroom was toasty warm, heated from below in the traditional Korean fashion. My bed was a two-inch thick foam mattress, and the "pillow" consisted of a three-inch wide, 15-inch long tube of plastic beads wrapped in a piece of coarse cloth. The situation would have been comical if I'd had someone to share it with, but I was alone, except for my multi-legged roommate just a short crawl away. It took a while to fall asleep because I was half-sore from all the cross-legged sitting and not used to sleeping on the floor. The last thing I remembered was the soothing sounds of a light rain on the roof and the feeling that this was going to be a very worthwhile weekend.

I awoke at 3:40 a.m. to the sound of someone vigorously beating on a moktak, the wooden, fish-shaped percussion instrument that is used to announce the start of a new day and to summon everyone to morning prayer. I put on my baggy monk's clothes and stumbled out of the dorm and up the dimly lit stairs to the Main Hall, where I was greeted by the ever-smiling Vietnamese monk, moktak in hand, who looked as refreshed as someone who'd slept until noon. Tired as I was, I was jolted awake by the 40-degree night air—morning was still far off—and I stopped to enjoy the silence and gaze at the innumerable stars that graced the tranquil rural setting. It didn't get much better than this.

Our little group started with a few minutes of simple chanting, followed by the main event, 108 prostrations of repentance. It was cold in the temple, but I was sweating hard before we passed 30. The idea is straightforward: we have done a lot of bad things in our lives, and we are sorry. The prostrations reminded me of similar practices in Hinduism, Islam, Judaism, and some Christian sects. I'm not the sharpest knife in the drawer, but I got the point after maybe 10 prostrations—*We're, sorry, really sorry!*—and I wondered who had decided that 108 was the magic number. We just kept on going. Kneel down, flatten your back, forehead to the floor, palms up, rock up using just your legs—which I couldn't do, even with practice—then back down, again and again for 20 minutes, accompanied by continuous chanting.

I breathed a sigh of relief when we finished and contemplated a quick nap before breakfast, but we weren't even half done with our pre-dawn activities. We chanted for another 20 minutes and then walked to the adjacent hall, arranged our cushions so that we faced a blank wall (to avoid any distractions from our fellow devotees), and sat cross-legged for 30 minutes of silent meditation. I was exhausted, over-prostrated, over-stretched, over-meditated… and it was only 5:15 a.m. on a Saturday morning.

I spent the next day and a half meditating, reading, doing calligraphy (we traced the outline of Chinese characters on pre-printed paper, much like children with a paint-by-numbers kit), walking the two adorable puppies that lived at the temple, and chatting with the six other Westerners who arrived on Saturday afternoon. Otherwise, the program was exactly the same: early to bed, with the fat centipede still there to keep me company; even less sleep as one of my human roommates was a world-class snorer; being awakened by the moktak-wielding monk at 3:40 a.m.; chanting; meditating; and of course, 108 prostrations. I'd been with these monks for most of my waking hours since yesterday, and I wondered, *One hundred and eight prostrations? Again? What could these guys have possibly done in the last 24 hours to atone for?* Later I learned there are programs in which monks do 3,000 or more prostrations as a gesture of surrender, reverence, and awareness. Just the thought of this was enough to make me appreciate my 11-hour workdays back in Seoul. They seemed easy in comparison.

After returning to Seoul, I reflected on what I'd learned. I'd gained respect for the rigors of monastic life, and the realization that it clearly wasn't for me, except in small doses; greater awareness of the sanctity of all living things, including my 100-legged roommate; and an appreciation of the many good things about other cultures and religions. A few other impressions stayed with me for a long time thereafter.

First, after months of living in South Korea where armed conflict with the North was always a possibility, I thought about the state of affairs worldwide. Anyone with a lick of sense could see there was a lot that wasn't working: the ugly side of nationalism, global hatred, and civil and regional wars that followed one another as day follows night. Clearly, religious principles in most countries didn't seem to apply to national and international affairs. I remembered the adage, "Without inner peace, it's impossible to have world peace," and I wondered, *Which of today's world leaders has inner peace?* Most of them were religious people, or at least they attended religious services regularly, but their often hostile foreign policies certainly didn't show it.

Second, I felt a profound sense of humility. When I arrived at the temple on Friday night, I left all of my accomplishments and everything that represented "Bob" at the door—my medical and MBA degrees, experience in the business world, athletic ability (limited, but not bad for my age), and even the fact that I was a husband and a father of three children. I was a novice in every sense of the word. The most influential event of the weekend was meeting An. He didn't have my formal education or life experiences, but he had an overwhelming sense of inner peace. I knew that my life would be much happier if I could see the world like he did.

Finally, while sitting alone for hours in the Main Hall, no one knowing or caring that I passed for an important person in my world, I discovered that my views on a lot of issues were different, much different, once I stepped away from how Bob might see them. I had no idea where many of my earlier thoughts, opinions, and convictions had come from. Some were formed during 50 years of long-forgotten experiences, others were borrowed from friends and family, and some seemed to have been with me since birth—unquestioned and often totally unsubstantiated. Yet when I ticked through the beliefs I'd held at different times in my life—my ideas about God, religion, social concerns, and how to live a meaningful life—I had trouble finding anything that was absolutely and unequivocally true.

That weekend marked the time when I let go of my most tightly held views. I'll never forget how much clearer I thought as I sat alone in the temple, seeing the world through the eyes of non-

Bob. I still didn't know what I didn't know, but I understood that I didn't know it all—and never would—and that understanding made all the difference for how I've lived my life since then.

54

The Buddhist Who Helped
His Friends Become
Stronger Christians

Keeping Both Eyes Open to See the
Whole Truth: Life in the Middle Way

I love you, my brother, whoever you are—whether you worship in your church, kneel in your temple, or pray in your mosque. You and I are all children of one faith, for the diverse paths of religion are fingers of the loving hand of the one Supreme Being, a hand extending to all, offering completeness of spirit to all, eager to receive all.

—Kahlil Gibran (1883-1931), Lebanon[118]

After returning from a long stay in Korea, where I spent one evening a week at the orphanage with my classes of five- and six-year-olds, I realized I was hooked on teaching English as a second language. This was partly because I loved children, and partly because this activity gave me a feeling of happiness and fulfillment. A social service agency in Asheville arranged for me to work with a Hispanic family that needed help with English, and I started the following week.

I liked my new family immediately because they reminded me of my own life 50 years earlier. They were even poorer than I was as a child, plus they had the added disadvantage of being first-gen-eration immigrants in a new country. Juan and María, the parents, had low-paying service jobs, and it would always be that way for them, as it had been for my father and mother. Their two young children, Ana and Luis, spoke almost no English when we first met, so I spent a lot of time doing homework and reading with them. I wanted to do whatever I could to help them succeed in school so they could move up in the world. I was especially impressed when Ana would bring out one of her own books and read to me in Spanish. She was clearly an intelligent girl; what she needed was someone to help her during this critical phase of life.

Christmas was approaching, and I was eager to give my new family a few gifts to celebrate the holiday. I asked Luis about the traditions in his home country, especially about Santa Claus. His answer was heartbreaking. "Yes," he said, "Santa used to come where I lived before, but he only visited the rich children." Ana and Luis had never received a Christmas present from Santa Claus. Not one.

They were a devout Christian family who attended church twice a week, prayed together before meals, and real aloud from a Spanish-language Bible each night. I saw a golden opportunity to do something special, the kind of thing that people remember long after we're gone. I bought the family a few practical gifts, such as down comforters to keep them warm in their poorly heated home, and I got the children some of the same games that my family played when our kids were little: Life, Yahtzee, and Twister.

Then I visited the largest Christian bookstore in town. I still remember the excitement I felt when I walked through the door and into an enormous showroom filled with Bibles, religious DVDs, and inspirational music. (It was the same feeling of exhilara-tion that gripped me after my first exhausting visit to the Korean orphanage months earlier, when I dragged myself off the train, thinking of dinner and bed, only to be re-energized when I discovered the large selection of Korean-English books at the store near the subway station exit.) I bought two beautifully illustrated children's Bibles—one in Spanish for Ana and one in English for Luis —and carefully wrapped them with the other presents for the family.

I wasn't there physically on Christmas morning when the family opened their gifts, but I was there in spirit. Juan called me later in the day to thank me for my kindness to his family. The comforters and games were greatly appreciated, and the children were excitedly paging through their new Bibles. I was in tears when I hung up the phone, happy I was able to give the children a gift that would draw them even closer to the faith that was so important to their family, and thankful for being able to share in the lives of such wonderful people.

In many respects, my adopted family and I were much different. They were very conservative on social issues (I'm a little right of center from a European point of view, and a little left of center from a U.S. perspective), we came from different cultures, our socioeconomic circumstances were poles apart, and there was the matter of religion. After we got to know each other, Juan asked if I was a Christian. I was expecting this question—people who spent that much time attending church and reading the Bible were obviously committed to their faith—and I was worried that he might be uncomfortable with our different views on something so important to him. A puzzled look crossed his face when I said, "Buddhist," so I tried "*Soy Budista*" ("I'm a Buddhist"), which I'd learned the prior week in *Spanish for Gringos*. This didn't help either; he had no idea what a Buddhist was. But it didn't matter. We both had the same goal—helping his family learn English—and this was far more important than any differences we might have had on religion.

The "Bob" that I had known in the past was so much different from the one who hung up the telephone on that Christmas morning. The old Bob wouldn't have volunteered, wouldn't have seen the many opportunities to be kind to people in small ways, and would never have had close friends whose beliefs were so much different than his. I had grown less confident in what I knew, much more interested in helping others, and infinitely more understanding of people who had different ideas about life. Somehow, without making a conscious decision, I had been drawn to the Buddhist tradition of the Middle Way.

In the early years of Buddhism, the Middle Way referred to a path between the extremes of self-indulgence and self-denial. It seems that the world of 2,500 years ago contained two kinds of people: (1) the wealthy, who were preoccupied with the sense pleasures of the day, such as food, alcohol, sex, and every manner of good living that was possible at the time, and (2) the poor, who spent their days looking for food, clothing, and shelter. In other words, it was a world very much like today.

The meaning of the Middle Way evolved over millennia to represent an approach whereby the focus of life is on balance and moderation in all things, especially in one's beliefs. One of the principal tenets of Buddhism is that all systems of thought, *including Buddhist teachings themselves*, are guiding principles only, and not absolute truth or doctrine, and Buddhists are enjoined to avoid any theory, ideology, or view that limits their openness to other ideas.[119] (I'm especially fond of this last point. If I find myself becoming narrow-minded, judgmental, or self-righteous because of some perceived superiority of my beliefs and worldview, it's time for me to re-examine my position because I've forgotten one of the core principles.) This philosophy of openness to other ideas and beliefs is the main reason why Buddhism is one of the world's most tolerant belief systems.

Despite its nonconfrontational connotation, Middle Way doesn't mean ambivalent, middle-of-the-road, or indifferent. In fact, there are movements such as "Socially Engaged Buddhism" that are devoted to dealing with societal problems and taking a strong stand against oppression and injustice. But what's different about the Middle Way is its emphasis on finding solutions that are nonviolent, nonpartisan, and that respect the rights of people to be different.

It's easy to see what drew me to this way of seeing the world: people accept the ideas that work for them. For many of us, this means keeping the basic beliefs of our childhood or early adult life because they connect us to our families, friends, and social networks, and of course, because this is what we truly believe. In my case, I probably would have retained the traditional Christian views of my childhood family if I still lived in Omaha, as did all of my friends who stayed there. But I'd seen much during my life, so many different ideas that were totally at odds with each other, so many highly ethical people who tried to do the right thing, but in different ways. It simply wasn't possible for me to accept a single set of truths. So I chose a belief system that encouraged me to continuously re-evaluate my ideas about everything, including religion, politics, nationalism, and the divisive social issues that cause so much upheaval worldwide, and to update these ideas as I acquired more experience and wisdom throughout life.

The 19th-century philosopher John Stuart Mill had an insightful perspective on the pros and cons of positioning ourselves at different points along the spectrum of belief, particularly at either extreme. Speaking of the intense partisanship that characterized the political factions in his day (and certainly now, as well), he said, "For our part, we have a large tolerance for one-eyed men, provided their eye is a penetrating one: if they saw more, they probably would not see so keenly, nor so eagerly pursue one course of enquiry."[120] By this he meant that extreme views—politics, in this case, but equally applicable to religion, nationalism, and social concerns—are useful, even essential, because they allow impassioned believers to see deeply into an issue, vigorously pursue their goals, and teach us important lessons that we might never have learned on our own. But the downside is that a one-eyed view inevitably limits our ability to see different sides of the same truth that are known to people who see just as deeply as we do, only through the other eye.

Mill further observed, "No whole truth is possible, but by combining the points of view of all the fractional truths."[121] After having seen firsthand the broad spectrum of opinions, beliefs, convictions, and faiths that exist throughout the world, I, too, had come to the realization that the view of truth that can be seen from the extremes, and from every point in between, was only a partial one. A lifetime of experiences had taught me that I could see the most by keeping both eyes open and positioning myself firmly in the middle. From there I could benefit from the wisdom of others, including those at the ideological extremes, but not be so committed to any single belief that I closed my mind to new ideas. It was a life-changing attitude that led to happiness, inner peace, and greater awareness and concern for the people around me.

Do you remember the times when you realized you were wrong, that Ah-ha! moment when everything became clear? Maybe you picked the wrong political candidate, the wrong religion, the wrong job, or even the wrong spouse. With the passage of time, it seems so easy to see the truth in these matters. *It takes a person of uncommon wisdom to realize that you can just as easily be wrong about truth in the present as you were about truth in the past.* This is the real Ah-ha moment, when we realize that the truth of today is only a partial truth, and that the truth of tomorrow will change as we learn more about ourselves and the world we live in.

55

All Good Things Must Come to an End: The Korean Orphanage, Part 5

Six Strategies for Becoming a Better Believer

Be done with knowing and your worries will disappear. How much difference is there between yes and no? How much distinction between good and evil? Fearing what others fear, admiring what they admire—nonsense. Conventional people are jolly and reckless, feasting on worldly things and carrying on as though every day were the beginning of spring. I alone remain uncommitted, like an infant who hasn't yet smiled: lost, quietly drifting, unattached to ideas and places and things.

—Lao Tzu (6th century BCE), China[122]

Birthdays come and go, and as we get older it becomes more and more difficult to pretend to be excited when they occur. It was because of my low expectations that I was so surprised by what happened on the day I turned 57. It was one of the more memorable days of my life.

I had been commuting between South Korea and the United States for three years, and I'd spent almost every Sunday evening at the orphanage when I was in Seoul. In some respects, the night of my 57th birthday was no different. I taught two 45-minute classes, had dinner with a roomful of amazingly energetic kids, and sat on the floor with two- and three-year-old children who climbed onto my lap to be held until they fell asleep. And as usual, I arrived back at the hotel feeling tired and hungry, and wearing a big smile on my face.

What made this birthday special was that it marked a turning point in my life. My three-year contract in Korea had come to an end. There would be no more return trips to Seoul, no more hikes in the beautiful mountains that I so loved, no more meditating after work at the Jogyesa temple behind my hotel, and saddest of all, no more visits to the orphanage where I'd spent so much time during my stays in Korea. I was about to start a new chapter in life. I had no idea how it would begin or end.

Major life changes always make one reflective, and I spent hours later that night thinking about the past, the present, and the future. Foremost in my thoughts were my students at the orphanage. How would they turn out? Did I make a difference in their lives? In particular, what would happen to the three Parks—siblings Sungbin, Hyunju, and Jinsoo? When they were finally adopted, probably by three different families that would take them in three different directions, what would they be like as grown-ups? Would they be open-minded and understanding of others, or narrow-minded and unwilling to admit that the unique circumstances of their lives had had such a vast influence on what they believed as adults?

And why, I wondered, do I even care what other people believe? I'd grown accustomed to seeing the world in the non-judgmental Middle Way of Buddhism, and I no longer felt angry, threatened, or dismissive when I encountered different religious, political, and social beliefs. The reason was clear: I cared because people confuse belief and faith with certainty and truth, and they act accordingly. Clearly, practicing one's beliefs is a good thing when it leads us to actions that allow others to live their lives in a way that gives them meaning, happiness, and hope. However, not everyone is like this. Instead, armed with the imagined certainty of belief and freed from the caution and restraint that comes with not knowing, some of us use our words and actions in ways that make it difficult or impossible for others to live life as *their* beliefs dictate.

So I wrote this book—most of it during three years of weekends alone when I worked in Korea—to describe the long journey I'd taken from my roots as a conservative Christian American to a centrist Buddhist and a citizen of the world. My path included innumerable choices, wrong turns, and dead ends. Somehow I ended up here. Is the worldview I've described in this book right? Everyone needs to follow his or her own path in life, and this was mine. It's the reason why I'm so mindful, happy, and tolerant today. For me, clearly it was right.

Beliefs are important. On a personal level they determine if we're happy or sad, tolerant or self-righteous; from a societal perspective they're the reason some nations have domestic and foreign policies that stress peace and respect for differences, or quite the contrary. Given the importance of beliefs, I've listed my suggestions for how we can all become better believers. The goal of these six strategies is to bridge the gap between the ignorance of certainty and the wisdom of not knowing, and in so doing, move to a centrist position that retains our core beliefs while still acknowledging the value—and possible truth—of other ideas.

Six Strategies for Becoming a Better Believer

1. *Make "not knowing" one of your core principles.* Don't surround yourself with like-thinkers who echo your beliefs back to you; this might make you feel good, but it distorts reality by convincing you that your beliefs represent truth. Instead, expose yourself to differences every day. Befriend people, read books, view Internet sites, watch news programs, and listen to talk shows espousing ideas that

disagree with your current views. The intent of this wisdom-building exercise is to change thought patterns so that your mind, particularly your subconscious mind that continuously processes the information it receives, gradually loses its hold on the feeling of certainty. In effect, you begin to think differently—more broadly, more inclusively, and more humbly—which is the only way to break free of the illusion of certainty.

2. *Accept your emotional, spiritual, and intellectual limitations.* None of us has super powers and we never will, and accepting our physical limitations is a normal part of life. We also have emotional, spiritual, and intellectual limitations, although they're not as readily apparent. Specifically, thinking or feeling something deeply, knowing in our minds or in our heart of hearts that it is absolutely, unequivocally true, doesn't make it so, and it never will.

This isn't to say that all beliefs are equal; some views, ideas, and opinions have a great deal more supporting evidence than others. Nor does it mean that all beliefs—particularly about religion, politics, and social issues—require ironclad, irrefutable proof. But it does mean that it's often not possible for us to know if we're right or wrong. We may not have enough information, may never fully escape our biases, and may live at a time when the truth is unknowable. So if we choose to accept our beliefs as guiding principles in life, we also need to acknowledge our limitations, admit that others might be right, and do what we can to ensure that everyone has the freedom to practice his or her own beliefs.

3. *Acknowledge the influences of life.* It's not easy to admit that the "belief anchors" that we've set over the years may not be correct. This challenges our conviction that an external force, such as God, fate, or karma, intervened in our lives to make sure that we could find the truth if we searched for it, or that we're so intelligent, well-educated, and experienced in life that we were able to find the right answer on our own. Rather, our core convictions, beliefs, and faith would be different, maybe even *the exact opposite* of what they are

today, if life had taken us another way. This acknowledgment adds a huge uncertainty to the validity of our beliefs—which is precisely the intent.

4. *Spend time reflecting on your selfless nature.* Think long and hard about how you would see the world if you could step away from your age, gender, race, ethnicity, sexual orientation, nationality, occupation, religion, and political ideology. Instead, picture the world through the eyes of someone who was neutral in all of these characteristics. It's immediately clear that our opinions, beliefs, convictions, and faith—which are for most people the very foundations of "self" and the essence of who they are—are creations of our minds based solely on the experiences we've had thus far in life. Change a few things here and there, and our most fundamental beliefs would be different.

5. *Strive for centrist beliefs.* Learn to stand between opinions, not at the extremes, in order to see all sides of an issue. The more we think, dream, and imagine "What if things had been different in my life?" the more doubt, and the less certainty, we'll have. We gain respect for other points of view—not necessarily agree, but at least understand—and move closer to the middle.

6. *Embrace the uncertainty of spiritual belief.* I was a Baptist-Catholic early in life, and now I'm a Buddhist, my Saudi friend Ali is a Muslim, and my dear friend Mark was nonsectarian. Is only one of these belief systems correct? All? None of them? Did the true religion flourish in prehistoric times and die out because of lack of interest? Is everyone wrong and the real prophet will visit us in a million years—or a million centuries—and make everything clear? Or maybe we're on our own, a view held by over a billion people today. Who knows? It's not within my ability, or anyone else's for that matter, to know for sure.

These metaphysical questions, so divisive and unanswerable, distract us from the tasks at hand. Pick a religion, spiritual practice, or secular belief system that fits your culture, traditions, and temperament, live it and live it well, stop worrying about the unknowable, and let the other people in the world do the same. Regardless of what's ahead of us, we won't go wrong, in this life or the next.

I recommend meditation as one of the best ways to practice these six strategies. In the stillness of our minds, far from the rancor of competing claims about the knowable and the unknowable, we are free to suspend our beliefs, turn the mind's gaze upon itself, and consider the many faces of truth. This mental exercise, in which we examine our thoughts and look deeply into the emotional, spiritual, and intellectual parts of our minds, helps us understand that what we believe at this exact moment is only one example of what we might have believed if things had gone differently in our lives. We also learn that the mind is capable of escaping many of the confines of time and life experiences that so strongly influence what we think today. In particular, we understand that there are universal principles—justice, compassion, generosity, and the desire for peace and happiness—that supersede the religious, political, and social ideologies that happen to be popular at our time in history.

Finally, we realize that we're not who we think we are. Our essence is not defined by being Hindu or Muslim; black, white, or Asian; conservative or liberal; teacher or electrician; or even man or woman. These superficial characteristics merely reflect the times during which we live and the circumstances of our lives. If we follow their lead, they will limit what we think, say, and do as we become more and more convinced that our way of seeing the world is right.

Rather, we are human beings with the potential to leave behind the fixed ideas of who we are and what we believe, and instead focus on what we might become. This broader view—in which we understand that truth depends on one's perception of reality, and that acknowledgment of others' beliefs doesn't negate ours—starts us on the path to wisdom, happiness, and an appreciation for the interconnectedness of people worldwide who share the same desire for purpose and meaning in their lives, but who often start from much different places.

References

1　Biddulph D. *1,001 Pearls of Buddhist Wisdom* (San Francisco: Chronicle Books, 2007), 171.

2　Sheban J. *The Wisdom of Gibran* (New York: Philosophical Library, 1966), 74.

3　Alighieri D. *Divine Comedy, "Inferno."*

4　Smith H, Novak P. *Buddhism: A Concise Introduction* (New York, HarperCollins Publishers, 2003), 136-137.

5　Metcalf F. *What Would Buddha Do?* (Berkeley, Seastone, 1999), 77.

6　Mahatma Gandhi. http://www.globalstewards.org/motivational-quotes-simplifying.htm.

7　Biddulph, 87.

8　Sheban, 11.

9　Biddulph, 80.

10　Rothberg D. *The Engaged Spiritual Life* (Boston, Beacon Press, 2006), 176-9.

11　Biddulph, 127.

12　Biddulph, 230.

13　Yogananda P. *How to Be Happy All the Time* (Nevada City, Crystal Clarity Publisher, 2006), 29.

14　Maitreya BA. *The Dhammapada* (Berkeley, Parallax Press, 1995), 9.

15　Biddulph, 206.

16　http://quotationsbook.com/quote/2501.

17　http://www.goodreads.com/author/quotes/812826.Abigail_Van_Buren.

18　Daoren H (Translated by Thomas Cleary). *Back to Beginnings: Reflections on the Tao* (Boston, Shambhala, 1998), 34.

19　Biddulph, 311.

20　Biddulph D. *1,001 Pearls of Buddhist Wisdom* (San Francisco: Chronicle Books, 2007).

21　Brody JE. "Thriving after Life's Bum Rap," *The New York Times*, August 14, 2007.

22　Mipham S. *Ruling Your World* (New York, Morgan Road Books, 2005), 62.

23　Yogananda (2006), 69.

24　Biddulph, 224.

25　Dalai Lama, Cutler HC. *The Art of Happiness* (New York, Riverhead Books, 1998) 219-20).

26 Hanh TN. Dwelling Happily in the Present Moment: The Seventh Mindfulness Training of The Order of Interbeing. http://www. orderofinterbeing.org.

27 Hanh TN. Community and Communication: The Eighth Mindfulness Training of The Order of Interbeing. http://www. orderofinterbeing.org.

28 Brahm A. *Who Ordered this Truckload of Dung?* (Boston, Wisdom Publications, 2005), 132.

29 Das S. *Awakening the Buddha Within* (New York, Broadway Books, 1997), 130.

30 Modified from the Matthew 26:41 of the King James version of the Bible: "Watch and pray, that ye enter not into temptation: the spirit indeed is willing, but the flesh is weak."

31 Prentiss C. *Zen and the Art of Happiness* (Los Angeles, Power Press, 2006), 38.

32 Brown PL. "In the Classroom, a New Focus on Quieting the Mind," *The New York Times,* June 16, 2007.

33 Boykin K. *Zen for Christians* (San Francisco, Jossey-Bass, 2003).

34 Hanh TN. Dealing with Anger: The Sixth Mindfulness Training of The Order of Interbeing. http://www.orderofinterbeing.org.

35 Yogananda (2006), 56.

36 http://feelbetteraboutthings.com/quotes.html.

37 Machiavelli N. *The Prince.* http://www.giga-usa.com/quotes/quotes.htm.

38 Gracián B. *The Art of Worldly Wisdom* (Boston, Shambhala, 2000), 40.

39 Milton J, *Paradise Lost.* http://www.brainyquote.com.

40 Mipham, 58.

41 Ricard M. *Happiness* (New York, Little, Brown and Company, 2003), 162.

42 Biddulph, 206.

43 Carroll M. *Awake at Work* (Boston, Shambhala, 2006), 150.

44 Lao Tzu (Translated by Brian Browne Walker). *The Tao Te Ching* (New York, St. Martin's Press, 1995), 46.

45 Rivlin G. "In Silicon Valley, Millionaires Who Don't Feel Rich," *The New York Times,* August 5, 2007.

46 Biddulph, 110.

47 Maitreya, 2.

48 Das, 278.

49 Hanh TN. Non-Attachment to Views: The Second Mindfulness Training of The Order of Interbeing. http://www. orderofinterbeing.org

50 Franklin B. *The Autobiography of Benjamin Franklin.*

51 Yogananda P. *Autobiography of a Yogi* (Los Angeles, Self-Realization Fellowship, 1946), 1.

52 Burton RA. *On Being Certain: Believing You Are Right Even When You're Not* (New York, St. Martin's Press, 2008), 102-5.

53 Gracián, 74.

54 Sheban, 24.

55 Appiah KA. *Experiments in Ethics* (Cambridge, Harvard University Press, 2008), 110.

56 Yogananda (2006), 64.

57 Lim C, Putnam RD. Religion, Social Networks, and Life Satisfaction. American Sociological Review 2010; 75:914-933.

58 Tavris C, Aronson E. *Mistakes Were Made, but Not by Me* (Orlando, Harcourt, 2007), 17.

59 Newberg and Waldman (2006), 253-257.

60 Westen D, Blagov PS, Harenski K, et al. Neural Bases of Motivated Reasoning: An fMRI Study of Emotional Constraints on Partisan Political Judgment in the 2004 U.S. Presidential Election. *Journal of Cognitive Neuroscience* 2006; 18:1947-1958.

61 Ariely D. *Predictably Irrational* (New York, HarperCollins Publishers, 2008).

62 Bikhchandani S, Hirshleifer D, Welch I. A Theory of Fads, Fashion, Custom, and Cultural Change as Informational Cascades. *The Journal of Political Economy.* 1992; 100(5):992-1026.

63 Tierne J. "How the Low-Fat, Low-Fact Cascade Just Keeps Rolling Along," *The New York Times,* October 9, 2007.

64 Vreeman RC, Carroll AE. Medical Myths. *British Journal of Medicine* 2007; 335:1288-1289.

65 Slovic P. *The Perception of Risk* (London, Earthscan Publications Ltd, 2000), 185.

66 Haidt J. *The Happiness Hypothesis* (New York, Basic Books, 2006), 71.

67 Tversky A, Kahneman D. Judgment under Uncertainty: Heuristics and Biases. *Science* 1974;185:1124-31.

68 Bishop B, Cushing RG. *The Big Sort* (Boston, Houghton Mifflin Company, 2008), 36.

69   http://www.adherents.com/adh_branches.html.

70   http://www.adherents.com/Religions_By_Adherents.html.

71   Dalai Lama, 193.

72   The Question of God. PBS interview with Francis Collins. September 2004. http://www.pbs.org/wgbh/questionofgod/voices/ collins.html.

73   Tavris and Aronson, 81.

74   Orwell G. "In Front of Your Nose," First published in *The Tribune*, Great Britain, March 22, 1946.

75   http://skepdic.com/cognitivedissonance.html (last accessed December 19, 2008).

76   Ayres BD. "Families Learning of 39 Cultists Who Died Willingly," *The New York Times*, March 29, 1997.

77   Tavris and Aronson, 1-10.

78   Tavris and Aronson, 244.

79   Newberg A, Waldman MR. *Why We Believe What We Believe* (New York, Free Press, 2006).

80   Newberg A, Waldman MR. *How God Changes Your Brain* (New York, Ballantine Books, 2009), 83.

81   Newberg and Waldman (2006), 128.

82   Newberg and Waldman (2006), 167-190.

83   Lehrer J. *How We Decide* (Boston, Houghton Mifflin Harcourt, 2009), 204.

84   U.S. Religious Landscape Survey–Religious Affiliation: Diverse and Dynamic. Pew Forum on Religion and Public Life. February 2008. Pew Research Center, Washington, D.C.

85   Roberts S. "In a Generation, Minorities May Be the U.S. Majority," *The New York Times*, August 14, 2008.

86   Bishop and Cushing, 39

87   Bishop and Cushing, 231.

88   Hanh TN. Openness: The First Mindfulness Training of The Order of Interbeing. http://www.orderofinterbeing.org.

89   Rothberg, 120.

90   Allama Sir Abdullah Al-Mamun Al-Suhrawardy. *The Sayings of Muhammad* (Whitefish, Kessinger Publishing, 2004), IX.

91   Woodroof M. "Boost from Big Stores Has Religion Books Rising," National Public Radio (United States). Reported on January 22, 2007.

92   Brahm, 186.

93   Gracián, 40.

94   Boyd L. "Split Leads to New Congregation," *Asheville Citizen-Times*, December 4, 2007.

95   Goodstein L. "A Divide, and Maybe a Divorce," *The New York Times*, February 25, 2007.

96   Melton JG. *Encyclopedia of American Religions* (Gale, Farmington Hllls, 2003), 1.

97   Faith in Flux: Changes in Religious Affiliation in the U.S. Pew Forum on Religion & Public Life. April 2009. Sec 1.1, p. 1.

98   Associated Press. "Archbishop of Canterbury Hails Unity on Women," *The New York Times*, October 22, 1989.

99   Noll MA. *The Civil War as a Theological Crisis* (Chapel Hill, University of North Carolina Press, 2006), 199.

100   Das, 388.

101   *International Herald Tribune*, Asia-Pacific edition. December 31, 2007.

102   Mlodinow L. *The Drunkard's Walk: How Randomness Rules Our Lives* (New York, Pantheon Books, 2008), 4.

103   Appiah, 125.

104   Bokser BZ. *The Wisdom of the Talmud* (New York, Kensington Publishing Corp., 1951), citing Yerushalmi Sanhedrin 4:2, 8.

105   Sheban, 65.

106   Haidt, 152.

107   Newberg and Waldman (2006), 246.

108   Dalai Lama. "Our Faith in Science," *The New York Times* (Op-Ed), November 12, 2005.

109   Obst L. Valentine to Science. *Interview*. February 1996. (Carl Sagan quoting from a prior conversation with the Dalai Lama).

110   Stairs A, Bernard C. *A Thinker's Guide to the Philosophy of Religion* (New York, Pearson, 2007), 195-6.

111   Burton RA. *On Being Certain: Believing You Are Right Even When You're Not* (New York, St. Martin's Press, 2008).

112   Burton, 141.

113   Lupton D. *Risk* (New York, Routledge, 1999), 29.

114 Many Americans Say Other Faiths Can Lead to Eternal Life. The Pew Forum On Religion & Public Life. December 18, 2008.
115 Newberg and Waldman (2009), 10, 97.
116 Hanh TN. Freedom of Thought: The Third Mindfulness Training of The Order of Interbeing. http://www.orderofinterbeing.org.
117 Biddulph, 105.
118 Sheban, 17.
119 Hanh TN. The Order of Interbeing. http://www.orderofinterbeing org.
120 Muirhead R. *In Defense of Partisanship*. Harvard University Panel 1-19, "Alternative Sources of American Political Thought." Prepared for delivery at the 2003 Annual Meeting of the American Political Science Association, August 28-31, 2003, 20.
121 Muirhead, 19.
122 Lao Tzu, 20.

CPSIA information can be obtained at www.ICGtesting.com
Printed in the USA
266613BV00003B/7/P